Multilingual Universities
in South Africa

BILINGUAL EDUCATION & BILINGUALISM
Series Editors: Nancy H. Hornberger (*University of Pennsylvania, USA*) and Colin Baker (*Bangor University, Wales, UK*)

Bilingual Education and Bilingualism is an international, multidisciplinary series publishing research on the philosophy, politics, policy, provision and practice of language planning, global English, indigenous and minority language education, multilingualism, multiculturalism, biliteracy, bilingualism and bilingual education. The series aims to mirror current debates and discussions.

Full details of all the books in this series and of all our other publications can be found on http://www.multilingual-matters.com, or by writing to Multilingual Matters, St Nicholas House, 31–34 High Street, Bristol BS1 2AW, UK.

Multilingual Universities in South Africa
Reflecting Society in Higher Education

Edited by
Liesel Hibbert and Christa van der Walt

MULTILINGUAL MATTERS
Bristol • Buffalo • Toronto

Library of Congress Cataloging in Publication Data
Multilingual Universities in South Africa: Reflecting Society in Higher Education/Edited by Liesel Hibbert and Christa van der Walt.
Bilingual Education and Bilingualism: 97
Includes bibliographical references and index.
1. Education, Bilingual—South Africa 2. Language and languages—Study and teaching (Higher)—South Africa. 3. Language policy—South Africa. I. Hibbert, Liesel, 1956-
LC3738.S6M95 2014
378.68–dc23 2013046977

British Library Cataloguing in Publication Data
A catalogue entry for this book is available from the British Library.

ISBN-13: 978-1-78309-165-2 (hbk)
ISBN-13: 978-1-78309-164-5 (pbk)

Multilingual Matters
UK: St Nicholas House, 31–34 High Street, Bristol BS1 2AW, UK.
USA: UTP, 2250 Military Road, Tonawanda, NY 14150, USA.
Canada: UTP, 5201 Dufferin Street, North York, Ontario M3H 5T8, Canada.

Copyright © 2014 Liesel Hibbert, Christa van der Walt and the authors of individual chapters.

All rights reserved. No part of this work may be reproduced in any form or by any means without permission in writing from the publisher.

The policy of Multilingual Matters/Channel View Publications is to use papers that are natural, renewable and recyclable products, made from wood grown in sustainable forests. In the manufacturing process of our books, and to further support our policy, preference is given to printers that have FSC and PEFC Chain of Custody certification. The FSC and/or PEFC logos will appear on those books where full certification has been granted to the printer concerned.

Typeset by Techset Composition India(P) Ltd., Bangalore and Chennai, India.
Printed and bound in Great Britain by Short Run Press Ltd.

Contents

Contributors   vii
Preface   xi

Part 1: Policy Development and the Opening up of Implementation Opportunities

1. Biliteracy and Translanguaging Pedagogy in South Africa: An Overview   3
Liesel Hibbert and Christa van der Walt

2. The Emergence of a Favourable Policy Landscape   15
Ernst Kotzé

3. Multilingualism at Work in South African Higher Education: From Policy to Practice   28
Pamela Maseko

Part 2: Enhanced Student Performance through Biliteracy Pedagogy

4. African Languages as Languages of Teaching and Learning: The Case of the Department of African Languages, University of South Africa   49
Ingeborg M. Kosch and Sonja E. Bosch

5. Promoting Concept Literacy through Multilingual Glossaries: A Translanguaging Approach   68
Mbulungeni Madiba

6 Teaching Indigenous African Languages to Speakers of Other African Languages: The Effects of Translanguaging for Multilingual Development   88
Leketi Makalela

Part 3: Affective Aspects of Biliteracy Pedagogy

7 isiZulu–English Bilingualisation at the University of KwaZulu-Natal: An Exploration of Students' Attitudes   107
Andrea Parmegiani and Stephanie Rudwick

8 Dual Language Instruction: Its Impact on Attitudes Towards the Role of African Languages in Education   123
Sandiso Ngcobo

9 Tertiary Educators' Reflections on Language Practices that Enhance Student Learning and Promote Multilingualism   145
Nomakhaya Mashiyi

Part 4: Africanisation and Localisation of Content for Cultural Identification

10 An Exemplary Astronomical Lesson that Could Potentially Show the Benefits of Multilingual Content and Language in Higher Education   167
Lerothodi L. Leeuw

11 Literacy Self-Narratives as Constructions of Pre-Service Teachers' Multiliterate and Multilingual Identities   179
Adelia Carstens and Linda-Anne Alston

12 African Languages in Higher Education: Lessons from Practice and Prospects for the Future   202
Christa van der Walt and Liesel Hibbert

Subject Index   220

Contributors

Liesel Hibbert is Professor in the Department of Applied Language Studies at the Nelson Mandela Metropolitan University in Port Elizabeth in South Africa. She received her PhD in Linguistics from the University of Cape Town. Her research spans global trends in youth development and multilingualism, academic and language development in higher education, linguistic ethnography and South African writing, including children's literature. Her work has been published in *Review of Research in Education, English Today, The International Journal of the Sociology of Language, Mannheimer Beitraege zur Sprach und Literaturwissenschaft, Per Linguam* and a variety of other local journals.

Christa van der Walt is Professor in the Department of Curriculum Studies at Stellenbosch University in South Africa. She trains English language teachers and has introduced a module in multilingual education in the secondary school teacher certification programme. Her research interests are focused on the teaching and use of English in multilingual contexts, with specific focus on learning in bi- and multilingual contexts and the role of teachers' and students' bi- and multilingual practices in secondary and higher education classrooms, as her most recent publication, *Multilingual Higher Education: Beyond English-Medium Orientations* (Multilingual Matters) shows. She is also interested in the emergence of South African varieties of English and their use in education.

Linda-Anne Alston is a lecturer in the Unit for Academic Literacy at the University of Pretoria, South Africa. She has eight years' experience in teaching academic literacies – both generic and subject-specific. Her research foci are student support and using technology to facilitate language teaching.

Sonja E. Bosch is Professor in the Department of African Languages at the University of South Africa (UNISA) in Pretoria. In her position as Chair of the Department, she facilitated a multilingual approach to the teaching of African languages as from 2009. Her main field of interest is natural language processing of the Nguni languages (Zulu, Xhosa, Swati and Southern Ndebele) with specialisation in morphological analysis, and the development of supporting resources including underlying machine-readable lexicons. Her research projects on the technological development of the official languages aim to ultimately render automated services to citizens in their language of choice.

Adelia Carstens is Professor and Director of the Unit for Academic Literacy at the University of Pretoria, South Africa. She has a National Research Foundation rating, and holds two doctorates: one from the University of South Africa and one from the University of Pretoria. Carstens has published more than 50 papers in peer reviewed publications, and has delivered 45 papers at national and international conferences. She specialises in designing and developing curricula for undergraduate and postgraduate academic literacy interventions. Her research foci include multimodal meaning making and disciplinary writing in higher education.

Ingeborg M. Kosch is Professor in the Department of African Languages at the University of South Africa (UNISA) in Pretoria, where she obtained her doctoral degree in African Languages with a thesis entitled 'A survey of Northern Sotho grammatical descriptions since 1876'. She was part of the team that spearheaded a multilingual approach to the teaching of African languages in the department. Her research focuses on Northern Sotho linguistics, particularly morphology, which naturally feeds into her lexicographic interests. As editor of a scientific journal, she serves academics in the field of African languages and literature and has mentored many inexperienced authors.

Ernst Kotzé is Emeritus Professor, Nelson Mandela Metropolitan University, Port Elizabeth, and Research Associate and Postgraduate Contract Lecturer at Northwest University. Kotzé studied at the University of Cape Town, receiving a BA and BA(Hons) and an MA and PhD at the University of the Witwatersrand. He has lectured at University of the Witwatersrand (Johannesburg), University of Zululand, University of Port Elizabeth, Nelson Mandela Metropolitan University and Northwest University. Kotzé has been widely published in Afrikaans, Dutch, English, German, French and Japanese, with 43 books and chapters in books, 47 articles in accredited journals, 36 conference papers, five internet publications to his name. His research areas of interest are sociolinguistics, lexicography, language planning and policy, orthography, translation studies and forensic linguistics.

Lerothodi L. Leeuw is Professor at the University of South Africa where he is an astrophysicist and writer, whose short fiction won the Pringle Award from the English Academy of Southern Africa. Among his current research, he collaborates on an international astronomical study to assemble a large sample of gravitational lenses, study these systems and use them as a probe of the distribution and nature of dark matter in the Universe. At UNISA, he started an interdisciplinary community engagement project on the multilingual use and impact of planetarium in science education and outreach, one of the topics on which he researches and writes.

Leketi Makalela is Professor at the University of the Witwatersrand and he is an internationally known researcher in the field of language and education, particularly within the framework of multilingualism in South Africa. His special interest is translanguaging, with specific reference to African languages. He is also the current Editor-in-Chief of the journal *Southern African Linguistics and Applied Language Studies*.

Pamela Maseko is a senior lecturer in the African Language Studies Section of the School of Languages, and the former Co-ordinator of the South Africa–Norway Tertiary Education Development (SANTED) Multilingualism Project at Rhodes University in Grahamstown, South Africa. She holds a PhD that focuses on the intellectualisation of African languages. Her other research and teaching interests are Applied Language Studies, language policy and planning and language development.

Nomakhaya Mashiyi is Teaching-Learning Specialist in the Economic and Management Sciences Faculty at the University of the Western Cape in South Africa. She has extensive experience in the field of language education and teaching and learning in higher education. Her research interests include multilingualism, teaching and learning in higher education, the development of Graduate Attributes in curricula and information and communication technology-mediated support for staff to enhance teaching and learning. She holds a BA(Hons) and MEd in Second Language Teaching from the former University of Transkei and Rhodes University, respectively. She has a PhD in Education Policy Studies from the University of Pretoria.

Mbulungeni Madiba is Associate Professor of Linguistics and Co-ordinator of the Multilingualism Education Project at the University of Cape Town. He received his DLitt et Phil in Linguistics and an MA and BA(Hons) in African Languages from the University of South Africa. He is the recipient of fellowship awards as an Oppenheimer Fellow (University of London, UK) and

Mandela Fellow at Harvard University. His main fields of research include language planning and policy; politics of language, terminology and terminography, multilingual education, language and identity, corpus linguistics and human language technology. He has published numerous articles and book chapters.

Sandiso Ngcobo is Assistant Professor and Research Chairperson in the Faculty of Management Sciences at Mangosuthu University of Technology (MUT) where he lectures in the Department of Communication. He holds a PhD in linguistics and his research interests are in multilingual education, language attitudes, translation and the use of literature and technology to enhance the teaching of academic literacy and communication skills. In addition, he supervises postgraduate students in journalism and MBA. His research activities have been facilitated by funding from the National Research Foundation (NRF) Thuthuka Grant and MUT.

Andrea Parmegiani is Assistant Professor in the English Department at Bronx Community College of the City University of New York (CUNY). He received an MA in English (Creative Writing) from City College (CUNY), an MEd in Language and Literacy from the University of Cape Town, and a PhD in English from the Graduate Center (CUNY). He has done extensive research exploring language attitudes and practices in South Africa and their implications for identity construction and power relations. He has launched an integrated Spanish–English academic literacy development programme to increase retention and graduation rates among Latino students at Bronx Community College.

Stephanie Rudwick completed her MA in Linguistic Anthropology at the Ludwig-Maximilians University, Munich, and her PhD in Sociolinguistics at the University of KwaZulu-Natal (UKZN), Durban. She taught Linguistics at UKZN for five years and later held a post-doctoral fellowship from the South African National Research Foundation (NRF). In August 2013, she obtained a research position at Leipzig University, Germany, funded by the German Research Foundation (DFG). Her articles and book chapters, focusing mostly on language and identity, Zulu ethno-linguistics, and language policy, have appeared in several international Journals, including *World Englishes, Journal of Contemporary African Studies, African Studies Review*.

Preface

This volume provides a first-time overview of multilingual teaching and learning strategies tried and tested in a number of higher education institutions in South Africa. Detailed insights are provided into the case studies conducted and the implications this body of work has for further research. Situated practices by language and academic practitioners 'on the ground' demonstrate what is possible by drawing on students' available linguistic resources for strategic language development in the formal tertiary educational sector.

The focus is particularly on case studies, which include the use of African languages alongside English, and the resultant inter-discursiveness that constitutes successful cross-cultural communication for the purposes of intellectual pursuit.

Special Dedication

This book is dedicated to Neville Alexander, a mentor, teacher, politician and international activist who passed away in August 2012. Neville Alexander addressed the importance of developing African languages in South African Higher Education Institutions and warned against the negative effects of postcolonial language policies in Africa, which 'have made no more than nominal gestures towards equipping the indigenous languages of the continent with the wherewithal for use in powerful and high-status contexts' (2003: 14). He further expressed the belief that the constitutional recognition of 'the historically diminished use and status of the indigenous languages' and the call on the state to 'make practical and positive measures to elevate the status and advance the use of these languages' (South African constitution) serve as an example to the rest of Africa, where policy has generally continued to remain focused on the use of European languages for higher functions in society. The legacy of colonialism in Africa and continuing neo-colonial influence has resulted in sociolinguistic inequalities that threaten linguistic and cultural death among many minority language groups.

In addition, Neville was an academic, activist, a banned person, an author and an advocate for human rights for as long as we all knew him. The leadership and inspiration he provided at the Project for Alternative Education in South Africa (PRAESA) and at the Western Cape Language Committee have had, and will have, long-term repercussions for positive attitudes and the will to make things work in South Africa. In many ways, the research generated under his guidance changed the linguistic landscape in the education system and in government structures. He was an active member of ACALAN (African Academy of Languages) and was deeply concerned about the severe deterioration in education in the Eastern Cape Province, which prompted him to become involved in the Eastern Cape Economic Forum literacy arm, under Darryl Braam.

Acknowledgements

We would like to thank the following colleagues who assisted with the chapter review process:

Linda Kwatsha, Lyn Webb, Lee Kemp and Marcelle Harran at Nelson Mandela Metropolitan University; Mbulungeni Madiba at the University of Cape Town; Caroline Kerfoot and Felix Banda at the University of the Western Cape; and Cecile Jacobs and Michelle van der Merwe at Stellenbosch University. We would also like to thank Jenny Williams and Guy Rogers for assisting with the editing process.

Reference

Alexander, N. (2003) The African Renaissance and the use of African languages in tertiary education. PRAESA Occasional papers No 13. Cape Town: PRAESA.

The editors
11 June 2013

Part 1

Policy Development and the Opening up of Implementation Opportunities

1 Biliteracy and Translanguaging Pedagogy in South Africa: An Overview

Liesel Hibbert and Christa van der Walt

This book aims to showcase current multilingual teaching and learning innovations in higher education in South Africa. Although language-in-education policies for multilingual contexts have been in place for some years, and have been discussed and critiqued, there is no overview which highlights the processes and success stories of case studies conducted. We attempt to fill this gap by showcasing work done 'on the ground' by higher education practitioners as they develop ways of drawing on all available discourses and languages for strategic and systemically supported multilingual and biliteracy development in the formal tertiary education sector.

In the age of wide-scale global migration, language education discourses have been strategically geared for international economic participation, thereby favouring an English-only orientation in most instances. English is perceived as the world's lingua franca (Kim, 2009: 396) and higher education institutions (HEIs) that aspire to international recognition have to manage and plan for this perception. The way in which this happens is mapped out by Ritzen (2004: 39, *emphasis* added), the erstwhile rector of Maastricht University:

> [A]n international university then breaks away from the national ministry; *it adopts the medium of English for its education and research;* it establishes educational programmes based around issues of social, economic and cultural relevance to the wider international community.

These decisions are increasingly made in Europe (Marginson & Van der Wende, 2007: 5) as well as in South America (Gacel-Ávila *et al.*, 2005), China (Li & Wang, 2010) and India (Amritavalli & Jayaseelan, 2007: 78), to name a few, resulting in bi-/multilingual institutions. In Africa, the use of colonial languages offers a two-in-one solution: such languages act as instruments that should compel a national identity as well as access ready-made educational materials (Muthwii & Kioko, 2004: 2). English plays this role in Anglophone countries, but is also being introduced at HEIs that, in the past, used French, Portuguese and Arabic as languages of learning and teaching (LoLTs). In countries where English has been the LoLT for a long time, as in the USA, Canada, England, Australia and New Zealand, the transnational mobility of students has resulted in campuses becoming increasingly multilingual. As noted in van der Walt (2013: 15),

> The complexity of multilingual academic environments requires the acknowledgement that academic language itself is a particular variety of a standard language and as such favours those students who use a variety perceived to be close to the high-status LoLT. Furthermore, transnational HE students will already have developed academic literacy in another language as well as a degree of fluency in the LoLT that they will be using at another HEI. They cannot, therefore, be seen as 'language deficient' but should rather be seen as emerging bi-literates.

From this brief description, it is clear that higher education is becoming increasingly multilingual as a result of internationalisation drives, the expectations of transnational students and the effects of colonialism. Monolingual language policies or attempts to impose monolingual classroom practices in such an educational landscape can only be seen as relics of a bygone era.

This situation makes for interesting dilemmas in the analysis of localised discursive practices in formal tertiary education. The multilingual practices of students outside formal educational encounters (such as lectures, seminars and tests) find their way into the classroom, where students are able to draw on literacies that they may have developed to a high level at secondary school level. In view of the economic imperatives to improve throughput rates, HEIs can hardly ignore the existing literacies and competencies that students bring to their institutions. The challenge, as indicated by Blackledge and Creese (2010: 206), is to harness existing multilingual practices for pedagogical gain. The concept of *translanguaging* and its application to higher education classrooms is crucial in this regard.

The concept of translanguaging was first used by Williams (2002: 2) to describe a language practice that is widespread in education and, as he indicates, 'simply means (i) receiving information in one language and (ii) using or applying it in the other language'. The term is used widely now to cover a variety of multilingual practices, including code-switching, translation and simultaneous interpretation in multilingual classrooms, as the contributions in this book will show. What is important for all higher education practitioners to understand is that such practices will occur whether or not they are mandated by lecturers or policy makers, since students will use the strategies and literacies that they have developed up to that point to further their education. When such strategies are acknowledged and fostered, a climate is created in which languages are seen as resources (Ruiz, 1994) rather than as problems that need to be eliminated. Even when students' languages are not used for academic purposes, they can still be mobilised to explore and contextualise their academic studies.

In this regard, we argue that discourses in regulated and unregulated spaces, as indicated by Sebba (2007), should be viewed on a continuum, rather than as binary opposites. In this manner, discourses in unregulated spaces can provide scaffolding to support academic discourses, if mobilised strategically. Hornberger's *continua of biliteracy* (1989, and Hornberger & Skilton-Sylvester, 2000) provide a useful heuristic by means of which the interplay of languages (inasmuch as they can be enumerated) can be analysed, described and managed. The continua of biliteracy are presented by Hornberger (2007: 184) as sets of interconnected relationships where factors that play a role in multilingual contexts can be plotted on a continuum in terms of the contexts, media, content and development of biliteracy (see Mashiyi in Chapter 9 for a more detailed description). It is important to note that the continua are not limited to educational contexts, but when we interpret them in terms of higher education, they provide clues for the 'harnessing' (Blackledge & Creese, 2010: 206) of multilingual practices for pedagogical purposes. The communities within which students communicate on a daily basis, which can range from oral and multilingual at the one end of the continuum to literate and monolingual at the other, provide the two ends of the *context of biliteracy continuum*. The degree to which students are exposed to or confronted with language(s) is expressed in terms of the two ends of the *media of biliteracy*, with exposure to more than one language simultaneously at one end and successively at the other. The extent to which languages are available for academic purposes is denoted by the *content of biliteracy*, where students may move from minority to majority languages, from the vernacular to the literary. The final continuum involves the *development of biliteracy*, which, in higher education contexts will involve the acquisition of (at least) a second academic literacy as students move from reception to production, starting with the production of oral and then moving to written production, which Airey (2009) refers to as *bilingual scientific literacy*. At school level, Hornberger (2007: 186) argues that 'what is needed is attention to oral, multilingual interaction at the micro level of context and to learners' first language oral, and receptive language skills development (that is, to the traditionally less powerful ends of the continua)'. One implication of this argument is that even minoritised languages that are perceived to require development as academic languages have their place in higher education.

The value of this book is that it provides examples of how such efforts could lead to academic success. We display work that relates not only to the inclusion of African languages in HEIs, informally, but also as languages of learning, and the resultant inter-discursiveness and translanguaging. We also include chapters that demonstrate to what extent the creation of linguistic and social-affinity spaces, including the use of new technologies, benefit language development. In addition, chapters that focus on identity and identification processes in multilingual learning and teaching spaces emphasise the role of language and languages as identity markers.

The book includes a variety of approaches, that is, single-disciplinary and multi-disciplinary approaches that include discourse analysis with all its emanations (critical discourse analysis (CDA), socio-cultural discourse analysis, etc.), interactional sociolinguistics and pragmatics, as well as personal reflexive narrative accounts and auto-ethnography.

In an increasingly globalised higher education context, this collection is of interest to higher education practitioners, policy makers and academic development professionals; in fact, to anyone teaching or researching at a linguistically diverse institution of higher learning. As argued previously, the multilingual demands of internationalising drives and the resultant transnational student mobility have created a multilingual higher education landscape – whether existing policies acknowledge this or not. In the South African context, where an ambitious national multilingual Language Policy for Higher Education (2009) is a form of redress for minoritised African languages, HEIs actively attempt to include African languages. The South African case studies thus provide promising glimpses of multilingual pedagogies and practices that can be applied globally, particularly in cases where marginalised languages and communities are struggling to access higher education successfully.

South Africa is not the only country where multilingual learning and teaching is a feature of higher education. Some institutions, particularly those known as 'historically Afrikaans', use English and Afrikaans in ways that are similar to strategies used at, for example, the University of Fribourg,

Switzerland, where German and French are used, or the University of Ottawa, Canada, where French and English are used (see van der Walt, 2013 for a comprehensive overview). What makes South Africa unique, however, is the inclusion of minoritised languages and the fact that languages are not necessarily separated in classrooms. Code-switching, translation and interpreting take place in one classroom, supporting the translanguaging practices that students and lecturers are accustomed to employing outside the classroom too.

English is generally by far the most desirable LoLT globally, which means that a world population of speakers of other languages is accommodated because they are able to mobilise the intellectual skills they have in their primary languages, for academic purposes. At the moment, there are no competing titles and although loose-standing studies have been published in a variety of journals, no collection of South African case studies exists. In this volume, we seek to fill a unique gap in the market by drawing on practices developed locally, rather than drawing on studies from abroad for theory formulation and for the design of case studies, as has been the tradition for South African researchers and lecturers.

Our main aim is to showcase work done by a new generation of academics. The chapters were commissioned in an attempt to showcase practices that are valuable, but invisible, either because of the fairly underdeveloped research culture in some of South Africa's institutions of higher learning, or because of the pervasive conviction that multilingualism is simply a positive spin-off of deficient English language proficiency. We envision that the book will come across as a definite move away from endless policy discussions to cutting-edge experimentation at the interface of social and linguistic realities 'out there'. In the process, concrete modifications of institutional agendas are proposed in order to meet the challenges of these realities.

The case studies and narratives that follow are examples of bilingual pedagogy in action. Inherent in the conceptualisation of this book, as a whole, are two major points of departure from previous perspectives on the position of African languages, namely:

- A critique of the view of African languages as 'whole bounded systems' (as can be seen in the contributions by Kosch and Bosch, Makalela, Madiba and Leeuw);
- An alternative to English-only orientations, by showing how translanguaging and biliteracy promote the motivational, cognitive and linguistic development of students (as described by the abovementioned authors, as well as Maseko, Parmegiani and Rudwick, Ngcobo and Mashiyi).

The Next Generation: Innovation and Development

Studies on the use of language in higher education often focus on the introduction of English as a LoLT or on a deficit view of students' language proficiency. In this publication, we see language as a resource (Ruiz, 1994) and focus on the introduction of minoritised languages as languages of learning in higher education. In Africa, the debates about home languages in education focus mostly on primary school levels and that is why this book not only highlights the importance of language in mediating complex academic materials, but also makes the role of African languages more visible. As the new generation of South African scholars demonstrates, the increasing diversity in higher education needs to reflect the diversity of languages used by students who did not have access to higher education before the first democratic elections in 1994.

The contributions by these new voices demonstrate both a wide and a narrow focus on multilingual pedagogies, that is, the wide focus on the importance of indigenous languages in education on the one hand, and the particular case studies of transformational classroom practice, on the other hand. The theme that runs through all the contributions in this book is that informal language practices in society need to inform classroom language practices in higher education, not the other way around.

The case studies and narratives show that translanguaging and biliteracy pedagogy significantly influence student performance, that student and lecturer/tutor attitudes are shown as a major variable affecting language development and that Africanisation of content (curriculum transformation, which leads directly to institutional transformation) is a major factor influencing language development of the students.

Significantly improved student performance

Mbulungeni Madiba's chapter focuses on African language glossaries used as scaffolding for the acquisition of concepts in English. He demonstrates that translanguaging in practice by lecturers and students has clearly become the default norm in South African higher education, as it has been in the schools for decades. His findings show first, that the interactive online learning environment (e.g. blogs, podcasts, pictures and glossaries) appeals to the young because of easy access and is therefore ideal for the support of concept development. Second, such an environment shows that translanguaging is critical for making the concept one's own, in the psychological sense.

The difficulty of trying to control and manage language use is foregrounded by Makalela, who agrees with Shohamy (2006: 165) that:

We can try to create all kinds of controlling devices, rules, regulations, laws, correctness, categories, policies, impositions; in life, we also create ceremonies, anniversaries, prayers, ritual, insurances, and other devices, all through the desire to impose order; but it does not work.

Makalela reports on experimentation with the teaching of Sepedi, by getting students to explore their knowledge of terms and structures in related African languages to contrast and compare them with Sepedi equivalents/approximations. In this way, students discover common cultural backgrounds. The teacher trainees who are the recipients of this language acquisition programme have to learn at least one new language in order to qualify as teachers. This does not, however, mean that they have to teach the language, just that they are compelled to go through a language learning process in order to experience, first-hand, how African languages overlap in their cultural and linguistic characteristics. He calls this the 'Ubuntu language methodology' (The isiXhosa word *Ubuntu* is translated as 'I am because you are'), which is a departure from Linguistic Tribalism that was prevalent in the teaching of African languages in 1953–1990. The main finding of Makalela's study is that the students find the translanguaging pedagogy linguistically and culturally transformative and enabling, which correlates with the findings of Blommaert *et al.* (2005: 197).

Mashiyi focuses on the experiences of lecturers with the biliteracy continuum. The study leads to the conclusion that if lecturers integrate the continua of biliteracy model into their student-centred pedagogy, they not only challenge existing hidden discourses of power and language, but also visibly improve student performance. The findings here are that, first, integrating the less and more powerful ends of the continuum of biliteracy enhances teaching and learning, as well as student and language performance. Second, where the lecturer's and the student's languages are not the same, the situation becomes very challenging. Lastly, ideological stances of lecturers have an impact on student performance, as the next cluster of studies show.

Affective aspects of biliteracy pedagogy

Student and lecturer/tutor attitudes were identified as a major variable by Parmegiani and Rudwick, by Ngcobo, and also by Mashiyi. Parmegiani and Rudwick sound a word of warning, by showing that students should not be compelled to choose between powerful LoLTs, but that a dominant LoLT needs to be offered with local/community languages to build on the translanguaging practices of students. One of the major findings of their study is that students prefer to use isiZulu/English in the classroom, as they do off campus, rather than pure isiZulu, because they are sceptical about the marketability of pure isiZulu skills for career purposes and are also worried about losing opportunities to develop their English.

Linking up with Parmegiani and Rudwick, Ngcobo assesses attitudes to African languages in dual-language instruction (isiZulu–English), using teaching and learning course material for engineering students in a course of Academic Literacy and Communication Skills to assess if such instruction would have an impact on language-in-education attitudes of the participants. The difference between school-based models of bilingual education and multilingual classrooms in higher education is clearly demonstrated when he finds that lecturer's decisions about code-switching in the classroom need to be based on reflexive reports from students. Three findings came to light. First, biliteracy/translanguaging approaches should be informed foremost by the needs of students and studies such as those by Vygotsky (1986, 1994), revealing the relationship between language and education. Second, negative attitudes to mother-tongue instruction only change with experience of mother-tongue instruction over three years. Third, and most crucially, to meet the students' career path needs, a pedagogy that aims to develop academic biliteracy needs to ensure high quality exposure and language developmental opportunities for English.

Africanisation of content (curriculum transformation, which leads directly to institutional transformation) as a major variable

Pamela Maseko presents a discussion on teaching, learning and research in the African Language Studies Section of the School of Languages, Rhodes University. She explains how the section adopted the provisions of the national policy and institutional policy on language in turning itself into a source of intellectual vitality in the teaching, learning and research of isiXhosa.

This chapter clearly demonstrates that political will, as well as funding, addresses the backlogs in African language use and intellectual engagement (as was militated against in previous decades) much more rapidly than could have been anticipated by anyone at the onset.

The problematic way in which African languages were constructed in apartheid times is shown to have resulted in an artificial separation of related languages. Kosch and Bosch show how these distinctions resulted in a particular structure for the UNISA (University of South Africa), Department of African languages. They explain how the department has acknowledged the fact that African languages have evolved in ways that make particular distinctions among languages a fairly complex task.

Bosch and Kosch show how the curriculum has recently been developed to meet the 'needs out there'. They argue for Africanised content and delivery, and explain how African languages were historically taught as totally separate entities from 1873 onwards (as a result of the missionary transcriptions/interpretations of these languages). In 1946, a purely grammar-orientated comparative approach was used in which students had to show how well they could distinguish one language from another. After 1994, a huge drop in student numbers in African languages was experienced in the country, to such an extent that African language departments were virtually closed down or had to amalgamate with other language departments. This was owing to the perception that they had no place in the future. Bosch and Kosch describe the multilingual 'basket approach' used at UNISA, which constitutes an important contribution to social and political curriculum redress by bringing the programmes in line with general language practices. From 2006, online blended learning made it possible for African languages to be taught again, without having to employ too many staff.

In 2009, the Africanisation of learning material in African languages started being put in place at UNISA. Examples of courses which then emerged are Communication Dynamics in African Languages, Indigenous Knowledge Systems and African Languages and Creative Writing and Translation, thereby creating a properly engaged learning community.

The contribution by Leeuw links up with the ground-breaking work done by Ramani *et al.* (2007) and shows that the use of marginalised languages is not simply a matter of using translating in the classroom: African languages represent indigenous knowledge systems (IKSs) that are not generally familiar and therefore not recognised. In a description of the way in which the BaTswana people traditionally conceptualise terms in astronomy, the indigenous knowledge that Leeuw shares provides a fresh perspective on traditional male labelling of celestial bodies in Western paradigms, showing how BaTswana culture views constellations of stars and the moon as female entities.

Leeuw demonstrates how astrophysics can be taught, comparing a SeTswana IKS to Western interpretations of the night sky. This type of pedagogy (according to Banks, 2011: 38) includes first, the *transformative* approach, which gives the opportunity for the students to see the subject from several perspectives, perhaps even allow them to delve into the impact or usefulness of the added context on the mainstream subject. Second, the pedagogy includes the *decision-making* or *action* approach. Students have a chance to make decisions and take action based on the added content, and therefore the approach also helps the students to develop their thinking skills, empowers them and allows them to acquire a sense of their own role in knowledge production and hence a feeling of efficacy (Banks, 2011; Cumming-McCann, 2003).

In the chapter by Carstens and Alston they ask first, 'What multiliterate and multilingual identities do students construct for themselves?' and second, 'How can knowledge of these identities inform curriculum design and classroom practice?'. Carstens and Alston used pre-service teacher trainees as their subjects to collect data consisting of literacy narratives. The narratives were part of the academic literacy course. The assignment given to the students was to write about one or more types of literacy that have meaning for them. The students were asked to write an essay of 700 to 1000 words telling the story of how they had acquired one or more types of literacy that have special meaning for them. After analysing the essay corpus in terms of sponsor identities, Carstens and Alston found that there was a gap in current research which identifies the role of various sponsors in the language learning process. They suggest the implementation of curriculum changes, as well as classroom exercises, that would help teacher trainees to critically reflect on the roles that sponsors play in the literacy development of learners. In terms of evaluating this outcome critically, this finding points to the fact that if one is looking for data *only* from the learners in the formal school environment, one does not have the whole picture. An in-depth ethnographic approach is what is needed in identifying the role of all sponsors in the process.

The student narratives confirm the complexity of the nature–nurture acquisition debate. The author's use of the plant metaphors as an analytical tool to illuminate students' tacit knowledge of their own learning mode and style is highly original and makes this case study replicable.

Conclusion

Ouane (2009: 59, *emphasis* added) says of simplistic perceptions of multilingual contexts, that 'the monolingual habitus does not take into account the intermeshing of languages *within* multilinguals and in communities, across social domains and communicative practices'. The case studies and narratives in this book exemplify the determination of students and lecturers to exploit their multilingualism for learning and teaching. The chapters show the following three groups of results regarding translanguaging and biliteracy:

- That pedagogy significantly improved student performance.
- That student and lecturer or tutor attitudes constitute a major variable in attempts to include multilingual teaching and learning practices.
- That the use of IKSs leads to curriculum transformation and to institutional transformation in turn.

These studies describe first steps in developing a pedagogy of multilingual teaching and learning. The new generation of academics who use African languages in higher education empower their students to succeed at that level and they are the pioneers in this developing pedagogy.

References

Airey, J. (2009) *Science, Language and Literacy: Case Studies of Learning in Swedish University Physics*. Uppsala, Sweden: Uppsala University.

Amritavalli, R. and Jayaseelan, K.A. (2007) India. In A. Simpson (ed.) *Language and National Identity in Asia* (pp. 55–83). Oxford: Oxford University Press.

Banks, J.A. (2011) Multicultural education: Goals and dimensions. Blog. See http://education.washington.edu/cme/view.htm (accessed 15 January 2014).

Blackledge, A. and Creese, A. (2010) *Multilingualism*. New York: Continuum.

Blommaert, J., Collins, J. and Slembrouck, S. (2005) Spaces of multilingualism. *Language & Communication* 25 (3), 197–216.

Cumming-McCann, A. (2003) Multicultural education: Connecting theory to practice. *Focus on Basics: Connecting Research and Practice* 6 (B), 9–12.

Gacel-Ávila, J. (2005) Internationalization of higher education in Mexico. In H. de Wit, I.C. Jaramillo, J. Gacel-Ávila and J. Knight (eds) *Higher Education in Latin America: The International Dimension* (pp. 239–280). Washington: The World Bank.

Hornberger, N. (2007) Multilingual language policies and the continua of biliteracy: An ecological approach. In O. García and C. Baker (eds) *Bilingual Education: An Introductory Reader* (pp. 177–194). Clevedon: Multilingual Matters.

Hornberger, N.H. and Skilton-Sylvester, E. (2000) Revisiting the continua of literacy: international and critical perspectives. *Language and Education: An International Journal* 14 (2), 96–122.

Kim, T. (2009) Shifting patterns of transnational academic mobility: A comparative and historical approach. *Comparative Education* 45 (3), 387–403.

Language Policy for Higher Education (2009) Pretoria: Ministry of Education. See http://www.wsu.ac.za/campuslife/indaba/documents/Language%20Policy%20for%20Higher%20Education.pdf (accessed 15 January 2014).

Li, Y. and Wang, L. (2010) A survey on bilingual teaching in higher education institutes in the northeast of China. *Journal of Language Teaching and Research* 1 (4), 353–357.

Marginson, S. and Van der Wende, M. (2007) Globalisation and higher education (Education Working Paper No. 8). Paris: OECD Education Working Papers Series. See http://doc.utwente.nl/60264/1/Marginson07globalisation.pdf (accessed 15 January 2014).

Muthwii, M.J. and Kioko, N.D. (eds) (2004) Editorial: A fresh question for new language bearings in Africa. *New Language Bearings in Africa* (pp. 1–9). Clevedon: Multilingual Matters.

Ouane, A. (2009) My journey to and through a multilingual landscape. In K. Kwaa Prah and B. Brock-Utne (eds) *Multilingualism: An African Advantage* (pp. 53–61). Cape Town, South Africa: Centre for Advanced Studies of African Society.

Ramani, E., Kekana, T., Modiba, M. and Joseph, M. (2007) Terminology development versus concept development through discourse: Insights from a dual-medium BA degree. *Southern African Linguistics and Applied Language Studies* 25 (2), 207–223.

Ritzen, J. (2004) Across the bridge: Towards an international university. In R. Wilkinson (ed.) *Integrating Content and Language: Meeting the Challenge of a Multilingual Higher Education* (pp. 28–40). Maastricht, MA: Universitaire Pers.

Ruiz, R. (1994) Language policy and planning in the United States. *Annual Review of Applied Linguistics* 14, 111–125.

Sebba, M. (2007) *Spelling and Society*. Cambridge: Cambridge University Press.

Shohamy, E. (2006) *Language Policy: Hidden Agendas and New Approaches*. New York: Routledge.

van der Walt, C. (2013) Active biliteracy? Students taking decisions about using languages for academic purposes. In H. Haberland, D. Lønsmann and B. Preisler (eds) *Language Alternation, Language Choice and Language Encounter in International Education* (pp. 103–124). Heidelberg: Springer.

Vygotsky, L.S. (1986) *Thought and Language*. Cambridge: Massachusetts Institute of Technology.

Vygotsky, L.S. (1994) The development of thinking and concept formation in school-aged children. In R. Van der Veer and J. Valsiner (eds) *The Vygotsky Reader* (pp. 355–370). Cambridge, MA: Blackwell.

Williams, C. (2002) Extending bilingualism in the education system. Report by the Education and Lifelong Learning Committee, National Assembly for Wales. See http://www.assemblywales.org/3c91c7af00023d820000595000000000.pdf (accessed 15 January 2014).

2 The Emergence of a Favourable Policy Landscape

Ernst Kotzé

Introduction

Almost 20 years after the advent of democracy in South Africa (SA), in the changeover from a bilingual (English and Afrikaans) to a purportedly multilingual dispensation, accompanied by the constitutional recognition of 11 languages, a balance can be drawn up of the extent to which this recognition has been reflected by the implementation of education policies. In spite of empirical research into various aspects of the role played by language in education in this country, and proposals aimed at giving effect to the constitutional ideals, a tacit policy of monolingualism has been in evidence. In this policy background discussion, it will be argued that a linguistic social Darwinist approach, which applies the linguistic framework to Darwin's biological theories of the realm of human social relations (Dafler, 2005: 1), has been followed in the handling of language matters in education at large. Attitudinal factors therefore play (and will play) a decisive role in effecting a paradigm shift, not only among educational policy makers, but also within the minds of all role players. Such a paradigm shift, which is a prerequisite for generating the political will to effectively implement any proposals based on empirical research, can be shown to have taken root in the thinking of political policy makers at the parliamentary level. However, recognition of the realities of language in education is still lacking at the level of implementation.

By way of the case studies presented in this book, it is shown that much valuable implementation work is in motion on the ground. This is owing to the convictions and dedication of practitioners who have obtained experience and expertise, and have been teaching bilingually for perhaps decades, without waiting for any policy directives. The successful teaching methodologies of these practitioners have, however, not been sufficiently publicised in order to contribute to blueprints of 'best practice'. The case studies in this book testify to the sensitivity to African languages, heritages and cultural trajectories displayed by these practitioners. Compelled by their convictions, they have set pedagogical processes in motion, with or without the stamp of approval from above, whether it be the institution or the policy stakeholder group. The overview given here outlines the importance of this work from a theoretical perspective and in terms of trends in the wider matrix.

The point of departure is that language in education is one of the most sensitive indicators of the viability of a national policy of multilingualism. In this introductory discussion, the role played by attitudinal factors in the implementation of a multilingual education policy is highlighted. The focus is on a possible motivating force causing the resistance to vernacular language development and its effects on education, and certain changes in attitude that occurred in the course of the evolution of SAs fledgling democracy since 1994. The role players in this process will be identified and it will be shown how the changes in attitude became apparent through the tone and content of debates on the topic in an important policy-making body. At the same time, factors that seem to have a positive influence on the acknowledgement of the value of a multilingual approach will be identified, leading to the proposal of a reality-based approach to be followed to create conditions for the implementation of a viable policy of multilingual education.

Background

The political history of Africa, and in particular the process of emancipation from the status of colonies under the sovereignty of European nations to political independence, left its imprint in the form of rather similar language configurations in the ex-colonies. A common factor is namely that of both individual and societal multilingualism in African countries, in which a European language, such as English, Portuguese or French, plays a dominant role as the medium for higher functions. A second common factor, a corollary of the first, is that of sociolinguistic inequality between the erstwhile colonial language and the indigenous languages of the African country concerned. This inequality is nowhere more clearly seen than in the role historically played by language in education, from the earliest introduction of formal schooling until today. By saying this, we do not deny the important role of language in other spheres of society. However, it is probably an axiom that language habits and perceptions are formed during the cognitive development of the rising generations, that is, in the process of education, and old habits tend to persist. Furthermore, it is these language habits and perceptions that form the basis of language attitudes, both towards the vernacular used as a home, or first language and the erstwhile colonial language, which is used, almost without exception, as a language of learning in Africa.

Generalisations

Let us leave aside for a moment the reasons for the sociolinguistic inequalities between the vernacular(s) (henceforth the V-language) and the relevant European language (henceforth the E-language), and focus on the nature of language in education policies. This is no simple matter when one compares various countries on the African continent with each other. However, the language situation in the field of education could possibly be generalised to two basic situations:

- An E-language is regarded as the most important medium for higher functions in society (and consequently for education), while indigenous languages fulfil a subordinate position and only play a role in basic education (if at all), as in the case of African countries in the French, Portuguese and (in the most cases) English spheres of influence.
- One or more indigenous languages (V-languages) are, in principle, developed as far as possible on a par with the E-language or to a certain extent, and also used as medium of education, in various combinations (as in the case of Kenya, Tanzania, Nigeria and SA).

Of these two situations, the first represents the easiest route in terms of language planning, and in countries where the second situation applies, there seems to be a tendency (for reasons that will be discussed below) to yield, in varying degrees, to the easiest route and diminish the role of the V-languages.

A crucial decision is what the role of the V-languages as the medium of education should be in situations of multilingualism. The argument that the V-language should be the only medium is almost never an issue. A common practice is that the vernacular is used as a bridge to the adoption of the E-language (or dominant indigenous language, such as Swahili).

Motivating Force and End Results

The reason(s) for the preference for a colonial language have been the subject of discussion for many years. In a recent publication, Stephen May (2001: chaps 1 and 4) links this tendency to a combination of so-called linguistic social Darwinism and a resulting theory of modernity. He says:

> The promotion of cultural and linguistic homogeneity at the collective/public level has come to be associated with, and expressed by, individual monolingualism. This amounts to a form of linguistic social Darwinism and also helps to explain why language shift, loss or decline has become so prominent.

This argument articulates an evolutionary discourse, assuming that sociopolitical change and language shift occur through the aggregation of individual rational choices and that individuals freely endorse new sets of values to participate in the 'modernisation of society'. In the process, a series of dichotomies is established, creating hierarchies of values and norms, in which traditional values become obsolete and/or suspiciously irrational: modernity is equated with progress – and modern, urban, universal values are lauded and confer prestige – while traditional, rural, parochial values are stigmatised (May, 2001: 141).

If this process is left unattended and allowed to run its course, linguistic and cultural death can become inevitable. One of the clearest symptoms is the phenomenon of language shift, which is described as follows:

> [A] 'majority' language – that is, a language with greater political power, privilege and social prestige – comes to replace the range and functions of a 'minority' language. The inevitable result of this process is that speakers of the minority language 'shift' over time to speaking the majority language. The process of language shift described here usually involves three broad stages. The first stage sees increasing pressure on minority language speakers to speak the majority language, particularly in formal language domains. This stage is often precipitated and facilitated by the introduction of education in the majority language. It leads to the eventual decrease in the functions of the minority language, with the public or official functions of that language being the first to be replaced by the majority language. The second stage sees a period of bilingualism, in which both languages continue to be spoken concurrently. However, this stage is usually characterised by a decreasing

number of minority language speakers, especially among the younger generation, along with a decrease in the fluency of speakers as the minority language is spoken less and employed in fewer and fewer language domains. The third and final stage – which may occur over the course of two or three generations, and sometimes less – sees the replacement of the minority language with the majority language. The minority language may be 'remembered' by a residual group of language speakers, but it is no longer spoken as a wider language of communication. (May, 2001: 1)

There are many variations of this process, but it seems to be the most general symptom of linguistic social Darwinism on the African continent. Language planners, and particularly those involved in education, are often intuitively aware of this tide, and are increasingly also informed about the results of research confirming the mind-set of such language communities. If so, they are able to appeal to reason and influence the relevant role players.

Modernity and Language in Education in SA

The focus here will be on the dynamics of a multilingual situation in an African country where changes have taken place as a result of large scale political and social transformation, and where language and education have been in the forefront of the quest for modernity, that is, SA. With the adoption of 11 official languages in SA, the relative positions of all indigenous languages (including Afrikaans) changed completely. While English is the undisputed *de facto* language of preference in government (including the Department of Education), five of the V-languages (i.e. isiZulu, isiXhosa, Afrikaans, Northern Sesotho and Setswana) have larger mother tongue communities than English (Van der Merwe & Van der Merwe, 2006: 15) and are in principle sufficiently standardised to be used as media of instruction up to an advanced level of education, as are the remaining five, to varying extents. (The language provisions of the constitution (Republic of South Africa, 1996c, SA Constitution, Section 6.5, the activities of the Pan South African Language Board (PanSALB), and published language policies by the Department of Education are also in support of this objective.) However, conflict between language attitudes have led to an almost stalemate situation in promulgating legislation, which has been drafted and in existence for more than a decade, to give effect to a general recognition of accepted principles of multilingualism and of the value of first language education (as medium) in empowering the youth of this country.

Turning of the tide

We now briefly look at how attitudes have changed regarding language in education by noting the reports of meetings held by policy makers over a period of time. A drama of 10 to 11 years unfolded in the committee rooms of parliament, with the following dramatis personae:

(a) The parliamentary Portfolio Committee on Education, consisting of members of various political parties, where proposed legislation and policy are analysed and debated before being submitted to parliament as draft legislation.
(b) The Minister of Education.
(c) The executive officials of the Department of Education.
(d) PanSALB, the Pan South African Language Board, created by the SA Constitution (Republic of South Africa 1996c, SA Constitution, Section 6.5) to promote and create conditions for the development and use of all languages in the country.

As a run-up to the functioning of the Portfolio Committee, the Department of Education published two policy announcements in August 1997, that is, the *Language in Education Policy* (Department of Education, 1997) (in terms of the National Education Policy Act of 1996 (Republic of South Africa, 1996b) and the *Norms and Standards Regarding Language Policy*, in terms of the SA Schools Act (Republic of South Africa, 1996a). This policy was based on the NEPI (National Education Policy Initiative) report, a well researched 13 volume investigation into various aspects of education in SA, published in 1992 (Department of Education, 1992). In the policy, the promotion of multilingualism was stated as a prime objective, together with strong support for either home language or dual-medium education. Although the right to choose the language of learning and teaching (LoLT) lay with the individual, it was to be exercised against the obligation to promote multilingualism, and the LoLT had to be an official language(s) (refer to Appendix A for the wording of the policy statements).

After three and a half years, in February 2001, a meeting of the Education Portfolio Committee was held to discuss a PanSALB presentation and the recommendations to the Minister and the Department of Education on the implementation of the Language in Education Policy. (See Maseko's description of the relevant policy and legislative frameworks in Chapter 3.) It was noted by PanSALB that the policy had still not been implemented. In fact, a previous policy of switching to English after four years of home language education, already instituted in 1976 (the year of the Soweto uprisings), with disastrous results regarding the matric pass rate, had been continued, as under the apartheid rule. This was despite intensive research into the effects of an abrupt switch to English undertaken by various research institutions. The arguments and detailed recommendations by PanSALB were swept off the table by the Committee, including the then Director General of Education, who maintained that language was only a small element influencing results, and that poor performance was a class issue, where schools with a lack of resources fared poorly. A question to the Director General about the importance of mother tongue education in performance was disallowed by the Chairperson (Parliamentary Monitoring Group, 2001: 1).

In July 2006, a language colloquium was held in Cape Town, attended by the then Chairperson of PanSALB, the president of the Academy of Languages in Mali, parents of pupils and others, where the Minister confirmed the Department's intention to comply with the aims of the 1997 policy statement. An important statement made by the Minister was as follows:

> The benefits that language diversity confers on any society far outstrip any advantages that monolingualism may offer. All recent research confirms this view.

Further:

> It is also now conventional wisdom that a strong mother tongue foundation provides the best platform on which to base the learning of a second language; it makes it easier and faster.

Lastly:

> There is also mounting evidence that a correlation exists between mother tongue loss and the educational difficulties experienced by many learners using another language for learning. (Pandor, 2006: 2)

The 2006 colloquium in Cape Town, preceded by a change of political role players (although from the same parties) after a general election, led to a different approach and tone of debate in the Portfolio Committee.

From this point onwards, meetings by the Portfolio Committee took no issue with the right to be educated in the mother tongue while having access to a global language such as English, even though it countered the dominant view among teachers and parents that English should be the medium of education as early as possible. A summary of a meeting held in September of 2006 (Parliamentary Monitoring Group, 2006) reads as follows:

> [T]he Committee agreed that advocacy was needed to convince parents, school governing bodies and teachers of the advantages of home language education.

The major problem to be addressed by the Committee was a matter of attitude, a general attitude of 'you need to speak English and if you speak your mother tongue, it will slow down the development of your English' (Parliamentary Monitoring Group, 2006: 2). The power to change this mind-set did not lie with the Committee, but with the schools, and these were not convinced. The question now was how this mind-set was to be changed.

A two-pronged approach

Positive factors are: (1) that the Department's own reference base (e.g. Plüddemann *et al.*, 2004) and the Wits-EPU report of 2009 showed time and again that cognitive development and academic achievement were markedly superior in schools where the home language was used as medium of education, and (2) that the major role players who oversee education policy are in agreement, by and large, about the necessity to implement the policy principles, and about the need for advocacy so as to convince teachers and parents about the validity of these principles.

Negative factors are: (1) in addition to the mind-set conditioned by the element of linguistic social Darwinism, fewer and fewer prospective teachers specialise in indigenous languages, or they are simply not able to teach their subjects in the mother tongue, and (2) although a majority of teachers, particularly in rural schools where English is the LoLT, switch to the home language to make themselves clearly understood, examination papers still have to be in English. The ironic situation exists that in many, if not most, instances the teacher and the class share the same home language, but the tuition has to be in a language in which neither of the two parties is proficient. Even the accommodating gesture by the Department to translate some key examination papers into the mother tongues of candidates to provide more clarity to the learners was only partially effective, since the papers still had to be answered in English.

It seems to be clear, from an analysis of the series of events over the past 20 years and the pace of development towards the engaged recognition of the multilingual nature of education, that a two-pronged approach is necessary: (a) a long-term process in which positive attitudes towards the vernacular and an acknowledgement of its formative and economic value are inculcated; and

(b) a short- to medium-term approach that deals with the status quo at hand in the most appropriate way. The following remark by Webb and Kembo-Sure (2000: 7), regarding the results of non-mother tongue education in South African schools, supports the long-term approach: 'The decision of school authorities and parents to use English as the language of learning in schools (especially primary schools) has definitely contributed to the underdevelopment of the South African people'. One of the tasks that language practitioners in SA need to undertake is to persuade parents that the answer to their needs and those of the children lies in the language of learning that their children know well, together with high-quality teaching of English as a subject. While education policies addressing the needs of a multilingual society can be implemented at short notice at the primary and secondary school level (as has been the case with new policies in the SA context during the past decade), the end result can only be expected to filter through to the tertiary level after an extensive period of exposure to the new paradigm. A different approach is therefore needed to ensure that the maximum benefits of a multilingual policy are derived by universities in the short to medium term.

Current paradigms affecting language policy

Recent years have seen a shift from second language acquisition theories to one of cognitive and linguistic development embedded in social and discourse theory. The notion of additive and mother tongue-based bilingualism has largely been replaced by that of simultaneous biliteracy, namely what García (2007) advocates as 'dynamic plurilingualism'. She defines this as a two-way polydirectional bilingual education. Her emphasis is on translanguaging in the classroom. By this she means that the teacher and the learners move between two languages as a matter of routine. The aim of literacy development, regardless of language, is to empower communities and individuals linguistically in such a way that they can participate with a view to their own economic wellbeing, as described by Bourdieu (Carrington & Luke, 1997: 96).

The Way Forward

How should this be achieved? On the one hand, an essential step is to utilise the political will, as evident from the discourse around language in education in the Portfolio Committee mentioned earlier, to effect infrastructure spending in order to create stability, security, employment, increased earnings and enhanced sharing of resources. While these objectives can only be achieved by way of a more general language policy, a draft of which is purportedly under discussion at cabinet level, changes can already be initiated at institutional level by making use of the latent multilingual dynamics of the system. One example of this is the fact, as mentioned earlier, that teachers use vernacular languages in the classroom, despite English-only policies, something that also occurs, albeit to a lesser extent, at university level. This practice may be regarded, I believe, as a strong point in the system, and probably the backbone on which new policy can be built. This multilingualism 'on the ground' (as Parmegiani and Rudwick describes it in Chapter 7) needs to be introduced into the institutional realm through implementation, not only through officialisation. In terms of languages of learning and teaching in higher education in Africa, and specifically SA, the institutional ethos of institutions needs to be addressed before embarking on implementation of an inclusive framework for linguistic empowerment of students. The ethos is created through addressing diversity management and transformation, with the aim of community building, to increase inclusivity and improve the often poor quality of cross-cultural and cross-linguistic interaction. One step to take would be to acknowledge that some of the historically entrenched institutional racial, ethnic and linguistic divides are still intact, as the case study by Parmegiani and Rudwick (Chapter 7) so clearly shows. Some of these manifest themselves in old, established, strategically protected networks of power. Others are visible in what may be termed *ghettos*. The ghettos are those pockets of employment and participation that are occupied by those cultural and linguistic groupings, which remain persistently undervalued and economically marginal.

Conclusion

Addressing individual languages separately may be missing the point. Each African language needs to be viewed as one of many that speakers practice in different situations and apply for specific effects and results. Therefore, a bi- or multilingual learning situation in which all discourses embedded in African languages (including Afrikaans) are mobilised for learning is advocated. In this multiliteracies approach, supported by multimodal resources, languages are extended through pedagogy within an intellectual activity realm. This process will alter the perception that African languages are not suited for learning in higher education, and will also facilitate the inclusion of these languages in higher education. At present, 70% of the student intake at the Nelson Mandela Metropolitan University (NMMU) in Port Elizabeth is isiXhosa-speaking. However, this may change in time, with NMMUs increasing international and pan-African exposure, which means that in 10 or 20 years other considerations may come into play. Ultimately, economically sustainable models of language in education are the only valid ones. The present symbolic power of African languages in the South African imagination cannot be disputed, which is why it is the ideal historic moment to mobilise them in SA. Although research-based insights into the advantages of multilingual education run counter to the ingrained effects of linguistic social Darwinism and the quest for modernity, the political climate seems to be transforming itself in favour of a multilingual social structure/ethos. A major stumbling block remains attitudes 'on the ground', which, in order for democracy to be seen to be practised, have to be accommodated as far as language choice is concerned, although they are difficult to reverse. However, once policy makers have realised the linguistic reasons for the failure of programmes to ensure unfettered access to knowledge, there is no shortage of strategies to change attitudes by means of valorising African vernaculars at both school and university levels, while simultaneously empowering the community of practice to obtain access to the language of wider communication through bi- or multicultural proficiencies and literacy programmes.

Note

A longer version of this chapter has appeared in the journal *Alternations*, 2010, 17 (1). Permission to republish this article in another format has been granted.

References

Carrington, V. and Luke, A. (1997) Literacy and Bourdieu's sociological theory: A reframing. *Language and Education* 11 (2), 96–112.
Dafler, J.R. (2005) Social Darwinism and the language of racial oppression: Australia's stolen generations. *ETC: A Review of General Semantics* 62 (2), 137–150.
Department of Education (1992) National Education Policy Initiative (NEPI). See http://www.education.gov.za/Documents/policies/ (LanguageEducationPolicy1997.pdf.link) (accessed on 30 June 2009).
Department of Education (1997) Language in Education Policy. See http://www.education.gov.za/Documents/policies/ (LanguageEducationPolicy1997.pdf.link) (accessed on 23 July 2009).
García, O. (2007) *Imagining Multilingual Schools*. Clevedon: Multilingual Matters.
May, S. (2001) *Language and Minority Rights: Ethnicity, Nationalism and the Politics of Language*. New York: Longman.
Pandor, N. (2006) Address by the Minister of Education, Naledi Pandor, MP, at the language colloquium, Cape Town, July 2006. See http://www.info.gov.za/speeches/2006/06080114451001.htm (accessed on 30 June 2009).
Parliamentary Monitoring Group (2001) National Plan on Higher Education: Briefing. See http://www.pmg.org.za/minutes/20010904-language-education-policy-briefing-department (accessed on 11 August 2009).

Parliamentary Monitoring Group (2006) Language in education policy. See http://www.pmg.org.za/minutes/20060904-language-education-policy-briefing-department (accessed on 30 July 2009).

Plüddemann, P., Braam, D., October, M. and Wababa, Z. (2004) *Dual-Medium and Parallel-Medium Schooling in the Western Cape: From Default to Design*. PRAESA Occasional Paper No. 17. Cape Town, RSA: PRAESA.

Republic of South Africa (1996a) South African Schools Act, Act no. 84 of 1996. Pretoria, RSA: Government Printers.

Republic of South Africa (1996b) National Education Policy Act 1996. Pretoria, RSA: Government Printers.

Republic of South Africa (1996c) Constitution of the Republic of South Africa, Act 108 of 1996 (as amended). Pretoria, RSA: Government Printers.

Van der Merwe, I.J. and Van der Merwe, J.H. (2006) *Linguistic Atlas of South Africa – Language in Space and Time*. Stellenbosch, RSA: SUN Press.

Webb, V.N. and Kembo-Sure, E. (eds) (2000) The languages of Africa. In *African Voices* (pp. 26–54). Cape Town, RSA: Oxford University Press.

Wits-EPU (2009) *An Investigation into the Language of Learning and Teaching in Schools*. Final report submitted to the Department of Education, 27 March.

Appendix A

Language in Education Policy in terms of

(a) Section 3(4)(m) of the National Education Policy Act, 1996 (Act 27 of 1996), and
(b) Section 6(1) of the South African Schools Act, 1996 (Act 84 of 1996).

According to (a), in the Preamble, the government, and thus the Department of Education, is tasked ... to promote multilingualism, the development of the official languages, and respect for all languages used in the country ....

The policy, is meant to facilitate communication across the barriers of colour, language and religion, while at the same time creating an environment in which respect for languages other than one's own would be encouraged.

This approach is in line with the fact that both societal and individual multilingualism are the global norm today, especially on the African continent. As such, it assumes that the learning of more than one language should be general practice and principle in our society.

A wide spectrum of opinions exists as to the locally viable approaches towards multilingual education, ranging from arguments in favour of the cognitive benefits and cost-effectiveness of teaching through one medium (home language) and learning additional language(s) as subjects, to those drawing on comparative international experience demonstrating that, under appropriate conditions, most learners benefit cognitively and emotionally from the type of structured bilingual education found in dual-medium (also known as two-way immersion) programmes. Whichever route is followed, the underlying principle is to maintain home language(s) while providing access to and the effective acquisition of additional language(s). Hence, the Department's position that an additive approach to bilingualism is to be seen as the normal orientation of our language-in-education policy.

... Policy will progressively be guided by the results of comparative research, both locally and internationally.

The right to choose the language of learning and teaching is vested in the individual. This right has, however, to be exercised within the overall framework of the obligation on the education system to promote multilingualism.

The language(s) of learning and teaching in a public school must be (an) official language(s).

3 Multilingualism at Work in South African Higher Education: From Policy to Practice

Pamela Maseko

Introduction

Language policies published after the attainment of democracy in 1994, which are particularly applicable to HEIs, seek to guard against the use of language to perpetuate the inequalities and inequities of South African society in the past. The main goal of these policies is to promote linguistic and cultural diversity in HEIs as well as to prepare students to participate fully in our multilingual society, where multilingual proficiency is critical. English and Afrikaans are acknowledged as languages of research and scholarship in HE at present, but legislative policies applicable to language use and practices in HE make provision for preventing these languages from being used as a barrier to the access, retention and success of previously disadvantaged people (see Kotzé's detailed discussion in Chapter 2). The indigenous African languages, which have, until now, had a minimal role in HE, are seen as critical for the attainment of the goals of the language policies. As a consequence, legislation on language in HE recommends that HEIs should rethink the place of these languages and, in line with national policy, should develop their own policies and implementation plans on the advancement, promotion and use of these languages.

In this chapter, an analysis is done of language policy and other official documents related to language use in South African HE. Using Rhodes University (RU) as an example, I propose to demonstrate how indigenous African languages can be promoted, developed and strengthened to foster multilingualism and multiculturalism. I will describe the work of the University's School of Languages (African Language Studies Section) in promoting the research in, and teaching of, isiXhosa[1] as an additional language in vocational training disciplines, to support learning in certain disciplines, and as a subject.

Multilingualism in South African HE: National Legislation and other Promulgations

South African HEIs are multilingual. Rhodes University is the smallest campus in the country (with just over 7270 students in 2012), but the student body uses over 24 languages, eight of which are indigenous African languages. This multilingualism is entrenched in the South African Constitution (SA Government, 1996), which adopted 11 of the most spoken languages as official languages. The status and role of the various languages in South African HE is outlined in a number of official policy and other state documents. Those relevant to this work and discussed hereafter are as follows:

(a) Language Policy for Higher Education (LPHE) (Department of Education, 2002).
(b) Report on the Development of Indigenous Languages as Mediums of Instruction in Higher Education (Department of Education, 2003).
(d) The Charter for Humanities and Social Sciences' (HSS) Catalytic Project on Concept Formation in African Languages (Department of Higher Education, 2011).
(c) The Green Paper on Post-Secondary School Education and Training (Department of Higher Education, 2012a).
(e) Ministerial Advisory Panel on African Languages in Higher Education (MAPALHLE) (Department of Higher Education, 2012b).

Language Policy for Higher Education (LPHE) (Department of Education, 2002)

The LPHE makes the following provisions regarding the use of languages in HE:

(a) It acknowledges the current position of English and Afrikaans as languages of research and scholarship, but makes a point that it will be

necessary to work within the confines of the *status quo* until such time as other South African languages have been developed to a level where they may be used in all HE functions.
(b) It states that consideration should be given to the development of other South African languages for use in instruction, as part of a medium- to long-term strategy to promote multilingualism.
(c) It recognises that the promotion of South African languages for use in higher education will require, among others, the development of multilingual dictionaries and other teaching and learning support materials.
(d) Language should not act as a barrier to equity of access and success. In this regard, the Ministry of Education encourages all HEIs to develop strategies for promoting proficiency in the designated language(s) of tuition, including the provision of language and academic literacy development programmes. (Department of Education, 2002: par. 15)

In essence, the LPHE (Department of Education, 2002) recommends that universities make provision for assisting students who speak languages other than those of tuition to develop academic literacy and make plans regarding the academic role of indigenous African languages alongside other languages within the institution. It also mandates universities to undertake projects that focus on the development of all South African languages, such that they can be used across disciplines and as formal academic languages at HE level. It requires universities to encourage multilingualism by identifying and promoting the learning of at least one additional language to provide a comprehensive implementation plan regarding the development of relevant languages in each institution, a plan that should indicate how and when these languages will be developed to be used in their various teaching practices.

All these recommendations point to the need for the comprehensive development of African languages so that, in the long term, they can be taught and used at university to ensure equity of access and success to students speaking languages other than those used for teaching and learning at present, as well as to promote social cohesion.

Report on the Development of Indigenous Languages as Mediums of Instruction in Higher Education (Department of Education, 2003)

The Development of Indigenous African Languages as Mediums of Instruction in Higher Education, 2003 (the Report) is a report of a committee chaired by

Professor Njabulo Ndebele and commissioned by Professor Kader Asmal, the Minister of Education at the time. Its mandate was to look into the state of African languages with regard to HE, as well as to make recommendations in terms of actions that could be taken in facilitating their promotion and intellectual development at university, particularly their use as mediums of instruction. In essence, the purpose of the committee was to look at, as well as pursue, the recommendations of the LPHE regarding steps that could be taken in the development of African languages for use in HE.

The Report indicates that what is prevalent at South African universities is not nearly adequate to bring the indigenous African languages to the fore and to have them used fully as mediums of instruction or to support tuition presently given largely in English, the dominant language of teaching and learning at most universities. The Report further notes that the present conditions are not conducive to the growth of the African languages. It confirms the view of many other scholars (Alexander, 2005; Bamgbose, 1991, 2002) that for the languages to grow, they need wider literacy (expansion of vocabulary, development of scientific terms, etc.) and use, because languages grow as they are used and they are used more as they grow. The Report also states that it should not be enough that these languages are declared official languages, but that they should also receive recognition of their status. Their use at all levels of education is of paramount importance as this encourages investment in the language. Lastly, it states that with the era of technology, the use of languages in the technological field (and other so-called intellectual disciplines) is also significant to enable their growth.

In the context of the LPHE framework (as given above), the Report (Department of Education, 2003: 20) concludes by recommending that, in the promotion and development of indigenous languages in HE, South African universities should:

(a) Ensure the sustainability of all indigenous South African languages.
(b) Select, according to region, one or more indigenous languages to develop for use as medium of instruction in HE, as well as short-, medium- and long-term implementation frameworks.
(c) Promote communicative competence of students in at least one indigenous language and encourage the labour market to make such competence an imperative, especially for civil service or state institutions.
(d) Promote partnerships between HEIs and the private sector in identifying and translating key texts into indigenous language/s selected for development by that institution.

(e) Ensure institutional collaborations, especially where languages selected are common, to ensure acceleration of work and non-replication of effort.

Each HE institution is required to develop a language policy with an implementation plan that needs to be reviewed periodically for its effectiveness. The development plan of these languages should be within the provisions of the language policy of each institution. The Report suggests which specific indigenous African language/s each institution should focus on. Over and above the other legislation, this would require that it be done in the context of the provincial and regional legislation that exists on language. The linguistic composition of the region where the HE institution is situated should also be taken into consideration in selecting the language for development.

The Charter for the Humanities and Social Sciences' (HSS) Catalytic Project on Concept Formation in African languages (Department of Higher Education and Training, 2011)

The project is one of the six catalytic projects proposed in the Report of the Charter for Humanities and Social Sciences (Department of Higher Education and Training, 2011). It acknowledges the centrality of language and of indigenous African languages in particular, in learning in South African HE and recommends that strategies for integration of languages be designed to influence humanities and social sciences practice and theory in South Africa.

The project is described as:

> A national multidisciplinary project on how indigenous languages in South Africa could support the process of concept formation in the HSS, and furthermore, what know-hows in these languages could enrich social scientific thinking or pedagogy. (Department of Higher Education and Training, 2011: 20)

The activities of the project were conceptualised in November 2012, and Professor Russell Kaschula, who heads the RUs SARChI Research Chair on 'Intellectualisation of African Languages, Multilingualism and Education', and Dr Pamela Maseko are its leaders. The project works in collaboration with 10 South African HEIs across four provinces and involves six indigenous African languages. Its purpose is to provide a theoretical framework and implementation strategies for use of indigenous languages in encouraging conceptualisation in various disciplines, with a focus on those in humanities and social sciences.

The Green Paper on Post-Secondary School Education and Training (Department of Higher Education and Training, 2012a)

The *Green Paper on Post-Secondary School Education* (Department of Higher Education and Training, 2012a: par 6.10) recognises the unfortunate position of African languages in South African HE, and consequently, in the Departments of African Languages, and acknowledges this as a threat to linguistic diversity in South Africa, as well as to the survival of African languages. The paper provides for African languages to be taught across disciplines at universities, and therefore, the following is proposed (Department of Higher Education and Training, 2012a: 50):

(a) Inclusion of African language proficiency as a requirement in professional training (the Department of Higher Education and Training acknowledges that this is already a practice in some faculties of some universities, and that the department will look at how this could be implemented across faculties in all universities).
(b) Universities should provide teacher-training that focuses on mother-tongue education for teachers of African languages in order to implement properly the Department of Basic Educations mother-tongue policy for primary school learners.
(c) Universities should encourage students to take a course in an African language as part of their curriculum (for proficiency as well as to elevate the status of African languages in the country).

The Green Paper, as with the Humanities and Social Sciences Catalytic Project on Concept Formation, makes bold and concrete recommendations on how indigenous African languages should be strengthened and developed in HE. It moves slightly from simply justifying teaching of African languages in HE and instead provides possibilities for how they can be included in various curricula. It also acknowledges some good practices and commits the Department of Higher Education and Training to explore how these can be replicated in other contexts. There is, however, focus on African languages being taught as *additional* languages in university courses and in teacher-training. While this is important in facilitating social cohesion and effective mother-tongue-based education, first and foremost, the survival of African languages is based on these languages being taught at universities as *first* languages. Only then will their scientific status improve and they will be developed and taught as languages of learning and teaching (Obanya, 2004).

Ministerial Advisory Panel on African Languages in Higher Education (MAPAHLE) (Department of Higher Education and Training, 2012b)

Notice 103 of Government Gazette 35028 (10 February 2012) announced the establishment of a ministerial advisory panel on developing African languages as languages of scholarship at institutions of HE. The panel was constituted by the Department of Higher Education and Training to advise the minister on the current status of teaching, learning and research of indigenous African languages in South African HE. Further, within this context (current status of research, teaching and learning of additional languages) and that of the present language policy in HE, the panel was required to identify hindrances to promotion of African languages in HE, as well as to provide the minister with practical recommendations on the promotion and development of these languages. The panel was expected to report its findings and recommendations to the minister in June 2013.

The above are just a few of the policies and promulgations that guide language use and practices in HE. It is a cause for concern, though, that implementation of the policies, grand as they are, is not effectively monitored; a point made at length by Kotzé in Chapter 2. Bamgbose (1991: 133) and other prominent language scholars (Alexander, 2003; Kaschula, 2004; Webb, 2001: 182–3) have concurred that many African countries and institutions within them have sound language policies, but nonetheless lack sound implementation plans. Kaschula went on to say that language policies in Africa are characterised by lack of 'political will to drive the process' and thus 'much lip service has been paid to the implementation processes' to little effect (Kaschula, 2004: 11). As a consequence, policies and recommendations on implementation are published without any monitor having assessed, through monitoring and evaluation, the non-implementation of previous policies. Having said that, the Catalytic Project (Department of Higher Education and Training, 2011), the Green Paper on Post-Secondary School Education (Department of Higher Education and Training, 2012a) and the Ministerial Advisory Panel on African Languages in Higher Education (Department of Higher Education and Training, 2012b) seem to be more definite and provide concrete guidelines on scholarly work that needs to be undertaken to ensure implementation and the expansion of the role of language, and indigenous African languages in particular, in HE in South Africa.

Areas of Focus in Teaching African Languages in HE

Almost all the policy documents listed above have indicated that departments of African languages are the academic custodians of scholarship in African languages. These documents also signal the significant reduction in student numbers in many South African HEIs, with many departments of African languages being threatened with closure. As can be seen in the graph presented by Kosch and Bosch in Chapter 4, this situation led to drastic changes to the profile and curricula of the departments.

In the context of legislation and the arguments raised above for the use of African languages in HE, the following are some of the possible areas of research and teaching around which promotion and development of African languages can occur, areas that would encourage the strengthening of African languages in South African HE.

(a) Language learning programmes in African languages, undergraduate and postgraduate studies:
- African languages as additional languages to speakers of other languages, to equip students with communicative competence (general and vocation-specific), with a focus on both linguistic and cultural competence, as illustrated by Makalela in Chapter 6.
- African languages taught as subjects, in the medium of African languages, to mother-tongue speakers, as illustrated by Kosch and Bosch in Chapter 4.
- Other language-related subjects taught in African languages, initially those that can be offered in African languages departments, for instance, sociolinguistics, translation studies, lexicography, terminography, media studies, and so on (but see Leeuw who makes a case for its use in astronomy in Chapter 10).
- Certified short courses in communicative competence for staff in HE, focusing on both language proficiency and cultural awareness and sensitivity, as mentioned by Parmegiani and Rudwick in Chapter 7.

(b) Support teaching material in African languages: Develop, through translation and other language development strategies, resources to support cognition for students to whom English (the common language of learning and teaching (LoLT)) is a second/additional language, in different

subjects. The following are some of the resources that can be developed:
- Bilingual/multilingual term lists.
- Bilingual/multilingual glossary lists.
- Monolingual/bilingual/multilingual dictionaries.

(c) Piloting African languages as LoLTs: As indicated in the policy above, focus should also be on piloting the use of African languages as mediums of instruction in HE. In that regard, African languages departments, through collaboration with other subject specialists, can devise effective strategies to develop indigenous languages for use as LoLTs in various disciplines. Strategies adopted should take into consideration that African languages are developed in form but that they have not been developed to function in HE. Therefore, strategies need to be devised to capacitate them further in terms of function and form, so that they are able to capture the scientific discourse of HE (Wildsmith-Cromarty, 2008).

(d) Promotion of academic literacy: While English and Afrikaans are languages of academia in South Africa, students not having these languages as their mother-tongue should be supported to achieve academic proficiency in them. Such literacy should be grounded in the affirmation of the students' first language, where possible.

(e) Aesthetics and general culture in HE: Signage, communication with the public and general institutional culture should reflect and embrace the linguistic and cultural diversity of these institutions as represented by the demographics of the university community and the institutional, provincial and national policy on language.

In the following section, I discuss the Rhodes University Language Policy, and contextualise it within the policy guidelines. I also introduce the African Languages Studies Section of the School of Languages whose research, teaching and learning programmes are inspired by the university's language policy.

In arguing for a multliteracies approach, Kotzé refers, in Chapter 2, to the symbolic power of African language in the South African imagination. Noting the quest for modernity, he argues that, nevertheless, the political climate seems to be transforming itself in favour of a multilingual social structure/ethos.

He refers, however, to the attitudes on the ground, which need to be transformed if the tacit policy of multilingualism in this country is to be overcome.

One example where this is successfully happening is at Rhodes University.

Rhodes University Language Policy (2005)

The Rhodes University Language Policy was approved by Council in October 2005. It is presently being revised by the University Language Committee, established in 2012. The policy explicitly encourages multilingualism among both students and academic staff. It affirms the importance of language and culture and the promotion and respect of linguistic and cultural diversity. The relationship between language and learning is central to the policy, and the policy acknowledges that indigenous African languages are not developed fully enough to be used to support learning in high-level domains such as HEIs, but charges the Department of African Language to design strategies for the development and teaching of isiXhosa at the university. What follows are the main objectives of the Rhodes Language Policy. The Department of African Languages of the School of Languages drives the major aspects of the implementation, especially where provisions of the policy relate to isiXhosa. These objectives of the policy demonstrate institutional support for multilingualism and multiculturalism within the university. Accordingly, the university language policy (Rhodes University, 2005) presents strategies for:

(a) Recognising and advancing the academic viability and status of the three major languages of the Eastern Cape Province: isiXhosa, Afrikaans and English.
(b) The promotion of multilingualism and sensitivity in language usage in such a way as to create and foster a supportive and inclusive, non-sexist and non-racist environment in which all members of the University can feel they belong.
(c) Regarding policy implementation, the provision by the School of Languages to:
 - devise strategies to recruit students into courses in isiXhosa; and
 - to explore the feasibility of reintroducing a programme in isiXhosa at postgraduate level for mother-tongue speakers by offering incentives such as scholarships to such students.
 Furthermore, the policy states that:
(d) The Human Resources Division will devise strategies to encourage members of the university who do not speak isiXhosa to enrol for the short communicative courses in isiXhosa.
 Finally, the policy states, *inter alia,* that:
(e) Academic departments will encourage constructive debate about bilingualism, multilingualism and the role of language in learning (Rhodes University, 2005).

The Rhodes University Language Policy is located in the South African context, and more specifically, in the Eastern Cape context, where the university is located. Various aspects of it are positive and point to the university's commitment to making a contribution towards nation-building, promotion of multilingualism and further development of isiXhosa as a living language. This is aligned to the specifications of the National Language Policy for Higher Education (Department of Education, 2002).

Besides English being the language of HE in South Africa, using it as the LoLT correlates with the university's mission of being an internationally esteemed university. Its embracing of multilingualism is an indication of its dedication to its South African identity, while its commitment to development of academic literacy among the historically disadvantaged students shows its obligation to social transformation and matters of equity in tertiary education.

Teaching and Research Focus of the African Language Studies Department at RU

Similarly to other academic Departments of African Languages in the country, the African Language Studies Department at RU has experienced a huge decline in numbers of students over the last 10 to 15 years. This was the case in both courses catering for home language speakers of isiXhosa, as well as those to whom isiXhosa is an additional language. The drop in numbers was associated with curriculum and teaching areas, as well as the fact that isiXhosa was no longer perceived as an enabler in getting into the job market after leaving university. Many Departments of African Languages were, and are still, faced with threats of closures as a result of these low numbers.

The African Language Studies Department at Rhodes in 2006–2007 undertook to restructure and reinvent itself in the context of what was happening in the arena of African languages in the country. In 2006, after a wide consultation within and outside the university, and after a review by peers from other universities which saw it almost closed down, this section within the School of Languages brought out its new vision, mission and objectives. In its vision and mission, the African Language Studies section seeks to promote national unity and linguistic and cultural diversity, and further to intellectualise isiXhosa so that it can be used at various levels of education. The objectives of the section are:

- To promote and advance scholarship in African languages.

- To promote multilingualism through programmes designed to teach isiXhosa as an additional language.
- To contribute in facilitating student access and retention, particularly of historically disadvantaged students.

Broadly speaking, the Department of African Language Studies at RU recommitted itself to being an intellectual home for the promotion and development of isiXhosa in the country by providing learning programmes that advance scholarship in the language, are interdisciplinary in nature and will respond to social needs of society.

As indicated earlier, the African Language Studies section of the School of Languages is at the forefront of implementing aspects of the Rhodes Language Policy, especially those relating to isiXhosa. Interventions range from the teaching of isiXhosa as an additional language for staff and students, the teaching of isiXhosa as a subject, to the development of support material for students for whom English is an additional language.

The following are key research, teaching and learning areas of the department.

(a) Acquisition of isiXhosa as an additional language in vocation-specific or generic contexts, with a focus on language and culture:
- IsiXhosa generic course (a three-year major).
- IsiXhosa for Journalism and Media studies (two-semester course).
- IsiXhosa for Education (a two-semester course).
- IsiXhosa for Law (a semester course).
- IsiXhosa for Pharmacy (a three-term course).

(b) IsiXhosa as a home language (research, teaching and learning of isiXhosa linguistic, literary, sociolinguistic and applied language studies).

(c) Development of multilingual learning support material and piloting the use of isiXhosa as an additional teaching material in technical domains (computer science, political studies, geography).

(d) Postgraduate studies in the above areas with the aim of theorising the process of development and strengthening the use of African languages in HE and society at large.

Teaching and learning of isiXhosa as an additional language focuses on equipping mother-tongue speakers of other languages with both language and cultural proficiency so that they are able to communicate and be culturally aware and sensitive in conversations where isiXhosa is spoken. The knowledge and skills imparted in the courses not only contribute positively to the learning experience of the students, but prepare them to be responsible multilingual citizens. These courses are aimed to equip students with basic language skills, specific to their vocation, to be able to cope during interviews in their professions, in contexts where isiXhosa is spoken. For example, the course in journalism and media studies has a module titled *Negotiating unfamiliar environment in the process of news-gathering, especially in respect of working with an interpreter and identifying appropriate people to speak to for a 'story'*. Further, the courses provide students with knowledge and skills that will be necessary for them to understand and interpret cultural issues embedded in isiXhosa communication, especially those specific to their vocational contexts. Examples of cultural topics presented in the journalism and media course relate to traditional leadership, sacrifices/slaughtering, traditional healing, traditional marriages, initiation and so forth. This approach seeks to raise awareness of cultural issues relating to isiXhosa-speaking people and how these influence various professional contexts of the people they interact with in their professional lives. The ultimate aim of the additional language learning courses is to provide students with the language of, and cultural knowledge in, isiXhosa in order to add value to their learning experience at Rhodes, knowledge on which they can build once they leave the university.

The isiXhosa mother-tongue major is designed to facilitate the intellectual development of isiXhosa. Given the history of African languages in HE, the African Language Studies section has designed academic programmes that are relevant to general language study, but also have social relevance and are attractive to students. Thus, the section has moved away from structural approaches to sociolinguistic and applied language studies, which appeal to students and have social relevance. Such courses include literature and publishing, African languages and media studies, translation studies, African languages and globalisation, language planning, sociolinguistics, lexicography and terminology development, human language technology, orthography and writing skills. Pure linguistics (morphology, syntax, phonology, semantics, etc.) are still studied, but within the context of the studies above. The writing skills courses are necessary as the schooling system does not prepare students well enough in African language teaching, and so when they reach university, they are underprepared in dealing with demands of learning in the medium of isiXhosa and in the general language competencies of speaking, reading and writing.

The general objective of the mother-tongue curriculum in each of the language courses presented in the subject areas above is to raise awareness on the subject, with both South African and global focus, and to provide theoretical underpinnings critical in each subject area. The application of knowledge in local, national and global contexts in a manner where students are exposed to a community of practitioners in African languages, and isiXhosa in particular, outside the university is particularly beneficial.

The other teaching and research area of the department is the development of support teaching material, specifically multilingual glossaries. Multilingual glossaries (constituting core concepts in these disciplines) have been developed in political studies and computer science. Development of glossaries constitutes a large component of our postgraduate studies at Rhodes. Processes around strategies for concept formation in African languages, and implementing the use of these materials in HE learning contexts, are an integral part of our postgraduate research. These materials are published in print form and posted on the RU e-learning site.

The review of the mission and vision of the African Language Section, and its goal to promote multilingualism and multiculturalism, and to be an intellectual hub on indigenous African languages, coupled with the review of its curriculum, saw the Section grow from 85 students in 2005 to 512 in 2012. About 15% of the students were postgraduate students. This is an enormous growth, considering that numbers in many African Languages Departments in the country are alarmingly low.

Some Enablers in Development of Indigenous African Languages in HE

Some common elements seem to be pertinent in the promotion of multilingualism in HE, especially the development of African languages. In the RU experience, the following are some of these: national and institutional policy, funding, executive support, expertise of African language scholars, collaboration with other disciplines and other institutions, and advocacy.

Institutional policy is derived from national and provincial legislation. Most institutions that have been active in promoting multilingualism and development of multilingualism have institutional policies and bodies, for example, language committees, whose role, in differing degrees, is to monitor the implementation of the institutional policy.

The work of the Department of African Language Studies accelerated when it received a funding grant from the South Africa–Norway Tertiary Education Development (SANTED) Programme. Subsequent funding from the Department of Arts and Culture for postgraduate studies and from the university's Research Office consolidated our research and teaching activities.

Demands for development of indigenous languages for use in HE require expertise and knowledge, which past training in African languages has not provided. Retraining and reconfiguration of thinking around scholarship in African languages in this area is needed.

Scholars in other disciplines also place value on the importance of students' communicative competence in African languages (during their professional training) and are beginning to consider a relationship between students first language and the language of teaching and learning and to associate it with students' low success in their disciplines. These scholars do not only collaborate in such research, but also provide advocacy for the role of African languages in HE.

The development of African languages for use in HE needs to be accelerated and institutional collaborations, as recommended by the policy discussed above, need to be facilitated. This will not only accelerate the process, but will minimise the duplication of resources and effort.

Challenges, Opportunities and Prospects

One of the main challenges in the development of African languages in HE is at policy level. While an admirable policy exists, which, at a glance, should ensure development of African languages and promotion of multilingualism, the policy lacks a plan of implementation, as well as directives on who should *lead or drive its implementation* (at both national and institutional level). The other factor related to implementation is *monitoring*. The LPHE (Department of Education, 2002) and the report on the *Development of Indigenous Languages as Mediums of Instruction in Higher Education* (Department of Education, 2003), for example, state clearly what needs to be done by institutions in promoting the development of African languages. However, there is no monitoring of the extent of compliance with provisions of policy (at both national and institutional level). The simple example is that of the formulation of institutional policy and the institutions submission to the Education Ministry of their five-year plan regarding the development of African languages as mediums of instruction. The LPHE (Department of Education, 2002) requires that HEIs formulate their policy with an implementation plan, and publish it. The LPHE (Department of Education, 2002) also stipulates that HEIs should provide the Ministry of Education, every five years, with a report that provides the extent of the implementation of its plan. While 19 of the 23 HEIs have their policies published, none have provided the Ministry with a report on the progress of implementation of policy. The essence of the argument here though, is that the policy could possibly be sufficient but lacks strategies and other means to monitor compliance to its provisions. As Kotzé points out in Chapter 2, it is crucially important for multilingualism to be introduced into the institutional realm 'through implementation, not only through officialisation'.

National policy is burdened with *limitation clauses* such as 'where possible', 'where practical', 'may' and so on. Policy at institutional level seems to take a cue from national policy and, as such, institutions seem to be able to escape some of their responsibilities towards use and development of African languages.

The study of African languages at university has been a challenge since the 1990s and therefore *African language departments have trained very few scholars* to sustain scholarship in African languages at university and to teach in schools. Very few students have been trained in conventional language areas such as linguistics, literature, morphology, phonology or in applied language studies such as translation studies, interpreting, sociolinguistics and others (Maseko, 2011). This presents threats to sustained scholarship in African languages in a number of ways:

(1) *Low interest in postgraduate studies*, including teacher training, in African languages. An informal survey conducted by the author links this low interest to lack of funding, which has been named as an 'enabler' in the section above.
(2) The states *funding* grid for languages places languages towards the bottom in terms of states subsidy. This needs to be reviewed such that all state policy provides synergy for development of African language for use in universities.
(3) Frequently, *institutional priorities* do not include development of African languages.
(4) The *poor state of the teaching of African languages at schools* means that universities inherit students who do not possess the expected competency for further study of these languages at university.

All the above have an impact on the *kind and quality of research* that emerges from the African languages department.

The challenges listed above need to be understood and weighed up against the opportunities and prospects that favour development of African languages in HE. A general national interest in African languages exists in HE. Also, initiatives supported by institutional executives, or by individual within institutions, have been implemented. Research shows a growing consciousness from scholars in other disciplines who have an interest in the link between language and effective learning, and promotion of social cohesion in acquisition of additional languages in professional/vocation-specific disciplines. All these initiatives will be possible if the study of African languages is made more easily available to students. Contrary to popular belief, students want to study African languages but funding remains a challenge.

Conclusion

The process of the promotion of multilingualism and development of African languages in HE is an inherently difficult task, especially given the history of the use of these languages in South African HE and in society at large. However, even though difficult, it is necessary given the relationship between language and learning. The role of language in ensuring that one and all are able to 'participate fully in, and contribute to the social, cultural, intellectual, economic and political life of South Africa' (Department of Education, 2002: par. 6) means that the process has to be undertaken without delay.

The policy landscape in the South African HE is conducive to facilitating the meaningful integration of indigenous African languages in all teaching, learning and research practices of HE and in ensuring that English, as the present common LoLT in HE, does not exclude students who speak it as an additional language. Further, policy is clear on the way language should be used in HE to cultivate multilingualism, and cultural awareness and sensitivity in students as they engage with the community in their vocational training and beyond. While some examples of best practices exist in HE, in terms of implementing the clauses of policy, these need to be extended across universities and across different languages. The amount of work to be done needs a harnessing of resources, knowledge and expertise from all, especially African language scholars and experts, scholars from other disciplines within the universities, the government and the private sector. Moreover, the process of the promotion and development of indigenous African languages (as subjects, as additional languages, as support teaching material), and the manner in which these languages can be used to enhance learning in HE, needs to be intellectualised. Hypotheses emerging from research on best practices need to be offered.

Note

(1) IsiXhosa is an indigenous language spoken by over 75% of the population of the Eastern Cape, where Rhodes University is situated. It is also the second most widely spoken language in South Africa, after isiZulu. In 2012, the statistics published by the Data Management Unit at Rhodes University indicated that 1400 (about 18%) of the student body had isiXhosa as a first language.

References

Alexander, N. (2003) *The African Renaissance and the Use of African Languages in Tertiary Education*. PRAESA Occasional Papers No. 13. Cape Town, RSA: PRAESA.

Alexander, N.E. (ed.) (2005) *The Intellectualisation of African Languages: The African Academy of Languages and the Implementation of the Language Plan of Action for Africa*. Cape Town, RSA: PRAESA.

Bamgbose, A. (1991) *Language and the Nation: The Language Question in Sub-Saharan Africa*. Edinburgh: Edinburgh University Press.

Bamgbose, A. (2002) *Language and Exclusion: The Consequences of Language Policies in Africa*. Hamburg, DE: LIT-Verlag.

Department of Education (2002) *Language Policy for Higher Education*. Pretoria, RSA: Government Printers.

Department of Education (2003) *Development of Indigenous Languages as Mediums of Instruction in Higher Education*. Pretoria, RSA: Government Printers.

Department of Higher Education and Training (2011) Report commissioned by the Minister of Higher Education and Training for the *Charter for Humanities and Social Sciences*. Pretoria, RSA: Government Printers.

Department of Higher Education and Training (2012a) *Green Paper for Post-Secondary School Education and Training*. Pretoria, RSA: Government Printers.

Department of Higher Education and Training (2012b) *Report of the Ministerial Advisory Panel on African Languages in Higher Education (MAPAHLE)*. Pretoria, RSA. Government Printers.

Kaschula, R.H. (2004) South Africas national language policy revisited: The challenge of implementation. *Alternation* 11 (2), 10–25.

Maseko, P. (2011) Intellectualisation of African languages with particular reference to isiXhosa. Unpublished PhD thesis, Rhodes University, Grahamstown, RSA.

Obanya, P. (2004) *Learning In, With and From the First Language*. PRAESA Occasional Paper No. 19. Cape Town, RSA: PRAESA.

Rhodes University (2005) *Language Policy*. Grahamstown, RSA: Rhodes University.

SA Government (1996) *South African Constitution* (Act 106 of 1996). Pretoria, RSA: Government Printers.

Webb, V. (2001) *Language in South Africa: The Role of Language in National Transformation, Reconstruction and Development*. Philadelphia, PA: John Benjamins.

Wildsmith-Cromarty, R. (2008) Can academic/scientific discourse really be translated across English and African languages? *Southern African Linguistics and Applied Language Studies* 26 (1), 147–169.

Part 2
Enhanced Student Performance through Biliteracy Pedagogy

4 African Languages as Languages of Teaching and Learning: The Case of the Department of African Languages, University of South Africa

Ingeborg M. Kosch and Sonja E. Bosch

Introduction

The aim of this chapter is to give an overview of multilingual teaching and learning at institutions of higher learning, using the Department of African Languages at the University of South Africa (Unisa) as a case study. As such, it elaborates on the policy setting provided by Maseko in Chapter 3, while illustrating its effects on one particular department. Various approaches to teaching and learning that have been adopted by this department over the years will be critically investigated, such as teaching in language groups, teaching all African languages as separate languages and finally the multilanguage 'basket' module approach.

We will address challenges that all departments of African Languages in South Africa were confronted with during the rapid decline of student numbers during the first few years of this century. Innovative solutions had to be found to keep the Department of African Languages at Unisa viable without curtailing the number of African languages it had been offering in the past.

Unisa, in line with its reputation as Africa's leading open distance learning (ODL) institution, is the only university in South Africa that offers open distance teaching and learning modes and methods, as well as student support, in eight of the nine official African languages, in its Department of African Languages (Unisa, 2011). These languages all belong to the Bantu language family and more specifically to Guthrie's Zone S (see Figure 4.1) (Nurse & Philippson, 2003: 609–610) in which the following language clusters are identified[1]:

(1) S20 Venda Group – Tshivenda [ven].
(2) S30 Sotho-Tswana Group – Setswana [tsn], Sesotho sa Leboa[2] [nso], Sesotho [sot].
(3) S40 Nguni Group – isiZulu [zul], isiXhosa [xho], SiSwati [ssw], Southern Ndebele [nbl].[3]
(4) S50 Tshwa-Ronga Group – Xitsonga [tso].

It is hoped that through the experiences of the Department of African Languages at Unisa, language practitioners will be inspired to find new ways of ensuring the growth and expansion of African language education in a multilingual society through an approach that is student-centred and technology driven with flexible learning opportunities. Having the advantage of an online learning platform such as *myUnisa*, lecturers in the department can

Figure 4.1 Location of Guthrie's Zone S

foster collaboration between students from different African language backgrounds. Students are afforded the opportunity to share their exploration of the subject matter and use fellow-students as the sounding board for their discoveries. This mode of learning ensures that lessons learnt will not easily be forgotten in the future. The relevance of our discussion is emphasised by the call of the Minister of Higher Education in April 2011 for the fast-tracked development of African languages at university level, in that every university student in South Africa could be required to learn at least one African language as a condition for graduating.

In the following section, the Department of African Languages at Unisa will be placed in perspective in terms of its origin, mode of tuition and delivery of study material as part of a distance education institution. The development of course content and medium of instruction will be reflected upon in subsequent sections. Innovative ways in which multilingual and other challenges were and are dealt with are analysed before the way forward is plotted in the final section.

The Department of African Languages (Unisa) in Perspective

From examining body to independent department

The University of South Africa, officially established in 1873, evolved out of the University of the Cape of Good Hope and initially functioned purely as an examining body, offering examinations but no tuition. By 1946, Unisa was transformed into a correspondence tuition university operating through print and post for non-residential students, thereby pioneering tertiary distance education in the Western world.

> For the next five decades, Unisa steadily built up an international reputation as an affordable, credible, accessible and flexible distance education institution. Recognition was achieved in 2002 when Unisa was endorsed by the Accrediting Commission of the Distance Education and Training Council (DETC) in the United States. (Unisa, 2012)

Subsequently Unisa progressed to a distance learning institution employing some degree of mixed media, including technologies with limited interaction such as computer-based instruction and videos, before becoming South Africa's dedicated ODL university that strives for multimedia with interactive possibilities aimed at 'bridging the time, geographical, economic, social, educational and communication distance between student and institution, student and academics, student and courseware and student and peers' (Unisa, 2008; Open Distance Learning Policy,). Currently, Unisa is the largest ODL university in Africa with student enrolment exceeding 300,000.

Within the greater Unisa picture, the Department of African Languages (known as the Department of Bantu Languages up to 1978) became an independent department in 1946 and, by 1959, plans were in place to provide tuition for the seven 'written languages of the Union' (Government of South Africa 1910–1960, before it became a Republic), namely isiXhosa, isiZulu, Sesotho (Southern Sotho), Setswana, Sesotho sa Leboa (Northern Sotho), Tshivenda and Xitsonga (Ziervogel, 1957: 33). It was not until 1992 that SiSwati was introduced. The reason for this delayed introduction was that SiSwati mother-tongue tuition at primary school level started in the late 1960s, but by the time prospective SiSwati language students were ready for tertiary education, no university was yet offering SiSwati as a subject. Unisa was the first university to provide the necessary infrastructure, namely study material, literary works and qualified lecturers (Taljaard et al., 2008: v). Shona undergraduate courses were also offered for a number of years, first introduced in 1952 for a short while and then reintroduced in 1980. A request had been received by the then minister of education in Zimbabwe to offer Shona through the Department of African Languages at Unisa, because Shona was not offered as a subject at tertiary level in Zimbabwe. The necessary study material was developed and courses were offered until student numbers dwindled in later years, leading to the phasing out of Shona by 2007.

Mode of tuition

When Unisa was still only an examining body, students had to 'prepare for examinations under their own steam or with the help of private correspondence colleges' (Olivier & Rossouw, 1989: 18). This was also what was expected of students studying African languages until the early 1920s when the Department of African languages started its tutoring activities through correspondence. Syllabi were drawn up and study material was provided in the form of lecture notes and tutorial letters. Only a few languages were offered at the beginning, namely Sesotho, isiXhosa, isiZulu and Setswana. For languages outside the borders of the country (Shona, Zimbabwe Ndebele, Nyanja and Swahili) the department continued to avail itself as an examining body in accordance with the university's original function.

Distance education has undergone revolutionary changes over the years, evolving:

from correspondence schools to delivery mechanisms such as independent study, computer-based instruction, computer-assisted instruction, video courses, videoconferencing, Web-based instruction, and online learning. Technology has played a key role in changing the dynamics of each delivery option over the years, as well as the pedagogy behind distance education. (Beldarrain, 2006: 139)

At Unisa, an online learning platform, *myUnisa,* was launched in 2006 to usher in online delivery of tuition and study material. Currently, a phased-in approach is being used to move towards online delivery of all modules. The university has identified four types of online delivery, divorced from paper-based tuition. The mode of delivery ranges from the most elementary online delivery method (the so-called 'paper under glass' approach) with no printed documents being posted to students (Group A), to the method using as many available electronic tools as possible (Group D). These include online learning activities and tasks (on *myUnisa,* as well as by means of blogs, wiki, drop boxes, Q and A, etc.), as well as new online learning experiences (podcasts, webinars, Web 2.0 tools and social networks). Content will be student-generated and in the assessment there will be an increased use of multi-media, student-generated videos and so on. One of the modules of the Department of African Languages offered at first year level (AFL1501 – Language through an African lens) is offered at an advanced level of online delivery. It was chosen by the College of Human Sciences as a so-called signature module that all students of the college have to include in their curriculum. The mode of delivery of the AFL1501 module serves as a benchmark for other modules in the department and in the college.

Multilingual delivery of study material

When study material first began to be developed by the department, this was done with more than one language in mind. The tutorial letters and guides were integrated to simultaneously cater for the learning needs of students within the same language group. The disciplines that were offered in this comprehensive manner were phonetics, prosodics, phonology, morphology and syntax. In their assessment tasks at second- and third-year level, students had to make an in-depth study of lexical and grammatical differences, not only between the dialects of their language, but also between their language and another language within the same language group. So, for instance, within the Sotho group of languages (Sesotho sa Leboa, Setswana, Sesotho), students of one language had to learn the main lexical and grammatical differences between their language and one of the other two Sotho languages as stipulated in their curriculum. For this purpose, literature books (novelettes) were prescribed for the different languages. They were used not for their literary merit or even for the story, but solely for comparative purposes.

The same principle applied to isiZulu and isiXhosa, which are part of the Nguni group of languages. Tshivenda and Xitsonga, however, were dealt with separately as they do not belong to a language group of related languages.

As student numbers increased, each language section started developing its own study guides. Administratively, this proved to be advantageous, and one could gauge the interest of students in particular languages by the number of enrolments. At that time the department had the capacity to handle over 100 undergraduate modules. Rising student numbers justified the proportionate appointment of staff members. The department grew so big, in fact, that at one stage, there was talk of breaking up the department into different independent language departments. Fortunately this did not materialise as it would have had a negative impact on the effective functioning of the department, where lecturers relied on each other's knowledge across languages, especially at postgraduate level. In fact, lecturers had to be multilingual to be able to assist with the design of study material in specific disciplines across the languages, since not every language had a specialist in, for example, phonetics, phonology, morphology, syntax and so on. The increase in student numbers at undergraduate as well as postgraduate level was a vote of confidence in the lecturers' collective knowledge, which resulted from the sharing and pooling of their resources within one department. Furthermore, if it had not been for this enabling multilingual collaboration between lecturers, students would have been restricted to studying only languages of their region and discouraged from 'understanding the close linguistic relationship that exists among African languages in southern Africa' (Dowling & Maseko, 1995: 101).

After the new millennium, student enrolments for African languages displayed a significant drop, not only at Unisa (see Figure 4.2), but also countrywide (see also Maseko in Chapter 3). Wright offered the following as one of the main reasons why there was such a decline in student numbers:

> The crux of the matter is economic. The job market has opened up for the previously disenfranchised.... Both English and African languages enjoy social and economic utility in different contexts, but for those starting out the overall economic value of English far outweighs that of the African languages. (Wright, 2002: 4)

In a report compiled by the Ministerial Committee appointed by the Ministry of Education (Department of Education, 2003: 19), it is stated that

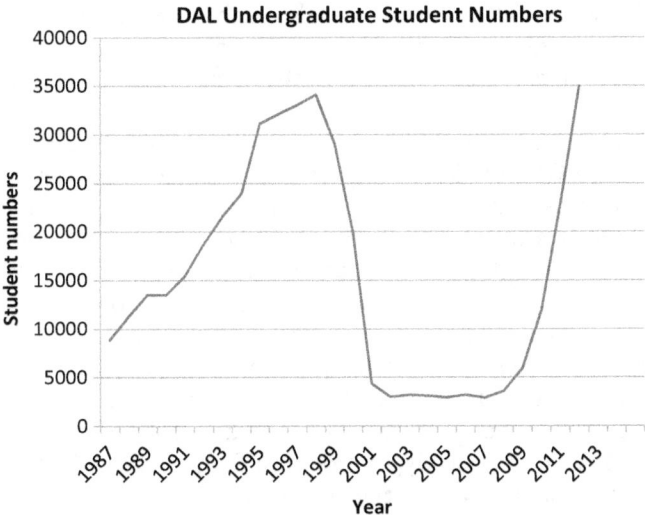

Figure 4.2 Undergraduate student registrations in the Department of African Languages at Unisa from 1987 to 2012[4]

'the number of student enrolments in official indigenous African languages at universities and technikons has recorded a dramatic decline of about 50% since 1999'. This trend resulted in many departments of African Languages having to close down or reduce staff. Some renamed their departments in accordance with the only language they were left to teach (e.g. Department of isiZulu). The African Languages Department at Unisa, despite losing a large component of its teaching staff, managed to continue offering the full spectrum of languages. Its designation as a Department of African Languages is thus not a misnomer, as it teaches eight African languages, with a ninth language, Southern Ndebele, on the cards for introduction in 2014.

Some modules in the Department were identified as non-viable because of the low or no student registrations. The Department was consequently caught in a university-wide drive to rationalise on the number of modules it offered. The challenge was to remain fully operational and to continue offering the whole spectrum of the official African languages. The rationalisation of modules was implemented from 2009 under a rigorous programme qualification mix (PQM) rationalisation process required by the Department of Higher Education and Training – new modules (with codes preceded by the uniform prefix AFL for 'African Languages') were phased in, while old language-specific modules were phased out. By 2011, a total of 114 modules had been phased out, and replaced by 12 new modules (10 for the major and two for beginners' modules). New methods of dealing with loss of human resources and reduction of modules necessitated a change in the mode of teaching and service delivery. The reduction of modules gave rise to the so-called multi-language 'basket module' approach and electronic service delivery, which will be discussed in more detail under the section dealing with multilingual challenges.

In the new PQM, students major in African Languages, not in individual languages such as isiZulu, isiXhosa, Tshivenda and so on. In the basket module approach, students are exposed to other languages besides their own target language through the discussion of examples from various languages in the core text, and by performing specific tasks that call for comparative investigations, for instance, in a level 2 module, students are shown how affixes and metaphor are used in Sesotho sa Leboa and isiZulu, respectively, to identify cattle. They are then given the task to describe alternative ways that are employed in other languages. This is also the approach that Makalela follows in Chapter 6. His Wits study of teaching Sepedi to students with other African mother tongues reveals the positive value in moving away from 'languaging tribes' and the hermetic sealing of languages into boxes and shows how this approach 'liberated the students from the negative stereotypes created by the systematic Balkanisation of Africans through language differentiation'.

Course Content before 2009

In this section, we look at the course content before the latest cycle of revision, while the next section will be focused on the revised material that has Africanisation of study material as one of its main aims.

Before the introduction of the revised major for African languages in 2009, the course content was generally divided equally between linguistics and literature. At level 1, there were two guides (one for linguistics and one for literature), while at levels 2 and 3, there were four guides at each level, two being more linguistically orientated and the other two dealing with literature.

In the linguistics modules, the content offered included phonetics, phonology, tonology, morphology, syntax, semantics, discourse analysis, the study of proto languages, language classification, dialectology and borrowing.

The teaching of general linguistics in departments of African Languages at South African universities (including Unisa) followed international trends, such as structuralism and the transformational generative approach (Dowling & Maseko, 1995: 101). The model of enquiry was analytic and focused on purely academic features, while applied linguistics was neglected. Wright concurs with the above observation by stating that:

> [r]ather than focus on African languages as living cultural media, the academic study of African languages in South African universities has in general followed the international pattern of change in the field of general Linguistics: briefly, grammatical studies on the lines established by C.M. Doke in the 30s, 40s and 50s were followed (belatedly) in the 60s by structuralism, pioneered in South Africa by E.B. van Wyk. The 70s saw work shaped by the transformational-generative approach. (Wright, 2002: 17)

In the literature modules, the following content was offered: theory of literature and analysis of prescribed literature works, folklore, novel, short story, essay, poetry, drama, translations, composition, literary analysis, comprehension tests and creative writing.

Africanisation of Study Material

In the latest cycle of revision (2009–2011), the undergraduate course material has been designed with the needs of contemporary African society in mind and in recognition of the development of knowledge that relates to the African continent: African scholars have mostly worked within frameworks of foreign (mainly Western) theoretical models. Analysing an African language from this angle invariably led to misrepresentations of certain intrinsic structures, values and norms of these languages. In linguistic analysis, for example, a morpheme, which has generally become known as the present tense morpheme, is actually not a marker of tense, but a syntactic marker distinguishing between old and new information (Kosch, 1988). Writing on the state of African literature, Swanepoel (1990: 48) is of the opinion that 'imported theories may cause one to disregard, or even to deny, culture-specific features'. Brock-Utne (2003: 42) rightly advocates that '[w]hat Africa needs is to develop its own courses, research, and publications, more directly suited to situations in Africa'.

The flagship module of the College of Human Sciences, which is also part of the major in African languages (AFL1501) is a clear example of a course that looks at language issues through an African lens and not through a Western filter. The colour system, for example, cannot be described from a universalist point of view, but has to be described and approached culture-specifically. The Western filter has erroneously adopted some African language terms to fill the gaps in the colour spectrum, not realising that by doing this, the true facts regarding colour recognition have actually been skewed (Louwrens, 1993).

Course content is aimed at empowering students to apply African languages (literature and linguistics/grammar) in a variety of real-life contexts. For instance, AFL2601 (Communication Dynamics in African Languages) prepares students to apply different discourse strategies for effective communication, while AFL3702 (Indigenous Knowledge Systems and African Languages) introduces an understanding of African conduct and perspectives (see Makalela on this topic in Chapter 6) and affords students access to terminology and activities of indigenous knowledge systems (see Leeuw on this topic in Chapter 10), with the purpose of developing African languages. AFL3705 (Creative Writing and Translation) aims at equipping students with practical skills to produce much needed original and/or translated literary texts in their mother tongues.

The nature of the course contents described above lends itself ideally to multilingual interaction and collaboration via a learning platform, such as *myUnisa*, which can lead to the creation of 'a stronger learning community where members can build expertise and develop problem-solving skills' (Beldarrain, 2006: 150).

Medium of instruction

For many years (from inception until the turn of the century), the language of instruction in the linguistics subjects was English (with parallel study guides in Afrikaans – the other official language of South Africa at the time – until the early 1990s), while literature was taught in the different African languages. Special provision was made at first-year level for students who were non-mother-tongue speakers who had passed the beginners' course. This group was known as the B-stream of students, whereas the A-stream consisted of students who had passed an African language as first language for matriculation. In order to prepare the B-stream students for study at the second level, the chapters in the vernacular were also presented in English for their benefit and to create a 'bridge' to study at the higher levels. At the higher levels (levels 2 and 3) the literature modules were presented mainly in the vernacular, but interspersed in an *ad hoc* fashion with extracts in English from relevant literature or a discussion/analysis of phenomena through the medium of English.

From 2000, the teaching of linguistics subjects exclusively in the vernacular was phased in over a period of three years. Student numbers had started decreasing gradually, and it was argued that instruction in the mother tongue in all modules, including the linguistics subjects, would attract more students. It was thus expected that there would be a sharp rise in student numbers after the material had been transformed into the different indigenous languages, but instead, student numbers declined further, one of the reasons probably being that glossaries for new terms had not been developed. Students were unfamiliar with some of the new terms that had to be created to express concepts such as 'vowel raising', 'apico-alveolar' and so on.

Apart from the dearth of appropriate terminology, mother-tongue instruction otherwise makes sense pedagogically, when considering the following observation by Brock-Utne:

> Another very important reason that underpins why rote learning exists and flourishes in African education has to do with the fact that teachers are forced to teach, and learners to learn, in a language they do not command well. This situation begs serious and important questions about issues surrounding language in higher education. How can you develop skills of abstraction and system thinking if you are required to do this in an unfamiliar language? (Brock-Utne, 2003: 44)

As far back as 1996 Msimang expressed himself as follows:

> The use of African languages as languages of tuition at university level is not yet 'appropriate' or 'immediately feasible'. Secondly, it is not desirable so long as prospective university students learn their subjects through the medium of English at **school level** [own emphasis]. However modernisation of these languages should be tackled as a matter of urgency. Universities should train lexicographers and terminographers in African languages. (Msimang, 1996: 11)

The Department of African Languages heeded the call for the training of lexicographers and terminographers by way of the development of a level 3 module aimed at developing the much needed skills in terminography and lexicography, with special reference to the African languages. This includes term creation strategies, basic dictionary typology and computerised lexicography.

With the enforced rationalisation of modules caused by university operations (from 2009), the department had to revert to English as the medium of instruction in all modules, as all languages had to be accommodated under specific (multi-language) module codes. During this phase, knowledge of the languages was developed through the medium of English, followed by adaptation of the core material in each of the African languages. The language-specific material is made available to students as 'Additional Resources' on the *myUnisa* learning platform as well as on a CD-Rom. One of the advantages of the parallel texts in English and the African languages is that students are exposed to multiple languages and can therefore compile their own glossaries, especially of discipline-specific terms not encountered in everyday communication. These terms need to be understood in context and may not be found in any dictionary; much like the adaptations that students can make to the subject terminology lists described by Madiba in Chapter 5. Hence, the texts are a valuable source for the expansion of terminology. Luckett (1995: 77) emphasises that in order to promote the development of African languages in education 'the African languages [as media of instruction] will need to be developed to carry cognitively-demanding content and concepts.... New curricula with interactive and communicative teaching methods will also need to be developed so that the African languages can be learnt as living second languages'.

The adaptation processes of study material into eight African languages involved extensive term creation, which not only facilitates the development of the languages, but also contributes to language resources such as multilingual parallel corpora that benefit terminology extraction, lexicography, language learning, as well as the study of translation processes.

Handling Multilingual Challenges

Since its inception, the Department of African Languages has had to find ways of handling the challenges of multilingualism. Initially, related languages were grouped together and offered in an integrated manner. Later in time, an increase in student numbers allowed the department to appoint more lecturers and to offer more modules, enabling it to teach all languages as separate languages. In the latest move towards rationalisation, the department had to adopt an approach that would cater for all the languages within only 10 modules for a major (and two modules for the beginners' courses) in African languages – an approach that popularly became known as the multilanguage 'basket module' approach (see Figure 4.3). This approach differs from the earlier one (grouping together of closely related languages) in that study material is presented in parallel with other languages, whereas it was integrated in the earlier model. Technology has played a key role in providing unique opportunities, not only to expose students to multilingual study material, but also to promote interaction among them, particularly via the *myUnisa* learning platform.

The basket approach was pioneered for the two beginners' modules in 2009. Students who need to include an African language in their curriculum,

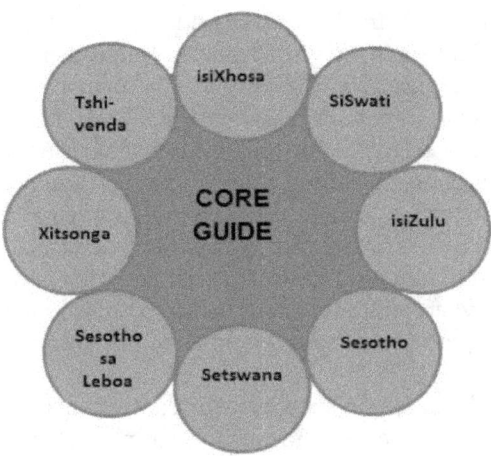

Figure 4.3 Diagrammatic representation of the multi-language 'basket module' concept

but who are in doubt as to which language would be the most appropriate for them in their area, can make an informed decision by browsing through the languages offered on a CD-Rom. This raises their awareness of differences and similarities between the languages, and even though they are required to choose only one language for the course, the full spectrum of other languages is available to the keen student wanting to learn more than one African language. In a multilingual context such as South Africa, where individuals need to communicate across speech communities, the 'basket module' approach with its multiple languages enables the student to gain insight into 'synergies and cross-fertilisation of languages which are a feature of "true" multilingualism' (Ouane, 2009: 59).

The multi-language CD-Rom was the only logical pedagogical approach to follow in order to accommodate all the languages under one module code. It represents both a technological solution and a pedagogical innovation. With computer knowledge and technological skills having become part and parcel of the graduate skills required of students when seeking employment, this course provides adequate integration of computer technology and the teaching process. The teaching approach on the CD-Rom aims to support creative learning environments by providing hyperlinks to pronunciations and interactive sound tracks.

Likewise, for the modules that form part of the major, a CD-Rom was the solution to cater simultaneously for all the languages offered. Students enrolling for a module are free to choose in which language they would like to study. To ensure that the offerings in the different African languages in a particular module maintain the same standard, core guides in English were developed first. Over time, they were 'translated' and then customised for each of the languages and placed on the *myUnisa* platform as well as on CD-Rom. The English core texts were not expected to be literally translated, but were to be used as a frame of reference for the development of African language-specific material. This entailed finding, for example, suitable poems and novels in all languages for analysis. The framework thus served as a benchmark and was not meant to be restrictive or prescriptive. The availability of the study material in multiple languages also leads to interesting and challenging tasks (as explained elsewhere in the chapter), whereby different African languages contribute to inter-comprehension, as explained by Ouane:

> To function adequately in such multilingual set-ups, there is a need to go beyond one's own speech community, to interact with other language groups and to be able to carry out survival transactions in other languages. (Ouane, 2009: 55)

Agnihotri (1995: 6) also refers to techniques in a multilingual classroom and suggests that a poem translated into different languages can lead to an appreciation of the similarities and differences between the languages. In this way, 'grammar, an otherwise hated aspect, could become both interesting and essential' (Agnihotri, 1995: 6). A comparative approach lends itself ideally to ODL. The multilingual approach has always been followed with regard to offerings at Honours level. Core guides in English are used to present the material and students need to apply the principles to their main language. Apart from this, they also need to be able to recognise the taught principles in other African languages.

Looking back, one realises that the department has actually come a long way in developing modes of tuition. As Beldarrain (2006: 140) observes, 'The rapid growth of online based distance education worldwide has prompted the need to revise delivery structures and re-think pedagogical practices that were once appropriate'. The basket modules may have been prompted by an operational challenge, but they also offer flexible learning opportunities, interaction and collaboration and are based on cross-pollination of knowledge between lecturers. Students are assessed in innovative ways, inspiring them to self-development and to discovering their own creativity, for example, in composing their own songs, based on characteristics observed through the analysis of traditional songs at beginners' level. At a more advanced level, students are, for instance, introduced to riddling and are tasked with comparing the different phrases in the different languages that are used in the introduction of a riddle.

The rationalisation of modules has also helped the less commonly used languages such as Tshivenda and Xitsonga to survive as student enrolment numbers in these languages would not have justified their continued existence. The marginalised languages were thus protected because they were incorporated into larger modules, with umbrella codes.

The department's drive then has been to achieve multilingual education through what Kotzé describes as a 'reality-based approach' (this volume).

Kotzé envisaged policy built on the backbone, as he put it, of vernacular languages used in the classroom as a means of instruction. As in the case of the Rhodes University study (Maseko, Chapter 3), Unisa's Department of African Languages is putting flesh on that backbone.

Way Forward

In order to stay abreast of ODL as a mode of delivery in higher education, and to bridge some of the more traditional constraints such as limited interaction and perceived distance, constant innovation is taking place within the multilingual environment of the Department of African Languages. A few examples, namely, open educational resources, full online delivery of study material and multilingual online terminology lists, are discussed in this concluding section.

Open Educational Resources (OERs)

Open Educational Resources (OERs) are teaching and learning materials that are available online, free of charge, and can be used by everyone whether they be lecturers, students or self-learners. Some examples of OERs include:

> full courses, course modules, syllabi, lectures, homework assignments, quizzes, lab and classroom activities, pedagogical materials, games, simulations, and many more resources contained in digital media collections from around the world. (Open Educational Resources infoKit, 2012)

Free online courses

An OER pilot project was run by the department in conjunction with the Directorate of Curriculum and Learning Development and the Sound, Video and Photography Department, whereby free online courses were developed, complete with video clips and interactive exercises (Free Online Courses Unisa, 2008) for five African languages (isiXhosa, isiZulu, Sesotho sa Leboa,

Sesotho and Setswana). This innovative and multidisciplinary project offers many prospects, which can be explored to enhance learning of an African language. In an environment of increased sharing of scholarship, the department will be revising its modules within an ODL framework and eventually aim towards designing materials for access on mobile devices, since currently more students are accessing the internet on mobile devices than on computers (McGreal, 2012).

Full online delivery

The Department of African Languages is becoming part of the repositioning of Unisa in the ODL sphere by participating in the so-called 'signature course' pilot project that promises dynamic innovation in terms of teaching and learning at Unisa. Courses in this project are developed for full online delivery (Mischke & le Roux, 2012). The focus of the signature modules will be 'mentorship, interaction, critical thinking, communication and media fluency, but they also reflect an appreciation for societal values and the establishment of social cohesion' (Mischke & le Roux, 2012). The signature course in African Languages has become a compulsory module for every student enrolling in the College of Human Sciences as from 2013. This module is taught according to a heutagogic approach, based on informal learning and peer teaching (students choose what is of interest to them within the discipline and teach each other). Essentially, students are taught to question themselves and to increasingly take responsibility for their own learning. It is incumbent on the lecturer to create conditions for the student to engage in situated learning and to co-create knowledge. The online mode of delivery encourages interaction and enhances critical and collective thinking.

Terminology

According to the Unisa Curriculum Policy (2010: 14–15), one of the activities relating to responsiveness to Unisa's *local* context is the inclusion of multilingual terminology lists in all modules. However, Mischke's (2010: 154) findings are that 'Academic departments largely teach in English with no multi-lingual terminology lists included in study material'. In response to the abovementioned policy, the Department of African Languages at Unisa has taken the lead in the development of African language terminologies through the teaching of, and research activities in, fields such as linguistics, lexicography, terminography, translation, literature, intercultural communication and so forth. In a recently approved inter-university project, funded by the DAAD (Deutscher Akademischer Austauschdienst), the aim is to fast-track the development of terminologies of African languages by means of an interdisciplinary team in which the South African linguistic expertise is complemented by German data management and programming expertise, in order to develop online terminologies and WIKI glossaries. The initial prototype will include two languages, namely isiZulu and Sesotho sa Leboa, and further languages will be included at a later stage.

Conclusion

In this chapter, the Department of African Languages at the University of South Africa (Unisa) was used as a case study in the investigation of multilingual teaching and learning of African languages at a tertiary level.

By reflecting on these learning and teaching experiences, the authors have attempted to portray best practices that emerged from the different approaches that have been followed from the past to the present, that is, teaching in language groups, teaching all African languages as separate languages and, finally, the multi-language 'basket' module approach, for the ongoing improvement of their courses.

Challenges, with which all departments of African Languages in South Africa were confronted during the rapid decline of student numbers during the first few years of this century, were addressed. Innovative solutions had to be found to keep the Department of African Languages at Unisa viable, without curtailing the number of African languages it had been offering in the past. This resulted in an adapted pedagogical approach, that is, flexible learning opportunities, interaction and collaboration, and exposing students to multilingual study material and assessment tasks.

Even though the South African Constitution explicitly protects and safeguards the equivalent linguistic rights of all official languages, the implementation of these rights cannot be taken for granted and hence the development and maintenance of the African languages need to be lobbied for constantly.

Notes

(1) We only list the South African languages within each group followed by their ISO 639-3 codes (ISO, 2012) in order to distinguish one language from other languages with the same or similar names and to identify the names of cross-border languages.
(2) Sesotho sa Leboa refers to Northern Sotho, a collective term for a variety of dialects of which Sepedi is the main dialect on which the standard written language is based (see Free Online Courses Unisa, 2008).
(3) Southern Ndebele will be offered as from 2014.

(4) It should be noted that student registrations as from 2000, when semesterisation took place, include registrations for both semesters 1 and 2.

References

Agnihotri, R.K. (1995) Multilingualism as a classroom resource. In K. Heugh, A. Siegrühn and P. Plüddemann (eds) *Multilingual Education for South Africa* (pp. 3–7). Johannesburg, RSA: Heinemann.

Beldarrain, Y. (2006) Distance education trends: Integrating new technologies to foster student interaction and collaboration. *Distance Education* 27 (2), 139–153.

Brock-Utne, B. (2003) Formulating higher education policies in Africa – the pressure from external forces and the neoliberal agenda. *Journal of Higher Education in Africa* 1 (1), 24–56.

Dowling, T. and Maseko, P. (1995) African language teaching at universities. In K. Heugh, A. Siegrühn and P. Plüddemann (eds) *Multilingual Education for South Africa* (pp. 100–106). Johannesburg, RSA: Heinemann.

Department of Education (2003) The development of indigenous African languages as mediums of instruction in higher education. See http://www.education.gov.za/LinkClick.asp x?fileticket=VVy05Mi9bJY%3D&tabid=452&mid=1036 (accessed 27 December 2013).

Free Online Courses Unisa (2008) [Xhosa, Zulu, Northern Sotho, Southern Sotho and Tswana]. See http://www.unisa.ac.za/free_online_course/index.html (accessed 5 June 2012).

ISO 639-3 (2012) See http://www.sil.org/iso639-3 (accessed 31 May 2012).

Kosch, I.M. (1988) 'Imperfect tense-*a*' of Northern Sotho revisited. *South African Journal of African Languages* 8 (1), 1–6.

Louwrens, L.J. (1993) Northern Sotho colour terms and semantic universals. *South African Journal of African Languages* 13 (4), 121–128.

Luckett, K. (1995) National additive bilingualism: Towards a language plan for South African education. In K. Heugh, A. Siegrühn and P. Plüddemann (eds) *Multilingual Education for South Africa* (pp. 73–78). Johannesburg, RSA: Heinemann.

McGreal, R. (2012) *Mobile Learning and Open Educational Resources: Challenge of the Future*. Address delivered on 25 April. Pretoria: Unisa.

Mischke, G. (2010) Towards effective curriculum design in ODL. *Progressio* 32 (2), 145–163.

Mischke, G. and le Roux, J.C. (2012) Analysing teaching presence in an open distance learning context. See http://www.unisa.ac.za/contents/conferences/odl2012/docs/submissions/ODL-021-2012_Final_MischkeG&leRouxJ.pdf (accessed 27 December 2013).

Msimang, T. (1996) The case for African languages. *Unisa Bulletin*, April: 11.

Nurse, D. and Philippson, G. (2003) *The Bantu Languages*. London: Routledge.

Olivier, J. and Rossouw, J.D. (1989) A portrait of Unisa. *Unisa Alumnus* 11 (November): 15–21.

Open Educational Resources infoKit (2012) See https://openeducationalresources.pbworks.com/w/page/24836480/Home (accessed 27 December 2013).

Ouane, A. (2009) My journey to and through a multilingual landscape. In K. Kwaa Prah and B. Brock-Utne (eds) *Multilingualism: An African Advantage* (pp. 53–61). Cape Town, RSA: Centre for Advanced Studies in African Society.

Swanepoel, C.F. (1990) *African Literature: Approaches and Applications*. Pretoria, RSA: De Jager-HAUM.

Taljaard, P.C., Khumalo, J.N. and Bosch, S.E. (2008) *Handbook of SiSwati*. Pretoria: J.L. van Schaik.

Unisa (2008) Open Distance Learning Policy. See http://www.unisa.ac.za/cmsys/staff/contents/departments/tuition_policies/docs/OpenDistanceLearning_Council3Oct08.pdf (accessed 27 December 2013).

Unisa (2010) Curriculum Policy. See http://www.unisa.ac.za/cmsys/staff/contents/departments/tuition_policies/docs/OpenDistanceLearning (accessed 27 December 2013).

Unisa (2011) African Languages. See http://www.unisa.ac.za/Default.asp?Cmd=ViewContent&ContentID=143 (accessed 27 December 2013).

Unisa (2012) The history of UNISA. See http://www.unisa.ac.za/Default.asp?Cmd=ViewContent&ContentID=19890 (accessed 27 December 2013).

Wright, L.S. (2002) Language as a 'resource' in South Africa: the economic life of language in a globalising society. *English Academy Review* 19 (1), 2–19.

Ziervogel, D. (1957) *We Present – Ons Stel Voor*. Unpublished manuscript. Pretoria, RSA: Unisa Archives.

5 Promoting Concept Literacy through Multilingual Glossaries: A Translanguaging Approach

Mbulungeni Madiba

Introduction

The focus of this chapter is on the role of multilingual glossaries in constructing scaffolding for concept literacy in different disciplines or content areas at tertiary level. The term *concept literacy* is fairly new in South African educational literature and is used here to refer to students' 'ability to read, understand and use the learning area-specific words, terms and related language forms which are part of knowledge formation in the different disciplines or content areas' (Young et al., 2005: 8). Learning new disciplinary concepts in higher education always poses a challenge to students. At the University of Cape Town (UCT), and perhaps in other English-medium universities, these conceptual difficulties are often experienced by English-as-an-additional-language (EAL) students who have limited proficiency in English, which is used in these universities as the medium of instruction. These EAL students experience problems at both conceptual and linguistic levels.

Linguistically, it is an accepted fact that an interdependent relationship exists between language and conceptualisation (Cummins, 1979, 2000; Pederson & Nuyts, 1997; Piaget, 1959, 1977). Thus, multilingual glossaries are seen as the panacea to the EAL students' language and conceptual difficulties. In fact, the development and use of multilingual glossaries in South

African universities is required by the Language Policy for Higher Education, adopted by government in 2002. UCT launched its multilingual glossaries project in 2007, in accordance with its Language Policy (University of Cape Town, 1999, revised 2003) and the Language Plan adopted in 2003 (University of Cape Town, 2003).

The aim of this chapter is to discuss the role of multilingual glossaries that are being developed at UCT and their use in building concept literacy. The argument presented in this chapter is that the use of multilingual glossaries, based on a translanguaging approach, constitutes an important pedagogic strategy to address EALs' conceptual and linguistic problems in South African English-medium universities such as UCT. However, the use of multilingual glossaries based on a translanguaging approach to developing concept literacy also raises questions of a theoretical, methodological and practical nature. Theoretically, while traditional multilingual glossaries were based on a pluralistic view of multilingualism, that is, the view of languages as discrete and separable entities (Makoni & Mashiri, 2007), translanguaging requires a different conceptualisation of both the constructs of 'language' and 'multilingualism'. With regard to methodology, the question is how translanguaging pedagogy can be used to support concept literacy through multilingual glossaries. The question of practicality concerns the number of languages used and a high linguistic diversity among students.

In this chapter, I seek to address some of the above questions. I have drawn insight from existing theories on translanguaging pedagogy and also from translanguaging practices that students and facilitators used during the multilingual concept literacy tutorials piloted at UCT. However, as the project is still in its pilot phase, the chapter will mainly provide a conceptual argument for the use of a translanguaging approach in providing scaffolding for concept literacy through multilingual glossaries. First, the UCT concept literacy project will be described, and then the pedagogic use of these glossaries to promote concept literacy will be discussed.

The Concept Literacy Project

The UCT Concept Literacy Project was initiated in 2007 as part of the implementation of the University's Language Policy (University of Cape Town, 1999, revised 2003) and the Language Plan adopted in 2003 (University of Cape Town, 2003). The Language Plan requires that multilingual glossaries be developed to support students for whom English is not their first language. As Maseko points out in Chapter 3, the development of bi-/multilingual glossaries and dictionaries are important to support cognition and for that reason these glossaries are aimed at building concept literacy in the different content-learning areas. The pilot project was focused on Statistics, Economics and Law. The first phase of the project was devoted to developing multilingual glossaries, and the second phase is focussed on using the glossaries to promote concept literacy. The multilingual glossaries will be discussed first and then their use in promoting concept literacy will be debated.

The compilation of the glossaries

The UCT multilingual glossaries are based on the special language corpora constructed for this purpose. These special language corpora are used as the main conceptual bases for the glossaries. The corpora are based on generally accepted criteria for designing special language corpora (Bowker & Pearson, 2002; Madiba, 2004). These criteria include size, text types, publication status, text origin, constitution of the texts, authorship, and external and internal criteria. With regard to size, special language corpora tend to be much smaller than general language corpora as a result of their content and the compilation process (Lawson, 2001: 293). A number of researchers have recommended at least 30,000 words for a small special language corpus (Bowker, 1996; Bowker & Pearson, 2002). Although the size of some of the UCT corpora is small, most important is the purposes for which they have been designed (Meyer & Mackintosh, 1996).

The extraction of terms was carried out by using WordSmith Tools. WordSmith Tools performs automatic term extraction on the basis of statistical analyses. A final wordlist was compiled – not solely on the basis of the number of occurrences or frequencies. Having gone through the basic list, lecturers and tutors in Economics were consulted, since some common words would normally have a high frequency of occurrence in specialised texts, while some terms would be of a relatively low frequency. After the compilation of the final wordlist, concordances were generated using WordSmith Tools and Multiconcord to identify the meanings or the sense of the terms in different contexts. The concordances were very effective in writing the definitions of the different terms. After the completion of the definitions, a professional translation company was commissioned to translate the glossaries from English into the other 10 official languages.

Multilingual glossaries hypermedia on Vula

The UCT multilingual glossaries were designed right from the start to be used as online resources. The University Online Environment for the glossaries was developed on Vula by the Centre for Education Technology and is

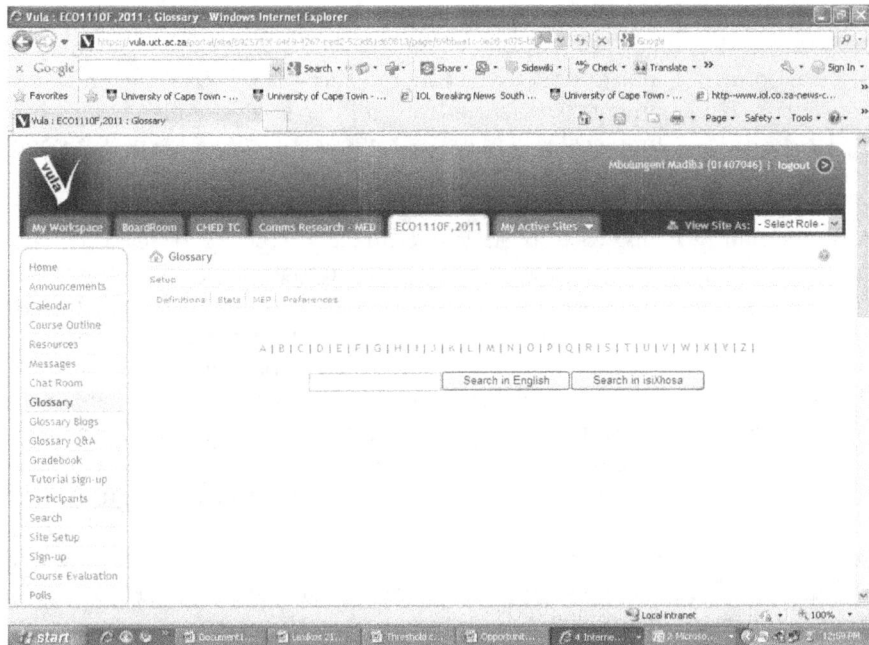

Figure 5.1 Economics online glossaries hypermedia on Vula

powered by Sakai. This networked Online Learning Environment provides students with easy access to the glossaries and other resources in different languages. The use of technology has made it possible to accommodate many languages and to provide a wide range of digital tools to enhance conceptual understanding, word meaning, contextual information and comprehension scaffolds to guide students' learning of the concepts. As can be seen from Figure 5.1 above, the Vula hypermedia system also includes multimodal mental representation of concepts that include visual (mental imagery), auditory (sound), perceptual (video) and kinaesthetic (sensory-motor).

A translanguaging approach to concept literacy

The pedagogic use of multilingual glossaries at university level raises questions of a theoretical, methodological and practical nature. Theoretically, the first question concerns the relationship between language and concept literacy. The relationship between language and concept literacy has been the subject of various studies, ranging from linguistic to cognitive/psycholinguistic and socio-cultural studies (Bakhtin, 1981; Cummins, 1979, 2000; Piaget, 1959, 1977; Vygotsky, 1986). Both Piaget and Vygotsky viewed concept learning to be developmental and constructive (Fosnot & Perry, 2005: 22). Piaget regarded conceptual development as essential for children's development of mental structures or certain logical schemata that allow encoding of aspects of content and their learning at deep level (Piaget, 1959, 1977). Vygotsky, who was a psychologist and a contemporary of Piaget, considered conceptual development as mainly owing to systematic and direct instruction of scientific concepts. Contrary to Piaget, Vygotsky (1986) argued that the learning of scientific concepts precedes the development of an established logical structure, and that such a development can be optimised through direct instruction. According to him, instruction of concepts does not need to wait for internal development. Rather, the instruction of scientific concepts should precede the development of an established logical structure as, according to Vygotsky, the development of mental structures is influenced by internal factors as well as external factors, such as social and cultural factors. Although he considered language as an important semiotic or mediation tool that children use to learn scientific concepts, and maintained that there is a direct relationship between thought and language, he did not address the issue of multilingualism or the use of two or more languages in developing the learning of scientific concepts.

The issue of multilingualism is complex as the meaning of the concept *multilingualism* has evolved over time. Early definitions of multilingualism were based on the view of languages as discrete and separate entities. Multilingualism was therefore viewed as a series of monolingualisms. Recent theories of multilingualism go beyond this view of multilingualism as a series of discrete separate languages to one which views languages as fluid and intermingling (García, 2009; Makoni & Mashiri, 2007). However, as Mick (2011: 38) points out, 'this does not mean denying the pragmatic sense of linguistic standards for communication in larger communities of practice', ... 'it means looking carefully at social power relations that are fostered and co-/re-/reproduced through ideologically motivated uses of "language" for social exclusion, domination or subordination'.

In regard to the role of multilingual glossaries in bolstering concept literacy, it is important to give a brief overview of the historiography of these types of glossaries. Multilingual glossaries have long been used as pedagogic tools to promote teaching and learning of concepts (Hüllen, 1989; Sauer, 2008). In the Middle Ages, for example, bi/multilingual glossaries were used to address difficult academic terms of foreign origin (Latin, Greek and French) by text producers and subject specialists and educators to explain these terms, first within texts and later outside their contexts as independent compilations. As Hüllen (1989) notes, within texts, the glossing notes were used to explain difficult terms and to provide translation equivalents. These words 'were copied, rearranged, e.g. from textual to alphabetical order, and extended, e.g. from bilingual to trilingual lists, and varied in other ways' (Hüllen, 1989: 101–102). Accordingly, in these lists, Old English terms were juxtaposed with (mostly) Latin, but also with Greek and Anglo-Norman terms, and were used as a helpful device for establishing word meanings. In this way, the glossaries promoted translatability between Latin, Greek and English, and the acquisition of Latin, Greek and English vocabularies during the Middle Ages. Thus, right from their emergence, multilingual glossaries were written down with the primary intention of providing academic support to multilingual students or readers of academic texts.

While early multilingual glossaries were based on monoglossic ideology, the development and use of multilingual glossaries since the 1980s is based on heteroglossic ideology. Bakhtin (1981) introduced the concept of *heteroglossia*, which according to Mick (2011: 24), 'challenges a materialist, essentialist ideology of singular, homogeneous and countable languages that is silently present in ideological interpretations of the concepts of bi-/multi-plurilingualism'. In the 21st century, the concept of heteroglossia has gained prominence and is supported by scholars such as García (2009), who criticises the monolingual and monoglossic approaches to language use in the academic learning environment. According to García, these approaches are no longer relevant as the academic learning environment has become linguistically more complex, especially in developing, multilingual countries, and thus requires the use of various linguistic resources in creative and innovative ways or what Makoni and Mashiri (2007: 71) refer to as 'multilingual networks'.

One of these creative ways of using different linguistic resources in the academic learning environment is what has now popularly become known as *translanguaging*. The term *translanguaging* (originally *trawsieithu* in Welsh) was first used in Welsh schools in the 1980s by Cen Williams (Lewis *et al.*, 2012b). In the Welsh context, translanguaging 'entails using one language to reinforce the other in order to increase understanding and in order to augment the pupil's ability in both languages' (Williams, 2002: 40). Thus, according to Williams, translanguaging is both a pedagogical theory and a practice. As a pedagogic theory, it is concerned with a cognitive process involving a two-language interchange, that is, 'the various cognitive processing skills in listening and reading, the assimilation and accommodation of information, choosing and selecting from the brain storage to communicate in speaking and writing' (Lewis *et al.*, 2012b: 644). Williams (1996, cited in Lewis *et al.*, 2012a) regarded translanguaging to be more than just translating as it moves from finding parallel words to processing and relaying meaning and understanding. An important distinguishing feature of translanguaging pedagogy is that it focuses on the child rather than on the teacher, that is, how a learner uses the available linguistic repertoires to develop deeper understanding of the subject. As a pedagogical practice, translanguaging is concerned with the practice employed to deliberately switch the language mode of input and output in bilingual classrooms.

The term *translanguaging* is now widely used and has been adopted for studies on multilingual education by various scholars (e.g. Baker, 2001, 2011; Canagarajah, 2011; Creese & Blackledge, 2010, 2011; García, 2009; Hornberger & Link, 2012). These studies clearly show that the use of translanguaging has many advantages in multilingual educational contexts. First, this approach resolves the tension that is often observed between 'students' heterogeneous life-world reality and an institutionally maintained ideal of single, holistic and unitary language' (Mick, 2011: 25), which tends to exclude the existing linguistic resources that students bring into the academic learning environment. Second, translanguaging allows 'multilingual speakers to intentionally integrate local and academic discourse as a form of resistance, re-appropriation and/or transformation of academic discourse' (Canagarajah, 2007: 56). Third, in concept literacy, it enables students to develop their own voice and engage critically with academic concepts rather than learning definitions by rote, much like the situation described by Kosch and Bosch (Chapter 4) when they note that 'these terms need to be understood in context and may not be found in any dictionary'. As Cazden (2005: 8) points out, 'there is a difference in "reciting by heart" and retelling in one's own words'. According to him, the words that are tightly woven with one's own words, awaken new and independent words that are organised from within, instead of remaining isolated and in a static condition. Lastly, translanguaging promotes a deeper and fuller understanding of the subject matter (Baker, 2011).

Translanguaging and the use of UCT multilingual concept literacy glossaries

The UCT multilingual glossaries were designed from the start to facilitate multilingual concept literacy. However, the development of these glossaries was not based on the translanguaging approach as described in the previous section. The main focus was on intertranslatability across languages as the glossaries promote access to concepts through the use of all the 11 official languages of South Africa. However, with hindsight from the previous section, it is clear that the multilingual and multimodal nature of the glossaries facilitates translanguaging. Figure 5.2 below shows multiple ways of accessing the concepts and their definitions.

Promoting Concept Literacy through Multilingual Glossaries   75

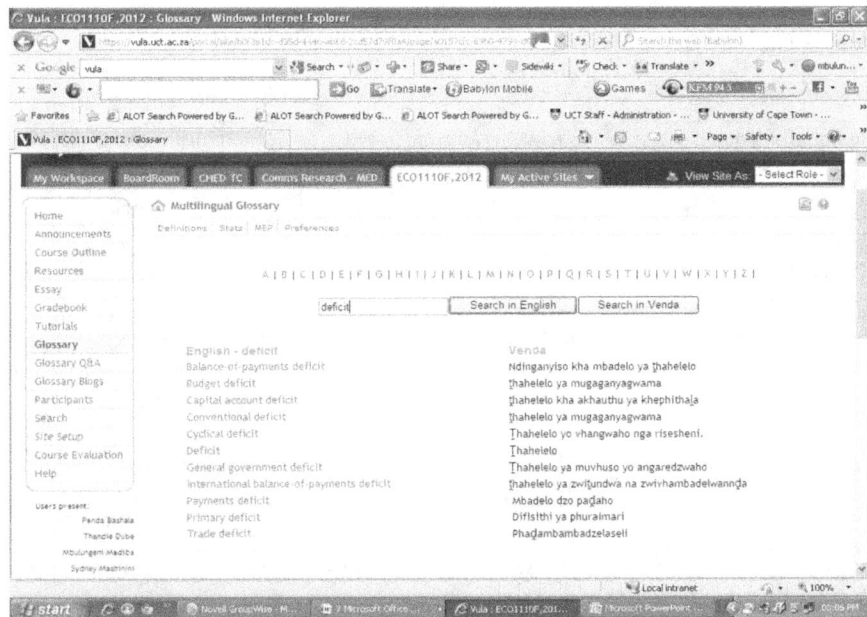

Figure 5.2 Economics online glossaries hypermedia on Vula

Figure 5.2 shows the various ways in which students can use the glossaries to search for terms and their equivalents in different languages. Students can search for the definition by entering a word or term in the space provided or using an alphabetical search by clicking on the relevant letter. The search conducted by entering the term, or part of it, is essential for concept literacy, as it brings together related concepts that enable students to understand the relationships among such concepts. The example, Table 5.1, extracted from the economics glossary on Vula, shows English multiword terms with the word 'aggregate' and their translations in Tshivenda and isiXhosa.

Although the examples above only show three languages, the glossary provides access to translation equivalents in all the 11 official languages of South Africa. Once the entry term is selected and its equivalents are identified, students can search in English and in all the other 10 official languages, as shown in Figure 5.3.

In Figure 5.3, the definition appears in both the source and the target languages. The list of other languages also appears at the bottom of the screen shot. When clicking on the language, the translation equivalent 'pops

Table 5.1 English multiword terms with the word 'aggregate' and their translations in Tshivenda and isiXhosa

English – aggregate	Tshivenda	isiXhosa
Aggregate demand	Ndilazwibveledzwadzo ṱhe	Umndililiwempahla (iyonke)
Aggregate demand – aggregate supply model	Tshiedziso tsha ṱho ḓeadzo ṱhe-na Nḓisedzodzo ṱhe	Umdilili onzinzileyo wendleko (AFC)
Aggregate demand for labour curve	Kheve ya ṱho ḓeadzo ṱhe dza vhashumi	Umndilili wokunyusa ixabiso
Aggregate expenditure function	ṱho ḓeadzo ṱhe dza zwibviswa zwo ṱhe	Umndilili okanye ukutwabuluka kwexabiso lesiqingatha sesazine semfuneko
Aggregate expenditure model	Tshedziso tsha zwibviswa zwo ṱhe	Umndilili wemveliso ephathekayo
Aggregate expenditures	Zwibviswa zwo ṱhe	Umndilili wemveliso (AP)
Aggregate expenditures – domestic output approach	Zwibviswa zwo ṱhe - maitele a u wana ndinganyiso	Umndilili wokuthambekela kusetyenziso
Aggregate-expenditures schedule	Sheduhuya zwibviswa zwo ṱhe	Umndilili wokutyekela kugcino/ulondolozo
Aggregate spending	Zwibviswa zwo ṱhe	Umndilili wezinga lerhafu yengeniso
Aggregate supply	Nḓisedzo yo ṱhe	Umndilili wengeniso (AR)
Aggregate supply curve	Kheve ya Nḓisedzo yo ṱhe	Umndilili wezinga lerhafu
Aggregate supply of labour curve	Kheve ya ndisedzo yo ṱhe ya zwa mishumo	Ukubeka ixabiso lomndilili
Aggregate supply shocks	Tshanduko ya tshihaṱu yanḓisedzo yo ṱhe	Umndilili wendleko iyonke

out' in that language, opposite the source language. A particular advantage of these online glossaries is the speed and the convenience with which students can make cross-linguistic searches. The glossary site also provides a space for the user to give feedback on the quality of the translation equivalents. The status of the translation equivalent is also shown as 'unassigned', 'draft', 'approved' or 'assigned'. This function is used to overcome the thorny problem of standardisation of translated terms in African languages. According to the traditional approach, standardisation should be top-down,

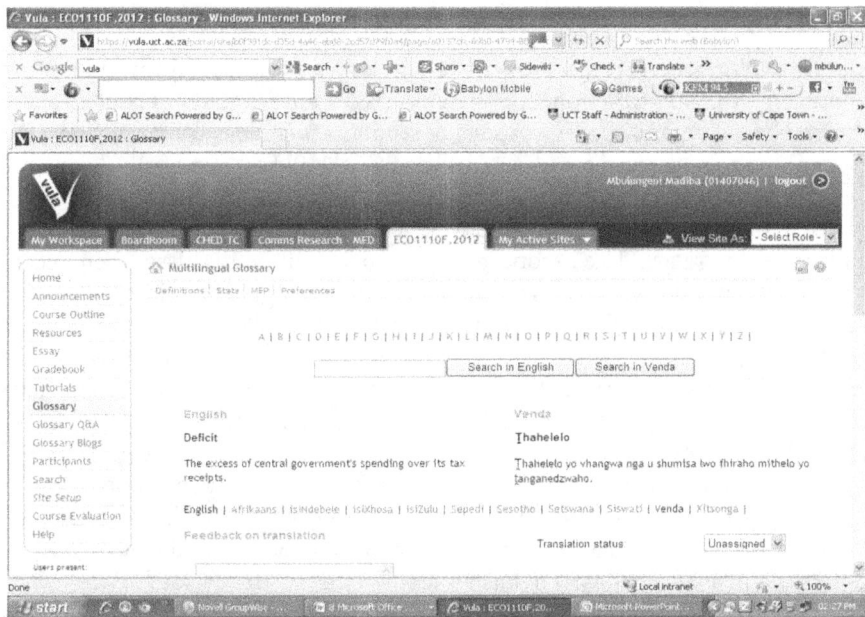

Figure 5.3 Multilingualism Education Project (MEP) online learning environment on Vula

that is, it should be carried out by authorised standardisation bodies such as the Pan South African Language Board (PanSALB) and its structures (the National Language Bodies) (Nkomo & Madiba, 2011). In the case of UCT, the power to standardise terms partly rests with the users, students and other professionals in the disciplines, and thus follows a bottom-up approach rather than the top-down approach adopted in the development of traditional multilingual glossaries. Because the approach adopted in these glossaries is not prescriptive, variant terms and synonyms are accepted provided they are useful in developing concept literacy.

The glossaries are based on a multimodal approach, and as such, the definitions can also be linked with tutorials, pictures, graphics and podcasts. The glossary site also includes other functions such as modules, blogs, chat room forums and a question-and-answer query function (Q and A). Using this online learning environment function, lecturers and students are encouraged to use their primary languages or mix them with English to describe their understanding of the meaning of the concepts. After students have completed their online tasks, feedback is given online or face-to-face in multilingual tutorials.

Translanguaging in multilingual concept literacy tutorials

To explore the effectiveness of the glossaries and the translanguaging approach in promoting concept literacy, two multilingual concept literacy tutorials were organised. Two groups of students were selected from first-year students who registered for ECO1110F or ECO1110H as part of the Academic Development Programme in the Faculty of Commerce. The first group comprised students who speak isiXhosa as a home language and English as an additional language. The second group, which will be discussed here, comprised students who speak Tshivenda as a home language and English as an additional language. The isiXhosa tutorial was a follow-up to the studies conducted previously, without the online multilingual glossaries, by Paxton (2007, 2009). Two tutorials (1 hour each) were organised for each group. Two tutors were also appointed to facilitate the tutorials. Only students who had studied an African language as Home Language in Grade 12 were selected. Two terms were selected for discussion in each session. Students were allowed to use both English and their home language in the tutorial discussions. The tutorials were recorded and then transcribed for analysis. Only the results of the Tshivenda tutorials will be discussed here because of lack of space.

The first Tshivenda tutorial focussed on the concept *deficit*. Seven students participated in this tutorial, which was facilitated by a post-graduate Tshivenda-speaking tutor. All the students selected for the project had studied Tshivenda as a Home Language in Grade 12 and were first-year students. These students participated in the tutorial voluntarily as this was just a pilot study.

The tutorial was first conducted online, where students were asked to log onto the glossaries website on Vula and complete a question and answer exercise. The exercise required students to look at the definitions of several terms, including the term *deficit*, and to define each in English and in their home language and give the equivalent term. This was followed by a face-to-face tutorial in which students were requested to write down their definitions of the term *deficit* in English and in Tshivenda on the sheet provided to them. The following are some of the definitions and their equivalents in Tshivenda.

Extract 1

Student 1

English: The shortage in the amount requested.
Tshivenda: Thahelelo kha zwine zwa khou diswa (zwine zwa khou todea). Thahelelo ine ya vha hone kha sia la masheleni nga

murahu ha musi vhathu vha tshi khou toda u renga thodea dzavho.

Student 2

English: A point at which a loss has been made, especially in the business situation wherein total expense exceeds total income.

Tshivenda: Ndi ndozwo ine ya bvelela nga maanda kha bindu hune ra wana mbuelo ye bindu la wana i thukhu kha ndozwo (zwe zwa shumiswa) nga maanda ro sedza tshelede, i.e. tshelede yo shumiswaho ndi nnzhi u fhirisa ye bindu la wana kana u bindulisa. e.g. bindu lo wana/ita ndozwo nwedzi uno.

Student 3

English: Deficit is when a country has overspent or used more money than it has. They have used more than the budgeted amount.

Tshivenda: Ndi musi wo shumisa kana huna ndozwo. Ndi musi vho shumisa tshelede i no fhira yo vheiwaho. Afurika Tshiepembe lo vha na ndozwo ya madana, avhili kha nwaha wa muvhalelano wa nanwaha.

Student 4

English: It means to be overpowered or loose [sic]/loss.
Tshivenda: Ndi u luza, loswo. Tsumbo, musi u na vhengele wa rengisa nga mutengo wa wa fhasi ha mutengo we vha u badela vha tshi renga zwi amba uri a vho ngo wana tshithu fhedzi vho luza.

Student 5

English: It means that a business is running at a loss or when a business is operating at a loss.

Tshivenda: Ndi musi bindu li sa khou wana mbuyelo, li tshi khou tshimbila nga ndozwo.

Student 6

English: A deficit is a loss that is suffered by business after they have conducted all their business acitivities [sic] and substracted [sic] their expenses out of their income.

Tshivenda: Ndi ndozwo ine ya wanwa kha mugaganyagwama nga murahu ha musi bindu lo no tusa masheleni ane a khou bva ngomu binduni kha masheleni ane la vha nao.

Student 7

English: It is a shortfall or loss in our budget, when expenditure exceeds own income.

Tshivenda: Ndi ndozwo ya masheleni kha mugaganyagwama ro wana zwituku kha masheleni e ra vha ro a lavhelela musi tshelede ine ra khou i shumisa i tshi fhira ine ra khou i wana.

From the definitions above, it may be observed that students tried to keep English definitions separate from the Tshivenda ones. They also tried to use standard Tshivenda as is used in school. They used loanwords such as *tshelede* (English 'money' or Afrikaans *'geld'*), *masheleni* ('shillings' or 'money') and *ndozwo* ('loss'). A term such as *budget* was replaced by a newly derived compound term *mugaganyagwama* (literally 'purse estimator'). It is also important to note that the English definitions are shorter than the Tshivenda ones. Some of the English definitions have spelling and grammatical mistakes. The English definitions also reflect students' surface understanding of the concept *deficit* and appear to be the result of rote learning. However, the aim of the tutorials was to deepen their understanding of the concepts rather than learning them by rote. To this end, students were engaged in debate and discussion to facilitate deeper understanding of the concept. As the facilitator, I, the author of this chapter, began by explaining the purpose of the tutorial and indicated to students to use English first and then Tshivenda. The following are the transcriptions of the multilingual tutorials facilitated by a Tshivenda tutor (T) and by me as I am also a speaker of the language. Each student was asked to present his or her definition(s) to the rest of the group, first in English and then in Tshivenda.

Extract 2: Definition of the concept of *deficit*

S1: IT IS A SHORTAGE
T: No i talutshedza nga ONLY ONE WORD
S1: *Ndi a balelwa* ACTUALLY *u tou li dzudzanya lothe lo fhelela,* BUT I KNOW *uri ri tshi khou ita* SURPLUS *na* [inaudible], *hu tou nga hu vha hu na* SHORTAGE *ya zwinwe zwithu, hu khou dimandiwa hu si na zwine zwa khou sapulaiwa.*

S2: *Nne ndo ri* DEFICIT IS A POINT WHEN A LOSS HAS BEEN MADE, ESPECIALLY IN A SITUATION WHERE EXPENSES EXCEED INCOME.

T: AS IS BUDGET, BECAUSE *heyo ndi* PROFIT. *Ndi* PROFIT OR LOSS

S3: THIS IS WHEN YOU HAVE USED MORE THAN THE BUDGETED AMOUNT.

S4: OK, IT IS THE SAME BECAUSE *nne na nne ndi zwi sedza* IN TERMS OF ACCOUNTING, SINCE I DID ACCOUNTING AT SCHOOL. IF EXPENSES *dzi tshi* EXCEED AN INCOME, IT IS A LOSS. THUS WHY I SAY DEFICIT IS A LOSS. THIS IS YOU HAVE USED MORE THAN THE BUDGETED AMOUNT.

T: *Ndi* LOSS IF *arali a khomphera* EXPENSES *ndi* LOSS *arali a khou i amba* IN TERMS OF ACCOUNTING, *habe hafho u khou i amba* IN TERMS OF ACCOUNTING.

S4: *A thi i pfesesi kha* ECONOMICS, *ndi i pfesesa kha* ACCOUNTING.

S5: *Nne ndo nwala uri* DEFICIT IS WHEN THE BUSINESS IS RUNNING A LOSS.

T: AGAIN, *no fokhasa* MORE *kha* ACCOUNTING, *ne*.

From this extract, it is clear that in their debates and discussions of the concept of *deficit*, the students were mainly concerned with meaning making or discourse rather than with the form. They use translanguaging to express their views. In some cases, a sentence starts in English and ends in Tshivenda or vice versa. This kind of language use would traditionally be referred to as 'codeswitching' (Lewis *et al.*, 2012b). However, as Makalela points out in this volume (Chapter 6), drawing from translanguaging theories of scholars such as García (2009), there is a difference between codeswitching and translanguaging. Codeswitching is based on the view of languages as separate entities, whereas translanguaging regards languages as fluid and intermingling (García, 2009; Lewis *et al.*, 2012a). This fluidity of languages is also evidenced by how students make use of English words within the Tshivenda grammatical system. However, it is interesting to note that the name of the disciplines such as 'Accounting' and 'Economics' were consistently used in Tshivenda sentences in their original English spelling.

Extract 3: The difference between 'deficit' and 'loss'

In this extract, students were asked to explain the difference between 'deficit' and 'loss' and this required them to demonstrate their comparison skills, which is a high-order thinking skill. Although students continue to use translanguaging, what is significant in the following passage is how the usage of Tshivenda increases in comparison to the previous extract.

Facilitator: What is the difference between 'deficit' and 'loss'?
Student: *Hmm, eish!*
[Hmm, exclamation.]
Facilitator: *Ni do ri ndi mini? Ambani nga Tshivenda.*
[What will you say? Speak in Tshivenda.]
Tutor: *Nne mara ndi khou vhona helo lauri zwi bva khauri ri khou amba zwi tshi khou elana na mini ndi zwone zwa vhukuma ngauri DEFICIT i na zwithu zwinzhi nga ngomu, hu na DEFICIT ya BALANCE OF TRADE na BALANCE OF PAYMENTS, hu na DEFICIT yeneyi ya zwisipotsokilabu, hu na DEFICIT ya TRADING STOCK DEFICIT, SO zwi do tou bva khauri ri khou i ambela gai.*
[I think that saying that it depends on the discipline under discussion is the correct approach because deficit has many meanings, there is deficit of balance of trade and balance of payments, there is also deficit of sports club, deficit of trading stock, so it always depend on the discipline under discussion]
Student: *Nne ndi khou vhona uri naho ri tshi khou ri hedzi DEFINITIONS dzo fhambana zwi tshi bva khauri ri khou i ambela gai, dzothe dzi vha dzi tshi khou amba LOSS, OVERALL ya zwithu zwothe zwi khou amba uri zwe ra vha ro lavhelela u zwi wana a ro ngo zwi wana, ndi loso, OVERALL ya zwithu zwothe kana ndi TRADE, kana mini, mara OVERALL, arali ri khou tou ri DEFICIT hu na LOSS.*
[In my view, even if these definitions are different depending on the contexts, all of them refer to overall loss of all things, implying that we did not get what we were expecting, and this is overall loss of all things, whether trade or whatever, but overall if we have deficit, we have loss.]
Student: *Loso ndi ya ACCOUNTING, hu tou vha uri kha ECONOMICS vha ri DEFICIT. Loso ndi LANGUAGE ya ACCOUNTING.*
[*Loss* is in accounting; it is only that in economics we say *deficit*. Loss is an accounting language.]
Student: *Zwi a CONFiyuza, nne na nne ndo thoma ECONOMICS fhano, hu na zwinzhi zwine zwi tshi ambiwa na kilasini vha ri ri tevhele heyi INFORMATION nga maanda, ngauri ri nga wana ipfi li la ACCOUNTING line na li shumisa kha ECONOMICS la vha li WRONG nga maanda.*

Promoting Concept Literacy through Multilingual Glossaries 83

	[This is confusing, I have also started to do economics here; there are many things which are warned to take into consideration, especially because you can find an accounting word which can be wrong when used in economics.]
Student:	*Zwi fana na CAPITAL, kha ACCOUNITNG IS MONEY, ngeno kha ECONOMICS i mitshini.* [It is the same with capital, in accounting it is money, whereas in economics it entails machines.]
Tutor:	*Mara OVERALL hu fanela u vha naho li tshi mina zwinwe zwithu zwine a li mini zwone, LIKE MAY BE arali ri tshi khou ri kha ACCOUNTING li mina hezwi, na kha ECONOMICS li mina hezwi, hunga si do ri kha ACCOUNTING ipfi a mbo di pfi POSITIVE ngeno kha ECONOMICS li tshi mbo di mina NEGATATIVE... arali ri tshi khou ri CAPITAL i ne ra khou ita yone zwino, CAPITAL i do vha uri ri khou ri OWNER o CONTRIBu-tha CAPITAL uri a kone u PRODU-sa kana u rana BUSINESS, zwino kha ECONOMICS i do da ya ri mini? OWNER u CONTRIBU-tha CAPITAL IN THE FORM OF mitshini uri a kone u PRODU-sa dzi-GOODS.* [But overall there needs to be similarity in meaning, that is, even if the terms means different things, for example, if we say the term in accounting means this, and something different in economics, the meanings cannot be directly opposite to each other, that is positive in accounting and negative in economics ... if we are talking about capital, we mean that the producer or a business person has contributed capital to produce or run the business, but in economics what will capital be? In economics the owner may contribute capital in the form of machines in order to produce goods.]
Facilitator:	*Zwi amba uri DEFICIT zwine ya amba zwone kha ACCOUNTING zwi do fanela u elana na zwine ya amba zwone kha ikonomi, zwi nga tou fhambanavho khamusi fhano na fhala.* [This means that the meaning of deficit in accounting should be related to what this term means in economics, the difference can only be here and there.]

From this extract, it is clear that translanguaging is used as a productive strategy to support discussion and deeper understanding of the two concepts. However, what is interesting to observe is the continuous use of the term *deficit* as in English. The term *loss* was often changed into a Tshivenda loanword *loso*, but sometimes used in its original English form. Another interesting strategy employed by students was to change only one part of the term into Tshivenda in words such as 'CON*fuza*', 'CONTRIB*u-tha*' and 'PRODU-*sa*'.

In sum, the two extracts clearly show the effective use of translanguaging to retain the economics discourse or register. Although no formal assessment of students' understanding of the concept *deficit* was done, their deeper understanding of the concept was quite apparent. Furthermore, that the students were, in the end, able to compare the concept *deficit* with other related concepts, such as *loss*, shows development or progression in their conceptualisation of the concept. The effect of translanguaging in students' understanding of the concepts has also been recognised in previous studies by Bangeni (2001) and Paxton (2007, 2009). Bangeni's (2001) project was focused on the use of students' first languages in a language course in Humanities. Paxton's (2007, 2009) studies, which were part of her pilot project on the use of multilingual glossaries at the School of Economics, in the same university, also established that the use of students' primary languages deepens their understanding of economics concepts and enhances their voices. The project also explored the use of a range of methods such as concept translation, code switching and multilingual tutorials.

Conclusion

The aim of this chapter was to show how a translanguaging approach can be used to provide a scaffold for concept learning among multilingual students in South African universities. The multilingual glossaries concept literacy project clearly demonstrated how multilingual students employ translanguaging to deepen their understanding of economics concepts. The use of translanguaging is critical at UCT as it enables EAL students to access the concepts in their own primary languages in which they have high proficiency and confidence. As Vygotsky (1994: 358) observes, '[t]he road leading from the initial familiarity with a new concept to the moment when the word and the concept become the child's property is a complex internal psychological process'. It is clear from the pilot tutorials that translanguaging allows multilingual students to integrate their primary languages and academic discourse with their discussion of the different economic concepts. Thus, the use of translanguaging also resolves the tension that is often observed between students' heterogeneous life and an institutionally monolingual English pedagogy in the classroom.

Although it is still too early to assess the success of this project, the interactive nature of the glossaries and associated elements, such as pictures, podcasts and blogs, provides implementation spaces for translanguaging in teaching and learning programmes. The main challenge, however, is in respect to assessment, which is always done in English only. However, as shown in this chapter, the advantage with a translanguaging approach is that it can also allow the use of different languages for different teaching and learning activities.

References

Baker, C. (2001) *Foundations of Bilingual Education and Bilingualism* (3rd edn). Clevedon: Multilingual Matters.
Baker, C. (2011) *Foundations of Bilingual Education and Bilingualism* (5th edn). Bristol: Multilingual Matters.
Bakhtin, M. (1981) *The Dialogic Imagination*. Austin, TX: University of Texas Press.
Bangeni, A. (2001) Language attitudes, genres and cultural capital: A case study of EAL students' access to a foundation course in the Humanities at UCT. Unpublished Master's Dissertation: University of Cape Town.
Bowker, L. (1996) Towards a corpus-based approach to terminography. *Terminology* 3 (1), 27–52.
Bowker, L. and Pearson, J. (2002) *Working with Specialized Language: A Practical Guide to Using Corpora*. London: Routledge.
Canagarajah, S. (2007) Lingua franca English, multilingual communities, and language acquisition. *Modern Language Journal* 91, 923–939.
Canagarajah, S. (2011) Codemeshing in academic writing: Identifying teachable strategies of translanguaging. *The Modern Language Journal* 95, 401–417.
Cazden, C.B. (2005) Describing classroom as hybrid spaces for the meeting of the minds: research planning in Singapore. In S. May, M. Franken and R. Barnard (eds) *LED2003: Refereed Conference Proceedings of the 1st International Conference on Language, Education and Diversity Conference*. New Zealand: University of Waikato.
Creese, A. and Blackledge, A. (2010) Translanguaging in the bilingual classroom: A pedagogy for learning and teaching? *The Modern Language Journal* 94, 103–115.
Creese, A. and Blackledge, A. (2011) Ideologies and interactions in multilingual education: What can an ecological approach tell us about bilingual pedagogy? In C. Hélot and M. Ó Laoire (eds) *Language Policy for the Multilingual Classroom* (pp. 3–21). Bristol: Multilingual Matters.
Cummins, J. (1979) Linguistic interdependence and the educational development of bilingual children. *Review of Educational Research* 49 (2), 222–251.
Cummins, J. (2000). *Language, Power and Pedagogy: Bilingual Children in the Crossfire*. Clevedon: Multilingual Matters.
Fosnot, C.T. and Perry, R.S. (2005) Constructivism: A psychological theory of learning. In C.T. Fosnot (ed.) *Constructivism. Theory, Perspectives and Practice* (pp. 8–38). New York: Teachers College Press.
García, O. (2009) *Bilingual Education in the 21st Century: A Global Perspective*. Chichester: Wiley-Blackwell.
Hornberger, N.H. and Link, H. (2012) Translanguaging and transnational literacies in multilingual classrooms: A biliteracy lens. *International Journal of Bilingual Education and Bilingualism* 15 (3), 261–278.

Hüllen, W. (1989) In the beginning was the gloss. Remarks on the historical emergence of lexicographical paradigms. In R.R.K. Hartmann (ed.) *Lexicographers and Their Works* (pp. 100–116). Exeter: University of Exeter.

Lawson, A. (2001) Collecting, aligning and analyzing parallel corpora. In M. Ghadessy, A. Henry and R.L. Roseberry (eds) (2001) *Small Corpus Studies and ELT: Theory and Practice* (pp. 279–310). Amsterdam, NED: John Benjamins.

Lewis, G., Jones, B. and Baker, C. (2012a) Translanguaging: Developing its conceptualisation and contextualisation. *Educational Research and Evaluation* 18 (7), 655–670.

Lewis, G., Jones, B. and Baker, C. (2012b) Translanguaging: Origins and development from school to street and beyond. *Educational Research and Evaluation* 18 (7), 641–654.

Madiba, M. (2004) Parallel corpora as tools for developing the indigenous languages of South Africa, with special reference to Venda. *Language Matters* 35 (1), 133–147.

Makoni, S. and Mashiri, P. (2007) Critical historiography: Does language planning in Africa need a construct of language as part of its theoretical apparatus? In S. Makoni and A. Pennycook (eds) (2007) *Disinvesting and Reconstituting Languages* (pp. 62–89). Clevedon: Multilingual Matters.

Meyer, I. and Mackintosh, K. (1996) The corpus from a terminographer's viewpoint. *International Journal of Corpus Linguistics* 1 (2), 257–285.

Mick, C. (2011) Heteroglossia in a multilingual learning space: approaching language beyond 'linguicisms'. In C. Hélot and M. Ó Laoire (eds) *Language Policy for the Multilingual Classroom* (pp. 22–41). Bristol: Multilingual Matters.

Nkomo, D. and Madiba, M. (2011) The compilation of multilingual concept literacy glossaries at the University of Cape Town: A lexicographical function theoretical approach. *Lexikos* 21, 1–25.

Paxton, M. (2007) 'You would be a master of a subject if taught in Xhosa': An investigation into the complexities of bilingual concept development in an English medium university in South Africa. *The International Journal of Learning* 14 (6), 61–67.

Paxton, M.I.J. (2009) 'It's easy to learn when you are using your home language but with English you need to start learning language before you get to the concept': Bilingual concept development in an English medium university in South Africa. *Journal of Multilingual and Multicultural Development* 30 (1), 1–15.

Pederson, E. and Nuyts, J. (1997) *Overview: On the Relationship between Language and Conceptualization* (pp. 1–12). Cambridge: Cambridge University Press.

Piaget, J. (1959) *The Language and Thought of the Child*. London: Routledge and Kegan Paul.

Piaget, J. (1977) *The Development of Thought: Equilibration of Cognitive Structures*. New York: Viking.

Sauer, H. (2008) Glosses, glossaries and dictionaries in the medieval period. In A.P. Cowie (ed.) (2009) *The Oxford History of English Lexicography*. Vol. I (pp. 17–40). General-Purpose Dictionaries. Oxford: Clarendon Press.

Williams, C. (1996) Secondary education: Training in the bilingual situation. In C. Williams, G. Lewis and C. Baker (eds) *The Language Policy: Taking Stock* (pp. 39–78). Llangefni: CAI.

Williams, C. (2002) *A Language Gained: A Study of Language Immersion at 11–16 Years of Age*. Bangor, Wales: University of Wales School of Education. See http://www.bangor.ac.uk/addysg/publications/Language_Gained.pdf (accessed 31 January 2013).

University of Cape Town (1999) (revised 2003) *Language Policy*. Cape Town, RSA: University of Cape Town.
University of Cape Town (2003) *Language Plan – Towards a Language Plan for the University of Cape Town: 2005–2010*. Cape Town, RSA: University of Cape Town.
Vygotsky, L.S. (1986) *Thought and Language*. Cambridge: Massachusetts Institute of Technology.
Vygotsky, L.S. (1994) The development of thinking and concept formation in school-aged children. In R. Van der Veer and J. Valsiner (eds) *The Vygotsky Reader* (pp. 355–370). Cambridge, M.A: Blackwell.
Young, D., Van der Vlugt, J. and Qanya, S. (2005) *Understanding Concepts in Mathematics and Science. A Multilingual Learning and Teaching Resource Book in English, Xhosa, Afrikaans and Zulu*. Cape Town: Maskew Miller.

6 Teaching Indigenous African Languages to Speakers of Other African Languages: The Effects of Translanguaging for Multilingual Development

Leketi Makalela

Introduction

The following extract reflects the orthodox language-teaching profession that has traditionally treated languages as isolated units in order to guard against cross-contamination between these languages, usually in favour of the target language or medium of instruction (García, 2009; Ricento & Hornberger, 1996; Shohamy, 2006):

> Language is like life, there is an aspiration for order, for control, for possession, driven by fear of the unknown, of the powers and sources of evil. But there is always the reality that language, like life, cannot be controlled. Language, like life, is bigger than any one of us. We can go through language, like life, we can be with language, like life, we can use it, but we cannot control it. We can try to create all kinds of controlling devices – rules, regulations, laws, correctness, categories, policies, impositions; in life, we also create ceremonies, anniversaries, prayers, ritual, insurances, and other devices, all through the desire to impose order; but it does not work. (Shohamy, 2006: 165)

This type of language 'policing' characterised the idealisation of the 'one nation–one language' ideology that permeated majority thinking in Europe in the 1820s, especially as seen in the influential works of Von Humboldt (Ricento, 2000: 198). In contradiction to this dominant thought, however, recent scholarship on bilingualism and multilingualism has revealed that imposition of monologic practices among multilingual learners is an exercise in futility, and, as Shohamy (2006: 165) correctly observes, 'it does not work'. Framed in the view that humans have complex identities that extend beyond pre-designed linguistic boundaries, it has increasingly become important for classroom practices, curricula and policies to build on the multiple, mobile and communicative repertoires of the learners (Hornberger & Link, 2012: 161) and to acknowledge the linguistic fluidities that are embedded in one another (García, 2011; Li Wei, 2011). Yet, this is not the case in African languages pedagogy.

South Africa is a typical African country that has had a history of 'boxing' or compartmentalising languages, which has invariably resulted in African languages becoming isolated into 'linguistic tribes', or even 'ghettos', as Kotzé uses the term in Chapter 2. I use the notion of linguistic tribes here to describe the Bantustan homeland system from 1953 till the early 1990s, in which 10 reserves were founded on perceived language differences and restriction of mobility of the speakers of indigenous African languages (Makalela, 2009a). While these boundaries have been *de jure* eliminated in the new socio-political dispensation that started in 1994, discrete linguistic units are still used administratively as strong identity markers, which are not to be conflated in African language classrooms. It is for this reason that the constitutional (Republic of South Africa, 1996) commitment to 11 official languages was viewed with skepticism, by some linguists, as an 'artificial construction' (Makalela, 2005) and 'disinvention' (Makoni, 2003) of linguistic entities that will perpetuate monologic pedagogical practices.

In more than 15 years of the constitutional commitment to multilingualism and enshrinement of several legislative frameworks, such as the Language Policy for Higher Education (Department of Education, 2001), it has remained difficult to implement the objectives of the multilingualism policy, as has been stated repeatedly in this book. The higher education sector, in particular, has seen a stalemate in multilingual practices in historically English-medium universities, even though there is an encouraging progress toward bilingual universities in historically Afrikaans-medium universities (Du Plessis, 2009; Makalela & McCabe, 2013). More conspicuously, the pedagogy of African languages, especially for teaching African languages to speakers of other African languages as additional languages in higher education, is relatively unexplored to date, with the Unisa approach (Kosch & Bosch,

Chapter 4) a notable exception. In this chapter, I report on the effectiveness of using a fluid communicative language practice among Nguni language speakers learning Sepedi as a second language in a higher education institution. This flexible phenomenon of using available linguistic repertoires in speech events is referred to as translanguaging, and as formally defined, it is 'a purposeful pedagogical alternation of languages spoken and written, receptive and productive modes' (Hornberger & Link, 2012: 262). I describe this phenomenon in detail in the next section and explain how it was used in the Sepedi class, followed by its effects that are highlighted through oral narratives and metacognitive reflections of the Sepedi students. In the end, I propose a framework that draws on translanguaging as an effective strategy for teaching African languages at higher education institutions and chart future research areas in similar contexts.

Translanguaging as a learning and teaching strategy

The post-modern school of thought that links sociology, political science, sociolinguistics and ecology has recently questioned our understanding of language as a static category with clear boundaries that separate different languages. Studies by García (2009, 2011), Hornberger and Link (2012), Makoni (2003), Makoni and Pennycook (2007), Mignolo (2000), Li Wei (2011) and Shohamy (2006) have all revealed that old notions of additive bilingualism and stable diglossia have lost space in the global world owing to their separatist orientation towards languages.

As a pedagogic strategy in bilingual classrooms, the idea of translanguaging can be traced back to the work of Cen Williams who studied Welsh–English bilingual secondary school learners' language practices in Wales (Williams, 2000, see also Madiba, Chapter 5). As understood from its earlier version based on Williams' work, the phenomenon referred to a language communicative function of receiving input in one language and providing output in another language. This process allowed bilingual learners to use their home language and develop positive experiences at school. García (2009: 45) extended this practice to include multiple discursive practices where, unlike a bicycle with two balanced wheels, the discursive practices are perceived as 'more like an all-terrain vehicle whose wheels extend and contract, flex and stretch, making possible, over highly uneven ground, movement forward that is bumpy and irregular but also sustained and effective'. Li Wei (2011: 1223) looked further at the creativity and criticality of multilingual speakers, using a psycholinguistic notion of 'languaging', which refers to the process of using language to gain knowledge, to make sense, to articulate one's thought and to communicate about using language. For Li Wei, translanguaging 'is going on between different linguistic structures and systems, including different modalities and going beyond them' (2011: 1223). She refers to the social space for multilingual language users as 'translanguaging space', which is an ongoing space created for language practices, where multilingual speakers are constantly involved in making context-sensitive, strategic choices about the language systems they use to achieve a particular communicative goal (Li Wei, 2011: 1). All of these ideas, taken together, suggest that classroom language practices restricted to monolingualism can be detrimental to multilingual students and limit their transformative, creative and critical values.

Noteworthy is that translanguaging assumptions depart from the 20th century views about classroom language practices of bilingual learners. Research shows that, in the name of maintenance bilingual education, teachers have always encouraged monologic classroom practices and, in turn, achieved no more than creating two monolinguals in one body (Blommaert, 2010; Li Wei, 2011). García (2011) elucidates the teachers' and language practitioners' roles through her use of a flower garden metaphor. She compares strict separation of languages, as in the case of maintenance bilingualism, to a flower garden, where each flower plot is differentiated according to the colours of the flowers. In the same way that a gardener would prune overlapping flowers, use of the learners' home languages in multilingual classes were devalued and prohibited. She observes the outcomes of such language separatism as follows:

> It was the strict separation of languages that enabled language minorities to preserve what was seen as their 'mother tongue', their 'ethnic language', while developing a 'second language' that would never be a 'first' or a 'native' one, for those designations were reserved for the language majority which inhabited a separate space. (García, 2011: 7)

The main argument here is that a separatist view of language and classifications of 'first', 'second', 'mother tongue' do not fit the socio-linguistic realities of the majority of speakers in the 21st century. In order to match a more complex account of language use to multilingual spaces appropriate to this century, classroom language practices of multilingual learners should be characterised by a discursive practice of 'languaging'. According to García (2011: 7), languaging refers to 'social features that are called upon by speakers in a seamless and complex network of multiple semiotic signs'. From this standpoint, language maintenance may not be a desirable end because it perpetuates strict definitions of language as autonomous and pure as used by a specific group of people whose identity depends on it (Shohamy, 2006). This stance towards language maintenance goes further to claim the purity of a language before it came into contact with other languages and before the diaspora came into being (García, 2011; Pennycook, 2010). Because such conservation of languages in their purest forms is not tenable, what is needed is sustainability, which is dynamic and future oriented. This conception of sustainability, according to García (2011), means a renewal of the past language practices to meet the needs of the present without compromising those of future generations.

One important distinction made in the translanguaging scholarship is its relationship with code-switching. While code-switching relates to this concept (see Madiba, Chapter 5), translanguaging does not refer to the use of two separate languages, or the shift of one language or code to the other as is the case with code-switching (e.g. García, 2011; Hornberger & Link, 2012). Instead, 'languaging' speakers 'select language features and soft assemble their language practices in ways that fit their communicative needs' (Garcia, 2011: 7). Furthermore, code-switching often carries language-centred connotations of language interference, transfer or borrowing of codes. On the contrary, translanguaging shifts the lens from cross-linguistic influence to how multilinguals intermingle linguistic features that are administratively assigned to a particular language or variety (Hornberger & Link, 2012: 263). In brief, code-switching treats language systems as discrete units, while translanguaging is speaker-centred and assumes unitary language systems (rather than differentiated systems). These unified language features are pooled together and treated as a single linguistic system from the point of view of the speaker, especially among speakers who grow up in balanced multilingual contexts.

Research on classroom and programme practices has revealed a myriad of benefits that show the need for translanguaging pedagogy in multilingual contexts. Researchers have observed that programmes in multilingual and bilingual education in the US and elsewhere have been accepting learners with different language profiles that do not fit past monolingual structures (Blommaert, 2010; García, 2011). In these new multilingual schooling contexts, notions such as additive bilingualism and transitional bilingualism have become questionable because they use a monoglossic curriculum that privileges one language over the other (García, 2011: 6). By extension, the language-in-education policies that favour monolingualism as the target norm, irrespective of the changing language context, place a huge constraint on multilingual learners' linguistic flexibility.

Despite restrictions placed on bilingual children by dominant monolingual practices, bilinguals have the tenacity to transform restrictive monolingual landscapes. In a British monolingual schooling culture, for example, Li Wei (2011) investigated translanguaging spaces where she used a combination of observation of multilingual practices and metalanguage commentaries by Chinese youths. A moment analysis, which is an analysis of language behaviours of the multilingual speakers on the spur of the moment, in this study revealed that the Chinese learners created critical and creative spaces for themselves using the resources they had (Li Wei, 2011: 1234) despite the dominant monolingual context in which they were expected to operate. Schools that have accepted translanguaging, on the other hand, recorded success with their programmes. Creese and Blackledge's (2010) study revealed the benefits of a flexible bilingual pedagogy in British complementary schools as follows:

- Use of bilingual label quests, repetition and translation across languages.
- Ability to engage audiences through translanguaging and heteroglossia.
- Establishment of identity positions.
- Recognition that languages do not fit into clear bounded entities and that all languages are 'needed' for meaning to be conveyed and negotiated.
- Endorsement of simultaneous literacies and languages to keep the pedagogic task moving. (Creese & Blackledge, 2010: 113)

While translanguaging presents an opportunity to understand the world view of the speakers of African languages in their plurality and advance their pedagogy based on languaging practices, there are practical challenges. The most serious one, according to Plüddemann (2011: 11), is for students to broaden their standard varieties to include speech forms not traditionally associated with them. In their current form, these languages are treated in separated units, with teaching following strict orthographic inscriptions of the missionary linguists of the 18th century (Makalela, 2009a; Hibbert & van der Walt, Chapter 1). Expansion of standard variety forms will, in this context, involve broadening translanguaging spaces to assess creativity and criticality (Li Wei, 2011) of their multilingual speakers. There is therefore a need for a systematic enquiry on 'languaging' pedagogical practices to establish the extent to which these varieties are permeable in classroom interactions. This study reports on the efficacy of using the translanguaging phenomenon in teaching African languages to speakers of other African languages. It is guided by this question: do 'languaging' practices among student teachers learning an African language affirm their complex identities and accelerate vocabulary development and metalinguistic/cultural awareness of the target language?

The Study

This is a practice-based enquiry that involved a population of 21 Sepedi additional language-student teachers from an intact class at the Wits School of Education, University of the Witwatersrand. The student participants included 14 females and 7 males, and they had a mean age of 20 years and 6 months. The students are mother-tongue speakers of several Nguni languages: isiZulu, siSwati, isiXhosa and isiNdebele language varieties and the majority of them came from KwaZulu-Natal where they had very little, if any, prior contact with speakers of Sotho languages.

In order to promote multilingualism as proscribed in the Language Policy for Higher Education Act, the Division of Languages, Literacies and Literatures in the School of Education has undertaken a comprehensive programme that trains language teachers to major in any of these five official languages: English, Sesotho, Sepedi, isiZulu and Afrikaans. In addition, the Division introduced new languages courses for all students who are required to take an additional language outside of their home language cluster in their second year of study. These students are further restricted from taking the languages in which they have had formal school exposure to their literacies. The overriding goal of the new languages programme is to ensure that every student teacher masters at least one new language so that they are prepared for multilingual classrooms. The new language instruction thus provides the student teachers with basic conversational, reading and writing abilities so they are equipped to work with learners from languages other than the ones from their own language clusters. They are, however, not expected to teach these new languages.

The course: Sepedi as a new language

Sepedi Additional Language is a one-year course that aims to develop basic communication skills among non-mother-tongue speakers of all Sotho languages. The first semester is geared toward development of receptive skills in listening and reading Sepedi texts, and the second semester focuses on productive skills (speaking and writing). A more communicative approach is used, with a focus-on-forms strategy (Long, 1991). This means that the instructor reacts to grammatical items as they emerge in actual language use. As I described elsewhere in English second-language classes of students from remote rural areas (Makalela, 2009b), this teaching method is a focus on *forms* as opposed to a more grammar-based focus (focus on *form*) that was used traditionally in foreign language classes (Barbieri & Eckhardt, 2007).

Departing from the grammar-translation method often used in African languages classes, the communicative approach used in this class is embedded within a functional–notional syllabus that includes thorough engagement with culturally sensitive content, such as greeting friends, elders; asking and giving directions, autobiographies and expressing ownership.

While inducing language use through this content, these notions are compared and contrasted with the students' home or other languages during the lessons.

In order to increase the pool of vocabulary items for the students, digital social networks were used to get the students interested in using the language via technology. A Sepedi Facebook group, 'A re boleleng', was used as an open multilingual space to extend language use beyond the classroom. While Sepedi was the main medium of writing in the group, other languages were used to express thoughts, which would not have been possible to do in Sepedi as it depended on individual levels of proficiency. Moreover, each student was expected to fill up a vocabulary list of 15 words acquired from any encounters they have had in the week and place this in their individual blogs. The blog had a secondary function, to help the students to chart their intellectual journeys through the use of Sepedi, their home languages and English – what I termed *multilingual blogs*. The students were also encouraged to draw from examples from other related African languages they knew to expand their linguistic repertoires. As in Kosch and Bosch's case study (Chapter 4), 'technology has played a key role in providing unique opportunities not only to expose students to multilingual study material but also to promote interaction among them'.

In order to use the students' language background, the instructor's teaching approach approximated 'translanguaging' where languages, such as isiZulu, isiXhosa, siSwati and isiNdebele, were encouraged, especially in discussion groups. The matrix language of communication still remained Sepedi, with English embedded sufficiently in the first semester and less so in the second semester. Their home languages were preferred to English, with the instructor directly calling for the use of other languages to explicate concepts, such as plural markers versus referents to respect in a greetings genre. I will henceforth refer to this strategy as *contrastive elaboration*, which relies on students crisscrossing between all home (or known) languages and multilingual spaces to extend their understanding of concepts or ideas introduced in the target language. This yielded creativity and critical assessment of their own learning process, while using all multilingual repertoires available to them as resources.

Data collection

The study relied on data collected from two sources: self-reflections and an interview schedule. After general ethical clearance for classroom-based research was obtained, these data collection procedures were carried out at least twice, first in the first quarter and next at the end of the second quarter of the academic year. Self-reflection notes were inscribed at the end of each week to reflect on successes of experimenting with the translanguaging teaching model.

With regard to the interview schedule, regular conferencing with each of the students was conducted to assess their understanding of the course content and their acquisition development trajectories of Sepedi as a new language. The students were asked standardised questions that included the following: (1) Say what you have learned from the course so far – give details, (2) How do you feel about learning a new language? (3) Say something about the approach used for learning and teaching the language, (4) Are there any difficulties or golden moments you would want to share while studying Sepedi as a new language? The interview data were derived from six student participants representing three proficiency levels: low, intermediate and high based on their quarterly examination results.

Data analysis

Three procedures were used in analysing the data for the study. The personal reflective notes were read several times to gauge salient moments that revealed some of the principles of translanguaging. Second, data collected through the interview schedule were analysed using a universal reductionist approach. The categories and themes that emerged from the data were drawn and supported by examples from verbal reports.

Results

Personal reflections

The self-reflective notes show the use of various strategies to enhance multilingualism in the classroom. The instructor provided culturally rich writings for the students to read and compare the cultural nuances with their own Nguni cultural practices. One of the best moments of the course was the use of a *contrastive elaboration* technique that allowed students to see commonalities among Sotho and Nguni languages. The students realised that death, wedding, initiation and burial procedures (e.g. readings from a primary school teacher's text entitled *'Moeno le Setšo sa Bakgakga'*) were not as different as they initially thought in these two language clusters.

Second, the students identified with a range of Sepedi cultural practices, such as various greeting categories stratified according to age. It became apparent to the students that age and respect are culturally embedded in the language. Learning to speak this language thus revealed cultural cross-overs and realisation of fluid cultural boundaries between Sepedi and other African languages. As a result, the motivation level of the students who were initially reluctant to learn the 'language based in Limpopo', improved over time as they expanded their pool of linguistic and cultural repertoires throughout the course.

With regard to differences, there were a number of cases where commonalities could not be discerned in culture-specific concepts. It emerged in the conversations about travelling to other parts of the country that initiation schools were not necessarily available in the isiZulu culture and that the equivalent word for someone not initiated, *lešoboro*, was not available in isiZulu. Its sister language isiXhosa, on the other hand, had an equivalent: *inkwenkwe*. When students traversed from one language to another, they observed various cultural aspects of the source language and their target language. In doing this, they learned the language within a rich context as they compared and contrasted their cultural orientations with sister languages and the target language at the same time. It became my contention that this complex language acquisition space was made possible in a fluid environment of languages without boundaries. My classroom teaching thus became a microcosm of a larger convergence of pedagogically isolated language systems. It also became a translanguaging space for creative thoughts and critical engagement that is concomitant with learning a language in heteroglossic milieus of the 21st century (Garcia, 2009).

Student views

Six students representing three proficiency levels were asked questions to reflect on the course at the end of the first semester. The results of the interviews are presented below.

Identification with target language culture

One way of learning a new language is to develop instrumental motivation through identification with the culture of the target language. The student participants' responses showed development of strong identity ties with the culture of the target language as revealed in Excerpt 1.

Excerpt 1

I realize that learning the language reminds me of similar culture I have in my language. I can identify with Bapedi people better now.

In this excerpt, the participant is able to connect his cultural practices with that of the Bapedi people (speakers of Sepedi) and could envision himself as a part of their culture. Learning Sepedi has given the participant another lens to reflect on his own language and culture. The teaching of Sepedi has thus shown an interwoven network of cultural continuity beyond learner language boundaries. It appears that segmentation of identities according to home languages will in this particular case limit the holistic and broadened sense of self within intercultural fluidity of expressions (García, 2011; Shohamy, 2006). The finding revealed in this excerpt tallies with earlier observations that indigenous African languages have in fact been 'disinvented' (Makoni, 2003) and that their perceived boundaries are 'artificial' (Makalela, 2005).

Ubuntu *and greetings*

The students were introduced to greetings in Sepedi and, while practising various levels of greetings in the language, they were asked to compare various levels of meanings of greetings to their own languages in order to explicate some of the nuances (contrastive elaboration) that could best be revealed through other African languages. Their responses during the interviews showed various conceptualisation of plurality relating to the *ubuntu* world view that cuts across their home languages and Sepedi as in Excerpt 2.

Excerpt 2

> For greetings, we also use plural markers like *sanibonani* to refer to someone we respect or older and not necessarily many people. So Sepedi and isiZulu show me that as Africans we see people in totality ... you and those around you.

This student has compared the meaning of generic Sepedi greeting: *Dumelang* and *Thobela*, which are equivalent to *Sanibonani* in isiZulu to refer to greetings of more than one person in one context. However, in another context, the same word is used to greet a single person who is either an elder or highly regarded as the case may be in other non-Bantu languages. The third meaning is read within the Ubuntu world view of '*I am because you are*'. In this case, the person greeting perceives the greeted as an embodiment of a larger clan or community to the extent that the one greeted is not seen in isolation from the rest of the clan or community. A typical response to this greeting prompt would indeed include a recount of the number of family members and their well-being. This greeting exchange both reflects and reinforces a communal orientation of African people or the 'totality' as pronounced in Excerpt 2 above. The fact that both greeting procedures and meanings are equivalent in both languages made the students see the interconnectedness of their languages and enhanced their motivation to learn with their affective filters lowered, that is, with less resistance.

Greater motivation to learn the new language

Most students in the interviews expressed their renewed desire to learn Sepedi owing to the similarities of the cultural orientations of the target language. The students developed self-efficacious attitudes and expressed intentions to learn more, as seen in Excerpt 3.

Excerpt 3

I see connections between *'botho'* and *'ubuntu'* and realize that the concept of 'I am because you are' is similar in both languages. During the course of the semester, I have come to see how close we are to Bapedi even though I had initially thought that they are different from us. I now feel motivated to learn their language and listen to radio Thobela.

This excerpt echoes the ideas expressed in Excerpt 2 above and goes further to show future intentions to engage in activities that will reinforce their learning of the new language. Radio Thobela, a prominent Sepedi national radio, was singled out as one important resource to continue to learn and appreciate the aesthetic values of the language. Also noteworthy is that the student participant here had thought that there was a big distance between Sepedi and Nguni languages and its speakers as remotely distanced from her own. From this statement above, it appears that attending the Sepedi course has bridged the perceived distance that could have been a barrier to learning African languages.

Mutual intelligibility in the seSotho language cluster

The data showed an understanding that the seSotho language varieties are mutually intelligible through dialogues of some of the students who picked up similar words and expressions in these languages. Although they learned Sepedi in class, the students often got confused at first when they heard Setswana and Sesotho utterances resembling Sepedi closely. This was one of the unintended consequences of teaching a language closely related to others. This is expressed in Excerpt 4.

Excerpt 4

Now I also realize that Sepedi, Setswana and Sesotho are not different. I was confusing words for each of these languages, but when I speak to any speaker of these languages, we just go along without them correcting me that I say *tš* instead of *ts*, for example. Now I can say I know three languages even if I still need to polish them.

Degrees of mutual intelligibility among clustered African languages have been pointed out through linguistic research (Prah, 1998) in studies by Progress for Alternative Education of South Africa and Centre for Advanced Studies in African Society. In particular, Sotho languages were consistently proven to have more commonalities than differences to the point that they could be considered one language in writing (Makalela, 2005, 2009a). While traditional native speakers of these languages might refuse to be associated with speech communities of a closely related language in order to maintain their separated identities, it is instructive that mutual intelligibility is expressed by new language students who pick it up from the languaging phenomenon in heteroglossic communicative practices. The student realises that variation between these languages is phonetic; that is, pronunciation of the same sound at two different points of articulation in the oral cavity: alveolar / *ts* / and palatum/ *tš* / – something not unique in any dialect continuum.

Local translanguaging: Towards an *Ubuntu* language methodology

The main research question for the study was whether using indigenous African languages of student teachers as resources in the teaching of Sepedi as a new language would enhance accelerated development of skills and motivation in learning Sepedi. The results of the study have shown that there was a fast-tracked development of speaking and language competencies through the translanguaging pedagogic approach. In particular, it was shown that vocabulary development among the students has increased through extended use of multiple discursive resources in and outside of the classroom space; these included Facebook, multilingual blogs, classroom languaging experiences and further contact with native speakers of related languages. This could be attributed to the efficacy of translanguaging pedagogy that extends and affirms multilingual resources at the students' disposal (García, 2009, 2011; Li Wei, 2011).

One of the revealing findings of the study is that the students developed positive associations with the target language and, on their own, realised that cultural ethos can be extended beyond discrete language boundaries. Their positive motivation towards another African language became a strong indicator of how well they performed in the language, without devaluing their own home languages. In addition, the students noted interconnections between sister language varieties: Sepedi, Sesotho and Setswana. This observation supports previous research conclusions on mutual intelligibility and harmonisation of African languages (Alexander, 1989; Makalela, 2005, 2009a; Nhlapo, 1944). Harmonisation, as understood from these studies, meant unification of orthographic representations of closely related languages without directly affecting the spoken varieties that are perceived to be mutually intelligible. The results of the study extend this view of mutual intelligibility as an externally experienced phenomenon in the new languages, in that the commonalities were experienced by non-mother tongue speakers who were learning one of the related language varieties – a very unique linguistic assertion. The experiences of the languaging phenomenon, thus, were not only with respect to differences and similarities between Nguni and Sotho languages, but also within these language groups. That is, the student teachers 'languaged' in Sepedi, Setswana and Sesotho as features of all the three varieties became readily available in their journey of learning Sepedi, both in and out of the classroom. In this connection, it is fitting to state that hermetic sealing of languages into boxes is not supported in heteroglossic environments as found through the students who registered for the course.

The results of the study also point to the need to re-conceptualise our view of language teaching in line with the recent scholarship on translanguaging (García, 2009; Hornberger & Link, 2012; Li Wei, 2011). As with other languages in most parts of the world, traditional views of teaching African languages as school subjects were based on Eurocentric models and definition of language, which relied on territorial inclusion or exclusion of the speakers (Shohamy, 2006). In order to move away from 'linguistic tribes' of the past, as exemplified in the Sepedi course, the pedagogy of African languages can be aligned with a cultural and epistemological conception of being. In effect, the translanguaging approach fits in well with the African worldview of ubuntu, which propagates a communal orientation and continuum of social, linguistic and capital resources under the mantra: 'I am because you are' to denote the interconnectedness of all human existence. This view of wholeness can be extended to the relationship between languages as they 'leak' into one another. The use of Sepedi in the context of other African languages typifies what I will refer to as the *'ubuntu language methodology'* and a higher degree of cultural unity between and within the two language clusters: Sotho and Nguni. This people-centred ubuntu lens recognises the wealth of multilingualism, the linguistic continuum of African languages and debunks the old ways of teaching African languages that were borrowed wholesale from monolingual approaches.

On the whole, the use of translanguaging approaches in the Sepedi class dismantles etho-linguistic divisions of the past with ten Bantustan homelands and creates opportunities for what García (2012) refers to as a 'pedagogy of integration'. This pedagogy of integration is liberating for historically excluded languages and affirms the fluid linguistic identities of their speakers. While these results show important developments in African language pedagogy, it is important to interpret the results within the context of the inherent limitation of the study; that is, being a reflective enquiry that used a small sample. However, the results give a lot of scope for further research in similar contexts of teaching African languages through a translanguaging approach and its locally appropriated version: *Ubuntu language methodology*.

Conclusion

This chapter described the use of translanguaging phenomena in teaching Sepedi as a new course for student teachers at the University of the Witwatersrand. Through accounts of personal reflections and student perceptions, this approach has proved effective. The study has established that students of African languages increase their pool of vocabulary and concept extensions. This is possible when multiple discursive resources are used and metalinguistic awareness is enhanced through a contrastive elaboration technique, which draws on multilingual repertoires that the students bring with them to the classroom.

Second, the study has shown that dynamic multilingualism can be harnessed as a methodology that is both linguistically and culturally transformative. What I described as *ubuntu language methodology*, which draws from a pool of other African languages, has liberated the students from negative stereotypes created by the systematic Balkanisation of Africans through language differentiation. The common understanding of a cultural ethos that is commonly shared between Nguni and Sotho groups and the realisation of mutual intelligibility of the target language with its sister varieties all explain the effectiveness of the languaging approach explored in the Sepedi class.

Although the findings of the study do suggest a neat fit for a translanguaging approach in an African language classroom in a higher education context, there is a need to extend the translanguaging experiences in other comparable African languages teaching environments and to augment conceptual frameworks, such as *contrastive elaboration* and *ubuntu language methodology* as explored in this study. In particular, there is a need for observation of spur-of-the-moment actions and metalanguaging data through a double hermeneutic, where the participants are trying to make sense of the world and the researcher is trying to make sense of the participants trying to make sense of their world (Li Wei, 2011: 1224). This double hermeneutic will increase our understanding of all social, psychological and cultural dimensions of translanguaging and its relationship with the teaching of African languages in multilingual spaces.

References

Alexander, N. (1989) *Language Policy and National Unity in South Africa/Azania*. Cape Town: Buchu Books.

Barbieri, F. and Eckhardt, S.E. (2007) Corpus-focused findings to form-focused instruction: the case of reported speech. *Language Teaching Research* 11 (3), 319–341.

Blommaert, J. (2010) *The Sociolinguistics of Globalization*. Cambridge: Cambridge University Press.

Creese, A. and Blackledge, A. (2010) Translanguaging in the bilingual classroom: A pedagogy for learning and teaching? *The Modern Language Journal* 94, 103–115.

Department of Education (2001) National Plan for Higher Education in South Africa. See www.education.gov.za/LinkClick.aspx?fileticket...tabid=188&mid (accessed 10 November 2009).

Du Plessis, T. (2009) From monolingual to bilingual higher education: the repositioning of historically Afrikaans-Medium universities in South Africa. *Language Policy* 5, 87–113.

García, O. (2009) *Bilingual Education in the 21st Century: A Global Perspective*. Miden: Wiley/Blackwell.

García, O. (2011) From language garden to sustainable languaging: Bilingual education in a global world. *Perspectives* 34 (1), 5–9.

García, O. (2012) Division of Languages, Literacies and Literatures Seminar. University of the Witwatersrand, Johannesburg, June 2012.

Hornberger, N. and Link, H. (2012) Translanguaging and transnational literacies in multilingual classrooms: A biliteracy lens. *International Journal of Bilingual Education and Bilingualism* 15, 261–278.

Li Wei (2011) Moment analysis and translanguaging space: Discursive construction of identities by multilingual Chinese youth in Britain. *Journal of Pragmatics* 43, 1222–1235.

Long, M.H. (1991) Focus on form: A design feature in language teaching methodology. In K. De Bot and C. Kramsch (eds) *Foreign Language Research in Cross-Cultural Perspective* (pp. 196–221). Amsterdam, NED: John Benjamins.

Makalela, L. (2005) We speak eleven tongues: Reconstructing multilingualism in South Africa. In B. Brock-Utne and R. Hopson (eds) *Languages of Instruction for African Emancipation: Focus on Postcolonial Contexts and Considerations* (pp. 147–174). Cape Town and Dar-es-salam: CASAS and Mkuki n Nyota.

Makalela, L. (2009a) Unpacking the language of instruction myth: Towards progressive language in education policies in Africa. In K. Prah and B. Brock-Utne (eds) *Multilingualism: An African Advantage* (pp. 170–194). Cape Town: Casas.

Makalela, L. (2009b) The role of feedback on L2 student writing: An experiment with form-focused feedback. In L. Makalela (ed.) *Language Teacher Research in Africa* (pp. 51–66). Alexandria, Egypt: TESOL.

Makalela, L. and McCabe, R.V. (2013) Monolingualism in a historically Black South African university: A case of inheritance. *Journal of Language and Education* 24 (4), 406–414.

Makoni, S. (2003) From misinvention to disinvention of language: Multilingualism and the South African Constitution. In S. Makoni, G. Smithermann, A. Ball and

A. Spears (eds) *Black Linguistics: Language, Society and Politics in Africa and the Americas* (pp. 132–149). London and New York: Routledge.

Makoni, S. and Pennycook, A. (eds) (2007) *Disinventing and Reconstituting Languages*. Clevedon: Multilingual Matters.

Mignolo, W. (2000) *Local Histories/Global Designs. Coloniality, Subaltern Knowledges, and Border Thinking*. Princeton, NJ: Princeton University Press.

Nhlapo, J. (1944) *Bantu Babel: Will the Bantu Languages Live?* Cape Town: The African Bookman.

Pennycook, A. (2010) *Language as Local Practice*. London and New York: Routledge.

Plüddemann, P. (2011) Crossing new frontiers with the translanguaging wagon. *LEAP* 29, 10–11.

Prah, K. (1998) *Between Extinction and Distinction. Harmonization and Standardization of African Languages*. Johannesburg, RSA: Witwatersrand University Press.

Republic of South Africa (1996) *The South African Constitution, Act 108 Of 1996*. Pretoria, RSA: Government Press.

Ricento, T. (2000) Historical and theoretical perspectives in language policy and planning. *Journal of Sociolinguistics* 4 (2), 196–213.

Ricento, T. and Hornberger, N. (1996) Unpeeling the onion: Language planning and policy and the ELT professional. *TESOL Quarterly* 30 (3), 401–426.

Shohamy, E. (2006) *Language Policy: Hidden Agendas and New Approaches*. London: Routledge.

Williams, C. (2000) Welsh-medium and bilingual teaching in the further education sector. *International Journal of Bilingual Education and Bilingualism* 3 (2), 129–148.

Part 3
Affective Aspects of Biliteracy Pedagogy

7 isiZulu–English Bilingualisation at the University of KwaZulu-Natal: An Exploration of Students' Attitudes

Andrea Parmegiani and
Stephanie Rudwick

Introduction

In this chapter, we explore some reasons behind students' scepticism towards UKZN's bilingualisation policy, which aims to promote isiZulu as a language of tertiary learning and teaching so that it can reach the 'institutional and academic status of English' (University of KwaZulu-Natal, 2006: 1). Our exploration will start from the following theoretical premises: in order to be successfully implemented: (a) language policies need to be supported by the speakers of those languages, and (b) in order to garner this support, it is crucial to understand how attitudes towards languages are inextricably related to complex processes of identity construction and of negotiation of power relations. Furthermore, in order to unravel this complexity in multilingual contexts, language should not be seen as a series of discrete 'whole bounded systems', but rather as continua across which speakers move in order to meet their communicative needs – a point that is made repeatedly about African languages in this book (notably

Kotzé, Chapter 2; Kosch & Bosch, Chapter 4; Madiba, Chapter 5; Makalela, Chapter 6).

We will begin with a brief discussion of the gap between LP and practice in South Africa and its implications for power relations. In this context, we will examine UKZN's bilingualisation policy as an attempt to bridge this gap, and also look critically at previous studies carried out by Moodley (2009, 2010) suggesting that there is little support for this policy on the part of isiZulu students and staff. After discussing our theoretical framework, we will use quantitative and qualitative data to examine the reasons behind students' scepticism towards using African languages as media of instruction. We will conclude by considering the possibility that the creation of biliteracy continua between English and isiZulu can bring UKZNs LP into better alignment with the language attitudes of its stake holders.

The Gap between Policy and Practice in South Africa

South Africa's language policies are arguably among the most progressive in the world (Paxton, 2009: 346), with the constitution granting official status to 11 languages and prescribing that 'every person shall be entitled to instruction in the language of his and her choice where this is reasonably practicable' (Republic of South Africa, 1996, Ch. 1, S. 6, Art. 5). Indeed, scholars such as Skutnabb-Kangas and Phillipson (2001: 143), who are in the forefront of language rights activism, have praised the work of South Africa's LP makers as exemplary for having succeeded at 'enshrining language rights in the constitution'. Unfortunately, however, several studies have shown that the sociolinguistic realities in the country are quite different from the constitutional ideal, with English occupying an unrivalled dominant position (Alexander, 2000, 2002, 2003; Heugh, 2000; Kamwangamalu, 2000; Webb, 2009).

It has also been pointed out that English has been appropriated by many Black South Africans who are using it as part of their linguistic repertoires to express themselves and negotiate power relations (Deumert, 2010; Janks, 1992; Parmegiani, 2008, 2009, 2010). Nevertheless, it cannot be denied that because English is spoken as a mother tongue by only 9% of South Africa's population, and because access to English proficiency as an additional language correlates with class, linguistic inequality is interrelated with socio-economic inequality. Fortunately, inroads have been made in the promotion of African languages in South Africa (Balfour, 2010; Deumert, 2010; Parmegiani, 2012), but there is no doubt that a lot remains to be done, especially in education where, in most cases, English remains the exclusive official medium of instruction after fourth grade (Webb *et al.*, 2010).

LP and implementations at the UKZN

The UKZN has been in the forefront in counteracting the dominance of English in tertiary education (Balfour, 2010) with the implementation of a LP that strives for the development of isiZulu as a LoLT, to the extent that eventually it will have 'the institutional and academic status of English' (University of KwaZulu-Natal, 2006: 1). The university's policy recognises English as the 'main international language of scholarship and the main language of administration and business' but, at the same time, it 'equally recognizes the importance of isiZulu as a custodian of culture, heritage, and tradition and as a means of communication' (University of KwaZulu-Natal, 2006: 1).

The UKZN has shown a strong commitment to the implementation of this policy, as evidenced by the following programmes. To address the need to develop isiZulu terminology for scientific concepts, the bilingual staff at the UKZN School of Nursing and Psychology have coined 1400 isiZulu terms for the discipline of Nursing and Midwifery (Engelbrecht et al., 2010: 266). At the same time, the *Masikhulume* [*Let's talk*] Programme has sought to equip academic and support staff with some isiZulu communicative proficiency (Ndimande-Hlongwa et al., 2010: 354). More importantly for the purpose of this chapter, a post-graduate Academic Literacy class has been offered in isiZulu since 2008 (Mashiya, 2010) and a new project is piloting an isiZulu-medium B.Ed Honours programme in Education, which is scheduled to run during 2012 over two semesters. A basic isiZulu course has been digitalised and made available to all staff members on an internal web programme.[1] Many articles in the monthly university-wide newsletter (*UKZNindaba*) are available in isiZulu. Several student and staff services at the UKZN have been bilingualised, for instance, the telephone services of the RMS (Risk Management Service) and ICT (Information and Communication Technologies). All Student Counselling programmes are now bilingual, and so are signs on campus.

These examples of successful implementation demonstrate that the UKZN LP has already received significant support from the administration authorities and, in fact, tick all the boxes for 'areas that would encourage the strengthening of African languages in South African higher education' (Maseko, Chapter 3). Nevertheless, an empirical study recently carried out by Moodley (2009) shows that scepticism towards the policy is widespread among students and staff. Her findings (Moodley, 2009: 28–30) can be summarised as follows.

- There is 'a collective notion of undesirability expressed by the majority of both staff and students toward bilingual education', with both groups

of respondents showing a strong preference for using only English as an official language on campus.
- The 'majority of staff and students never, or at best rarely, used isiZulu as medium on campus'.
- 'One possible reason for the unwelcome attitude of the university community towards isiZulu concerns their level of proficiency in the language', since many respondents reported nonexistent or 'substandard proficiency' in isiZulu.

It must be pointed out that Moodley's findings are of limited validity since her analysis, as thus far published, fails to take into account a crucial variable in shaping attitudes towards the LP, that is, whether respondents are native English speakers or whether they are native isiZulu speakers. While it is possible that native isiZulu speakers might have reservations about using their mother tongue as a LoLT, it is extremely unlikely that they would report a 'non-existent' or 'poor' command of their first language, let alone that they 'never, or at best rarely, [use] isiZulu on campus'. Moreover, Moodley's study does not delve into the reasoning behind these alleged negative attitudes towards bilingualisation, besides suggesting that they could stem from the fact that students and staff have limited isiZulu proficiency.

These findings (Moodley, 2009) should be taken with caution, but it is not unlikely that there might be scarce support for the use of isiZulu as a LoLT even among its native speakers, as this is a widespread phenomenon that is often lamented by language rights activists (De Klerk, 2002; Kamwangamalu, 1997). Some scholars have been rather dismissive of this scepticism, constructing it as 'false consciousness' (Alexander, 2000: 21) or 'colonization of the mind' (Ngũgũĩ wa Thiong'o, 1981), suggesting that Black South Africans are misguided in their strong preference for the exclusive use of English as a LoLT.

While it is important that parents, teachers and school administrators be informed of the benefits of mother-tongue education, it is also dangerous to be dismissive of Black South Africans' preference for English as a language of instruction, given that throughout centuries of racial domination, one of the rhetorical pillars of white supremacy was that the 'natives' are incapable of making decisions in their own interests (Teal, cited in Rose & Tumner, 1975: 213). One must also not forget that because of the poor legacy of Bantu education, African languages are associated with oppression and dysfunctional education. Historical considerations aside, we share Canagarajah's (2005) logical assumption that a LP promoting a particular language needs the support of the speakers in order to be successful. It is necessary to recognise that language needs are often the result of complex and interwoven beliefs, 'a composite of micro-identity traits that reflect biological characteristics, environmental influences, social discourses and constructions of the self', as Carstens and Alston find (Chapter 11). This is why we believe that it is crucial to understand the reasons behind the scepticism that characterises some students' attitudes towards using isiZulu as a LoLT, in order to find ways to garner support for the bilingualisation policy.

Theoretical Framework

In order to unravel the complexities of language attitudes among bi- and multilingual speakers, it is important to move away from the notion that languages are 'whole bounded systems' that can be associated with 'whole bounded communities'. As Heller (2007: 1–13) recommends, we should acknowledge that 'the constant emergence of traces of different languages in the speech of individual bilinguals . . . illustrate[s] the permeability of boundaries'. This approach is particularly relevant for South Africa, where first, the boundaries between the languages within the Nguni and Sotho clusters are often blurred, and second, English permeates the speech of most urban residents. It is well known that many Black South Africans, especially in urban areas, are more comfortable using hybrid forms of communication, such as contact languages, urban vernaculars, CS and code-mixing, rather than unadulterated versions of their mother tongues (Ndlangamandla, 2010; Paxton, 2009). Indeed, the very notion of *mother tongue* can be quite problematic in South Africa, as it is not uncommon for speakers to be exposed to a wide range of languages from birth (Mesthrie, 2002: 13).

What this could mean for language policies in education is that the use of a continuum of languages, dialects and literacies, rather than one discrete mother tongue, might be the most effective medium of instruction to help Black South African students succeed, as argued in Part 2 of this book. As Hornberger has argued, the more schools attended by multilingual students 'allow learners to draw from across the whole and of each and every continuum, the greater are the chances for their full biliterate expression' (Hornberger, 2004: 158).

A monolithic notion of mother tongue is problematic even in terms of understanding how the relationship between language, identity and power relations shapes language attitudes. Although language, in particular isiZulu, remains a clear marker of ethnic identity in South Africa (Parmegiani, 2008, 2009; Rudwick, 2004, 2008a, 2008b), it is important to problematise this relationship with 'multilayered, partial, transitory, and context specific' conceptions of identities (Ricento, 2002: 2). This is because during apartheid, language had been used in conjunction with race and ethnicity to create essentialised identities that sustained white supremacy (Malherbe, 1997), and the imposition of mother-tongue education on the Black population was part and parcel of apartheid's racial engineering. Hence, a major obstacle in the promotion of African languages as LoLTs is that speakers 'will stay tethered to essentialist notions of language, ethnicity and culture', which are often encapsulated in monolithic conceptions of mother tongue (Ricento, 2002: 3).

While we do not suggest that the notion of *mother tongue* does not play an important role in the construction of people's cultural identities and in the way they negotiate power relations in contemporary South Africa, we argue that the promotion of multilingualism requires a distancing from the assumptions of the 'birth right paradigm', that is, the notion that human beings can legitimately own only one language, and that language can only be inherited by birth (Parmegiani, 2010: 360). Hence, for the purpose of this chapter, it is particularly important to problematise the following two assumptions.

- A person's identity is rooted only in his/her mother tongue.
- A person has a better command of his/her mother tongue than his/her additional languages in any communicative situation (Parmegiani, 2010: 360).

Our study of language attitudes among isiZulu-speaking students will start from the premise that multilingual speakers own an extensive repertoire of languages, dialects and registers, rather than just the one 'whole bounded system' we often refer to as 'mother tongue'. With this approach in mind, we will use an empirical study to examine to what extent the UKZN LP meets the needs of isiZulu-speaking students in terms of learning, identity construction and empowerment aspirations.

Methodology

The data about language attitudes presented in this chapter were collected as part of a larger study carried out by Parmegiani (2009) aimed at problematising the assumptions of the birthright paradigm by investigating language attitudes and practices among students who had entered the UKZN through the Access Programme. This is a bridging programme whose goal is to increase the presence of students from disadvantaged backgrounds. The research questions of this study were much broader than the scope of this chapter, as they sought to investigate what role English played in Black South African students' identity construction and in their empowerment trajectories. Attitudes towards language policies formed a subset of this larger investigation. Also, these attitudes were not investigated specifically with respect to the UKZN LP, but with respect to the use of African languages as LoLTs in general. Nevertheless, students' responses provided very useful insights into why the UKZN's bilingualisation policy might have been met with scepticism by isiZulu speakers and these insights can provide a useful starting point for further research. Because the focus of this study concerned African students from disadvantaged backgrounds, this chapter does not provide data about the language attitudes of the UKZN's lecturers and administrators.

As recommended by Kirk and Miller (1986: 30) and Pavlenko and Blackledge (2004: 26), the data for this study were collected using a triangulated approach that involved both qualitative and quantitative methods. Triangulation is 'the combination of methodology in the study of the same phenomenon' (Denzin, 1978: 291) whose goal is to improve the reliability and the validity of the findings. As Johnstone (2000: 139) writes, 'each source of data requires a different caution but also provides a different kind of insight'.

The 'combination of methodology' for this study included a semester of ethnographic observations, in-depth interviews with a focus group of seven students and a questionnaire.

The ethnographic observations took place over a period of four months, during which the principal author interacted as a participant observer with a group of 25 students while they took English Language Development and Academic Literacy classes. As discussed elsewhere (Parmegiani, 2008: 114), this interaction will 'lay the groundwork for the mutual respect necessary for the interview process' (Seidman, 2005: 38).

The interviews took place after the observations and after the questionnaire was administered, which allowed for a preliminary analysis of the quantitative data before the interview process began. During the interviews, students engaged in conversations about language practices and attitudes in the context of their lives and the sociolinguistic complexities of South Africa. The goal was to explore in more depth the trends that emerged from the questionnaire. The seven students who participated in the interviews were chosen to represent the broadest possible spectrum of views on the topic being researched. All respondents were native isiZulu speakers; three were female and four were male.

The questionnaire was administered at the end of the semester to 120 respondents, which constituted the majority of the students enrolled in the Access Programme. Its design did not emerge 'fully fledged', but 'it was created or adapted, fashioned, and developed to maturity after many abortive test flights' (Oppenheim, 1992: 47), which took place during the ethnographic study. Following Dörnyei's recommendations (2003: 167), a two-phase piloting project preceded the administration of the questionnaire. The final version comprised 37 multiple choice questions.

All the students who responded to the questionnaire were native speakers of an African language; 88% of them were isiZulu speaking; 65% of them were female and 35% were male. While interesting correlations emerged between gender and language, and attitudes and practices, they will not be discussed in this chapter as they have been discussed elsewhere (Parmegiani, 2013).

Findings

In the questionnaire, students were asked to choose the language that would make it easier for them to fulfill a series of communicative tasks.

Table 7.1 shows that students are not necessarily more comfortable using their mother tongue in any communicative situation, and they would rather use English, or a combination of English and their mother tongue, to carry out academic tasks. The only situations where the largest group of students feels that the exclusive use of the mother tongue would give them the highest level of expertise are emotionally loaded situations, such as having an argument (58%) or discussing feelings (37%).

The interviews revealed several possible reasons why, contrary to what is assumed by the birthright paradigm, students are not necessarily more comfortable communicating in their mother tongue in an academic setting. Several students reported that while they have a very good command of their

Table 7.1 Language(s) that give students the highest level of expertise in different situations

Situation	English	Combination English/mother tongue	Mother tongue	It depends on the situation
Writing an essay	60%	13%	11%	16%
Writing a letter to a friend	45%	39%	9%	7%
Reading a book	67%	17%	9%	7%
Having an argument	8%	25%	58%	9%
Talking about feelings	22%	33%	37%	8%
Discussing politics	31%	37%	17%	15%
Discussing what you learned in school	33%	45%	8%	14%

mother tongue in informal situations, they find it difficult and tedious to use it to carry out academic literacy tasks. A comment by Nobuhle, a student, captures this situation adequately:

> I know that I can speak Zulu. I use it in my family, but I never speak Zulu in an academic context.... It takes me a while to write Zulu and to read Zulu. I wouldn't read a Zulu novel as well as I would read a novel in English.

The difficulties that students refer to have to do with the fact that many of them did not have the opportunity to develop strong academic literacy skills in their mother tongue, which is not surprising, given that English is the official LoLT in secondary institutions and African languages are only taught as a subject.

Several students also commented that the standard varieties of the African languages are often removed from their communicative needs and their sense of self. To illustrate this idea, participants would often mention that rather than using the *'proper'* isiZulu term for cell phone, *umakala ekhukhwini* (literally translated 'it rings in your pocket') students would simply use the English lexical borrowing with the isiZulu i-prefix, thus *i-cell*, because that is, as they say: *'short and sweet'*.

In some cases, it was also argued that English makes it easier to discuss certain topics that would be considered taboo in their mother tongue. A male student named A.W. asserted:

> If you are going to say 'I am going to sleep with my partner,' nobody would mind if you say that in English. But if you said that in Zulu everybody would like sit back and say 'what are you saying?'

Ingenious, another male student, maintained that Zulu girls prefer to receive love letters in English because *'it doesn't sound very good or simple if things are written in Zulu'* and because the use of standard isiZulu projects an identity that is looked upon with suspicion by urbanised female Zulu speakers:

> If you are speaking proper Zulu, girls kind of think of you like you are going to take them to a very old fashioned life, and make them do all those old-fashioned things, like fetching water from a river.

The fact that students prefer English in certain situations does not mean that they are ready to discard their mother tongue; on the contrary, every single individual in the focus group demonstrated a high investment in isiZulu as a marker of cultural identity. The participants often expressed regret for not being able to have the same level of expertise in the standard variety of isiZulu as their elders or their peers who have grown up in rural areas. One student, Ingenious , explained:

> In a rural area you have to speak a very formal language. In townships you speak a little bit diverted Zulu ... a Zulu which is mixed with other languages. It's normally mixed with English.

Tables 7.2 and 7.3 show an interesting contradiction in students' attitudes towards the promotion of African languages. On the one hand, the vast majority of the sample believe that promoting African languages is at least as important as increasing access to English in order to empower Black South Africans; on the other hand, the majority of the respondents do not believe that it is important for African students to be able to do more of their school work in their mother tongue. The interviews confirmed that while students are in favour of promoting African languages in principle, they are sceptical towards a greater use of African languages as a LoLT.

Another student respondent, Bongani, expressed concern about the vitality of his mother tongue because of the tendency among African parents to send their children to so-called 'White' or 'English' schools where no African language is taught. The fact that the next generation of African language speakers may not conserve their language upsets him tremendously:

> I am very sad because losing language is like losing your identity, where you come from, your culture. It is not OK to speak just English ... I just imagine if all the families ... will all send their children to English medium schools where there is no Zulu. That will be the lost [sic] of African languages.

Table 7.2 Which LP is more important to promote empowerment?

Increasing access to English and promoting African languages are equally important	59%
Making English more accessible is more important	22%
Promoting a greater use of African languages is more important	19%

Table 7.3 Do you think it is important for African students to be able to do more of their school work in their mother tongue?

No	59%
I am not sure	29%
Yes	22%

Ironically, he might be contributing to the 'lost of African languages' himself by planning to send his children to a former White school *'where there is no Zulu'*. When I asked him to explain this contradiction, he claimed that given the realities of the linguistic market, native speakers of African languages do not have a choice:

> Where would I be employed with my Zulu degree in this world? Maybe in the government, but I don't know of any department where I can only speak isiZulu.

Other respondents raised similar objections, despite their strong commitment to isiZulu and Zulu culture. For example, student A.W. believes that:

> even if you can get a degree in Zulu, the opportunities for you are limited. But with an English degree, you can do many things; you can knock on many doors.

It must be noted that students' objections towards using isiZulu as a LoLT are not only owing to the dominance of English as a national and international lingua franca, but also to the fact that there are nine official African languages that need to be promoted in South Africa. Several students are uncomfortable with according a special treatment to isiZulu. *'I generally don't like the idea'*, claims A.W. *'What about the other languages? What about Xhosa, what about Sotho?'* Like other respondents, he believes that promoting all the nine official African languages would be too unpractical: *'South Africa is a very diverse country. If every language could be represented equally in every institution, we would be far behind.'*

It is precisely the multilingual character of South Africa that makes some respondents see English as a necessary language of national unity whose ownership belongs to all the people of South Africa, irrespective of their mother tongue. As Bongani, a student respondent, put it:

> English is our official language. This is an African language because we have English speakers in Africa. It is used by Indians. Nowadays English is their mother tongue. English is an African language. It's everybody's language.

Once again, it must be emphasised that whatever reservation students might have had towards using isiZulu as a LoLT did not result in the desire to give up their mother tongue. On the contrary, every single respondent expressed concern about the vitality of isiZulu and African languages in general. In fact, students tended to be very critical of people who use English instead of their mother tongue in situations where they do not have to. Respondent A.W pointed out, *'I get very annoyed when you see someone you knew in high school who is living here on campus. She'd be like speaking all English, when you're like 'but I know you are Zulu. How come you don't speak Zulu¿'*

There was virtual consensus about the idea that the vitality of marginalised languages lies in the hands of their speakers, rather than in the successful implementation of language policies. For example, student Prosperity claimed that:

> In order to conserve our African languages it's up to us Africans. We should teach the younger generation. They should know about the Nguni languages, where they come from. They should also be speaking them, even though they go to Model C schools, so that they don't disappear.

A.W. agrees that learning isiZulu is the *'biggest responsibility'* for a person of Zulu ethnicity, if he or she grew up without knowing the language because of his or her life's vicissitudes.

These students' investment in their mother tongues as markers of cultural and ethnic identities, combined with their scepticism towards language policies aimed at raising the status of African languages, points to a scenario where African languages continue to be extensively used in informal domains, while English continues to be the undisputed intra-national lingua franca in formal domains. Respondent Nobhule is aware of the diglossic relationship between her mother tongue and English:

> You know that you know your Zulu, that you won't stop knowing Zulu, because you are always communicating in Zulu with your family and your friends, but you are not using it in an academic way. Even if you go to the library you don't think about going to the Zulu section and taking a book to read because everything is like English, English!... We kind of take Zulu for granted. We know that we can communicate in that language, but then we don't pay much attention to it in an academic point of view.

She regrets having a limited command of academic literacy in isiZulu and wishes she had been able to develop these skills by using her mother tongue as a LoLT. Yet, when she reflects on her mother's choice to send her to an Indian school, where her exposure to isiZulu was even less than it would have been in an ex-Department of Education and Training school, she clearly agrees with that choice:

Zulu is as important as all other languages, but then, with English being the language that you need to succeed as a person, it's better to learn in English.

Conclusion

The results of this study suggests that although isiZulu-speaking students have a strong investment in their mother tongue and consider it the prime marker of their cultural and ethnic identity, there is scepticism towards using it as a medium of instruction. Part of students' scepticism towards isiZulu as a LoLT stems from their language proficiency and practices. For many students, the use of 'pure' standard isiZulu as a medium of instruction would not necessarily make it easier to carry out academic tasks, whereas using isiZulu in conjunction with English might. In addition, some of the identities projected by the use of pure isiZulu clash with some students' sense of themselves as modern, upwardly mobile young Africans. Undoubtedly, a lack of faith in isiZulu as a passport to socio-economic mobility is the major reason behind this scepticism. Students are also aware, however, that in a country where nine African languages have official status, promoting one African language in particular would not be fair to the native speakers of the other eight. English, on the other hand, is seen as a language of national unity that is helping to build a new South Africa.

I believe that it is crucial to address the reasons behind the scepticism towards isiZulu in order to garner support for the UKZN's bilingual LP. Given the role English plays in Zulu students' language practices, identity constructions and empowerment trajectories, it is essential that the promotion of isiZulu be complemented with the promotion of a higher level of English proficiency. As has been argued (Alexander, 2002: 11), promoting African languages and increasing access to English should not be seen as mutually exclusive empowerment measures. At the same time, as Ngcobo points out (Chapter 8), actual experience of mother tongue instruction can change language attitudes, as opposed to surveying attitudes towards the use of Black African languages where the respondents have been exposed only to teaching and learning resources that make sole use of English. Moodley (2009) rightly pointed out that reassuring the UKZN community that the university remains fully committed to the development of English language proficiency while promoting isiZulu as a LoLT is essential to address the reservations towards the bilingualisation process.

Analysis of the data gathered also suggests that establishing language and literacy continua between English and isiZulu, rather than as 'whole bounded systems' might be a more effective way to help students succeed while creating more positive attitudes towards African languages as media of instruction. Courses where *both* English and isiZulu are used as resources would be more aligned with students' language practices and are likely to facilitate the acquisition of concepts in both languages.

Note

(1) It is questionable, however, whether UKZN staff members have thus far made use of this service. While time-constraints have been identified as a major problem for most staff members, it is no doubt also a lack of prioritising the acquisition of isiZulu.

References

Alexander, N. (2000) *English Unassailable But Unattainable: The Dilemma of Language Policy in South African Education*. PRAESA Occasional Paper No. 3. University of Cape Town, RSA: PRAESA.

Alexander, N. (2002) Linguistic rights, language planning and democracy in post-apartheid South Africa. In S. Baker (ed.) *Language Policy: Lessons from Global Models* (pp. 116–129). Monterey Institute of International Studies.

Alexander, N. (2003) *The African Renaissance and the Use of African languages in Tertiary Education*. PRAESA Occasional Paper No. 13. Cape Town, RSA: PRAESA.

Balfour, R.J. (ed.) (2010) Mind the gaps: Higher education language policies, the national curriculum, and language research. A special issue on languages in higher education in South Africa. *Language Learning Journal* 37 (3), 293–306.

Canagarajah, S. (2005) Ethnographic methods in language policy. In T. Ricento (ed.) *An Introduction to Language Policy* (pp. 153–169). Malden: Blackwell.

De Klerk, G. (2002) Mother tongue education in South Africa: The weight of history. *International Journal of the Sociology of Language* 154, 29–46.

Denzin, N. (1978) *The Research Act: A Theoretical Introduction to Sociology Methods*. Columbus, OH: McGraw-Hill.

Deumert, A. (2010) Tracking the demographics of (urban) language shift – an analysis of South African census data. *Journal of Multilingual and Multicultural Development* 31 (1), 13–35.

Dörnyei, Z. (2003) *Questionnaires in Second Language Research. Construction, Administration, and Processing*. Mahwah and London: Erlbaum.

Engelbrecht, C., Shangase, N., Majele, S.J., Mthembu, S. and Zondi, Z.M. (2010) IsiZulu terminology development in nursing and midwifery. *Alternation* 17 (1), 249–272.

Heller, M. (ed.) (2007) Bilingualism as ideology and practice. *Bilingualism: A Social Approach* (pp. 1–22). New York: Macmillian.

Heugh, K. (2000) *The Case Against Bilingual and Multilingual Education*. PRAESA Occasional Paper No. 6. University of Cape Town, RSA: PRAESA.

Hornberger, N. (2004) The continua of biliteracy and the bilingual educator: Educational Linguistics in practice. *Bilingual Education and Bilingualism* 7 (2), 155–171.

Janks, H. (1992) Critical language awareness and people's English. *Southern African Journal of Applied Language Studies* 1, 64–73.

Johnstone, B. (2000) *Qualitative Methods in Sociolinguistics*. Oxford: Oxford University Press.
Kamwangamalu, N. (1997) Multilingualism and education policy in post-apartheid South Africa. *Language Problems and Language Planning* 21 (3), 234–253.
Kamwangamalu, N. (2000) A new language policy, old language practices: status planning for African languages in a multilingual South Africa. *South African Journal of African Languages* 20 (1), 50–60.
Kirk, J. and Miller, M.L. (1986) *Reliability and Validity in Quantitative Research*. Beverly Hills, CA: SAGE.
Malherbe, E.G. (1977) *Education in South Africa II (1923–75)*. Cape Town: Juta.
Mashiya, N. (2010) Mother tongue teaching at the University of KwaZulu-Natal: Opportunities and Threats. *Alternation* 17 (1), 92–107.
Mesthrie, R. (ed.) (2002) South Africa: A sociolinguistic overview. *Language in South Africa* (pp. 11–25). Cambridge: Cambridge University Press.
Moodley, D. (2009) Bilingualism gridlocked at the University of KwaZulu-Natal. *Nordic Journal of African Studies* 18, 22–72.
Moodley, D. (2010) Bilingualism at the University of KwaZulu-Natal: Staff and student preferences. *Alternation* 17, 328–354.
Ndimande-Hlongwa, N.P., Balfour, R., Mhize, N.J. and Engelbrecht, C. (2010) Progress and challenges for language policy implementation at the University of KwaZulu-Natal. *Language Learning Journal* 38 (3), 347–357.
Ndlangamandla, S. (2010) (Unofficial) multilingualism in desegregated schools; Learner's use of and views towards African languages. *South African Linguistics and Applied Language Studies Journal* 28, 61–73.
Ngũgĩ wa Thiong'o (1981) *Decolonising the Mind: The Politics of Language in African Literature*. Harare: Zimbabwe Publishing House.
Oppenheim, A. (1992) *Questionnaire Design, Interviewing, and Attitude Measurement*. London: Pinter.
Parmegiani, A. (2008) Language ownership in multilingual settings. Exploring attitudes at the University of KwaZulu-Natal. *Stellenbosch Papers in Linguistics* 38, 107–124.
Parmegiani, A. (2009) The power of English and academic literacy: Students' perceptions and theoretical, political, and pedagogical implications. A case study of students at the University of KwaZulu-Natal. Unpublished doctoral dissertation. The Graduate Center of the City University of New York.
Parmegiani, A. (2010) Reconceptualizing language ownership. A case study of language practices and attitudes at the University of KwaZulu-Natal. *Language Learning Journal* 38, 359–378.
Parmegiani, A. (2012) Language, power and transformation in South Africa: A critique of language rights discourse. *Transformation* 78, 74–97.
Parmegiani, A. (2013) Gender and the ownership of English in South Africa. Unpublished Paper, available from the author.
Pavlenko, A. and Blackledge, A. (eds) (2004) Introduction: New theoretical approaches to the study of negotiation of identities in multilingual contexts. *Negotiation of Identity in Multilingual Contexts* (pp. 1–33). Clevedon: Multilingual Matters.
Paxton, M.I.J. (2009) 'It's easy to learn when you are using your home language but with English you need to start learning language before you get to the concept': Bilingual concept development in an English medium university in South Africa. *Journal of Multilingual and Multicultural Development* 30 (1), 1–15.
Republic of South Africa (1996) *Constitution of the Republic of South Africa*, Act 108 of 1996 (as amended). Pretoria, RSA: Government Press.

Ricento, T. (2002) Introduction. *International Journal of the Sociology of Language.* 154, 1–9.
Rose, B. and Tumner, R. (1975) *Documents in South African Education.* Johannesburg: AD Donker.
Rudwick, S. (2004) 'Zulu – we need it for our culture': Umlazi adolescents in the post-apartheid state. *South African Linguistics and Applied Language Studies* 22 (3&4), 159–172.
Rudwick, S. (2008a) Coconuts and Oreos: English-speaking Zulu people in a South African township? *World Englishes* 27 (1), 101–116.
Rudwick, S. (2008b) Linguistic Culture and essentialism in South Africa. *Macrolinguistics* 2, 34–47.
Seidman, I. (2005) *Interviewing as Qualitative Research.* New York: Teachers' College Press.
Skutnabb-Kangas, T. and Phillipson, R. (2001) Reflections on scholarship and linguistic rights: A rejoinder to Jan Blommaert. *Journal of Sociolinguistics* 5, 131–155.
University of KwaZulu-Natal (UKZN) (2006) Language policy. See http://www.ukzn.ac.za/site-search?cx=011803114398820865437:ugpuxu4q8rq&cof=FORID:11&q=language%20policy (accessed 13 February 2013).
Webb, V. (2009) Multilingualism in South Africa: The change to below. *Language Matters* 40 (2), 190–204.
Webb, V.M., Lafon, M. and Pare, P. (2010) Bantu languages in education in South Africa: The absent owner. *Language Learning Journal* 38 (3), 273–292.

8 Dual Language Instruction: Its Impact on Attitudes Towards the Role of African Languages in Education

Sandiso Ngcobo

Introduction

The majority of South African Black[1] students do not experience success in higher education and drop out before they complete their studies. Scott (2009: 20–24) reports that a sector-wide study that was conducted by the Department of Education (DoE) to establish academic performance patterns of first-time-entering undergraduates found that about 70% of students drop out of universities, and 14% of the 30% that remain spend more years completing their studies than expected because of failure. Worse still, the graduation rate was below 5% in the 20 to 24-year age group among Black students. One of the factors that has repeatedly been identified as one of the major contributory causes of high failure and dropout rates among Black South Africans is their low academic literacy in the language of learning (i.e. English, which is their second language) (Dalvit & De Klerk, 2005; Department of Education, 2002; Deyi *et al.*, 2007; Pretorius, 2002; Weideman, 2006). Stubbs (2002: 65) says of this situation: 'educational failure is linguistic failure'. A possible educational approach that has been used successfully in other countries to address linguistic issues in education is that known as 'dual language' or 'two-way' programmes. This term refers to educational programmes or courses that provide instruction in and through two languages, which means some academic content is also presented in students' native or primary language (L1) in order to facilitate enhanced learning (Goldenberg, 2008: 11; Short & Fitzsimmons, 2007: 6). The term preferred by Plüddemann (2011: 11) in this regard is 'translanguaging' or the language integration approach, where there is a focus on students' right to use either of the two languages during lessons and assessments as well (see the contributions by Madiba and Makalela, Chapters 5 and 6, respectively, in this regard). Such an educational approach is aimed at ensuring that the pursuit of the dominant language of trade and commerce is not done at the expense of community languages; this approach facilitates learning and affirms students' identities within the educational system (Hibbert, 2011: 33).

The main challenge however, that concerns this study, is that mother-tongue literacy as an alternative or complement to literacy in the second language has inadequate access to educational materials (Hornberger, 2003) and is not often well received by the public (Gómez *et al.*, 2005; Watson, 2007). This implies that it would not be enough to simply develop bi-/multilingual materials, but that one would also have to take into consideration stakeholders' perceptions of such an educational approach, as Parmegiani and Rudwick show very clearly in Chapter 7. Hence, the research paradigm that informs this study is *educational sociolinguistics*, a subfield of sociolinguistics that examines the relationship between language and education (Mesthrie *et al.*, 2000: 354). In the study described in this chapter, I sought to longitudinally investigate students' perceptions of the use of L1 (isiZulu) within an educational approach commonly known as bilingual education; in this instance, the approach was to utilise a dual language instruction (DLI) pilot course.

Literature Review

To conduct a discussion on the use of L1 in academic literacy and communication skills development, one needs to consider the distinction between the following two sets of language competencies, as introduced by Cummins (2000, 2001, 2003): Basic Interpersonal Communication Skills (BICS) and Cognitive Academic Language Proficiency (CALP). A discussion of this distinction is important as it serves to clarify that the use of L1 in education does not automatically imply that all students will experience academic success. Rather, a particular level of language proficiency and associated competencies enables students, whether L1 or L2 speakers, to experience success in their education (Cummins, 2000). In making this distinction, Cummins (2000: 55, 2003: 322) defines BICS as being the conversational fluency or oral language skills used on a day-to-day basis in social situations. Cummins asserts that it is comparatively easy to develop BICS in a second language, particularly if the learner is in an environment where the target language is spoken frequently. According to Cummins, this can be attributed to the idea that BICS are not cognitively demanding, because the meanings are often supported by a wide range of non-linguistic or paralinguistic cues. These cues include the use of prosody (pitch, stress, intonation) and paralinguistic features (gestures, expressions). Moreover, meaning may easily be negotiated in the course of interaction (Matjila & Pretorius, 2004: 3).

In contrast to BICS, CALP entails the ability to use language in context-reduced communications, and includes those cognitively demanding skills that are required for formal academic learning (Cummins, 2003: 323). CALP reflects the registers of language acquired in school and which learners need to be able to use effectively if they are to experience academic success. The registers of language that promote academic success in the tertiary education context can be promoted by developing students' critical reading skills. Critical reading skills development should focus on the following: (a) developing vocabulary in context; (b) identifying coherence in a text; (c) knowing how to distinguish between fact and opinion; (d) interpreting different text types; (e) interpreting visual information; (f) identifying sequence in a text; and (g) identifying what counts as evidence for an argument (Weideman, 2006).

The same competencies developed during academic reading lessons may also be applicable to academic speaking, academic listening and academic writing. Cummins (2000) does however caution that mastering such academic proficiencies requires a great deal of time and support, particularly if they are being learned in one's L2. One of the ways in which support could be provided would be to employ the students' L1 as a linguistic resource to facilitate effective teaching and learning in what has come to be known as bilingual education (Alanis, 2000; Baker, 2001; Hoffman, 2001). In the discussion of the interdependence hypothesis and the threshold hypothesis, Cummins suggests that it might be beneficial to first develop CALP in the learner's L1 before it is transferred to the second language (Cummins, 1998, 2000, 2009). Although these theories were developed to be applied at primary school level and for immigrants in countries where a second language such as English is the dominant everyday language, Cummins's hypotheses can be taken to suggest that young adult tertiary students with problems in academic literacy competencies (CALP) might benefit from developing this skill to the required level of language proficiency through the use of their L1 as a resource alongside their L2.

However, this might prove to be a challenge if they also lack the basic conversational skills in their L2 as the result of a weak education system. This means that both language skills (BICS and CALP) should be addressed simultaneously within DLI material. The ways in which the students' L1 can be used is for support purposes, such as giving translations, discussing the subject during or after class, and previewing the material before a lesson in the L2 (Goldenberg, 2008: 11). The L1 may also be used to clarify concepts, introduce new ideas or provide explanations (Condelli & Wrigley, 2005: 17). The different ways in which L1 can be used alongside L2 demonstrate that, where theories of skills transfer are not applicable, there are other options that can be pursued in an endeavour to promote bi-/multilingual education. These different options can be particularly useful in situations where academic literacy has not been extensively developed in the students' L1. One possible approach that could be explored in this regard would be to develop course material in both L1 and L2. Such learning material could serve as a good point of reference for students, especially when the lecturers are not speakers of the students' L1.

On the one hand, Cummins' BICS/CALP theories have received support from various scholars (Heugh, 2002, 2005; Zwiers, 2005) who argue that when L2 learners enter school, they bring with them a wealth of cognitive, social and linguistic skills that they have developed in their L1. It is then to the advantage of the educational institutions to exploit these skills that learners possess in their L1 to make the learning of skills provided in L2 effective. On the other hand, Cummins' BICS/CALP distinction is not without its critics (Aukerman, 2007; Edelsky, 1996; MacSwan & Rolstad, 2003). MacSwan and Rolstad (2003: 334), for instance, object to certain properties that Cummins associates with academic language. Among these is the notion that school 'improves' language, and they question the perception that the language of the educated classes is in any sense richer or more complex than the language of the unschooled. The plausible argument put forward by MacSwan and Rolstad is that there is no relevant empirical evidence to support Cummins' claim. While it is important to keep such objections in mind, the focus of this chapter prevents any further engagement with this particular aspect of the BICS/ CALP distinction.

Irrespective of whether learners' available languages are characterised as 'developed' to the level of CALP or not, the development of bilingual learning material could exploit whatever resources are available in other languages when such materials are task-based and informed by an integrated approach to language and literacy development (Nunan, 2006). Were the material to adhere to the three stages of tasks (i.e. pre-task, during-task and post-task), it would provide opportunities for the use of L1 as a resource to facilitate learning (Ellis, 2006). This can take place at pre-task and during-task stages, when students are either provided with information that draws from their L1 to explicate the task ahead, or when they are engaged in a group discussion where they are likely to use their L1 to help negotiate meaning as they interact with each other, as Madiba shows in Chapter 5. Most importantly, the material and its tasks should not only be aimed at language development, but should also be integrated with academic content from students' disciplines as this could create an effective context for both language learning as well as the pursuit of overall academic goals.

The added benefit of such teaching material is that it could contribute towards a better understanding of attitudes towards the use of L1 in education among L2 learners. In this regard, the claim by Triandis (1971: 142) that by providing someone with new information the cognitive component of their attitude may be changed, appears appropriate as a basis for a study of this nature. This attitude change would however be determined by the perceived nature of experience in the presence of a new object towards which one has an attitude. The change in feeling might translate into support for any future behaviour that is directed towards the promotion of the subject, such as language use in education. One of the ways in which this relationship could be investigated is through the use of survey questionnaires. The survey questions could include self-reports on language use, language preference, the desirability of bilingualism and bilingual education, and opinions on shifting or maintaining language policies (Garrett *et al.*, 2003: 15; Ryan *et al.*, 1988: 7). Bangeni and Kapp's (2007) South African study posits that it is however important that such attitudinal research be conducted longitudinally because a shift can take place in attitudes during the course of students' enrolment at university.

Course material development

The teaching and learning material developed for this study uses isiZulu (it is estimated that 35% of the material is in this language) and English (estimated to comprise 65% of the material). The uneven use of the two languages is as a result of the fact that the use of isiZulu (L1) is for support purposes and aims to develop academic literacy and communication competency in English (L2). For this reason, the material is designed to try to provide a translation of every aspect of the content. The students' L1 is used to make clarification of essential and problematic concepts and tasks. In addition, certain tasks are organised such that they allow students to interact among themselves in their L1 while preparing to make presentations in the L2.

Sections of the material that employ translation of its content include the course outcomes and the assessment criteria. These sections are translated because it is considered important that students clearly understand what will be covered in the course and what will be expected from them.

Example 1 below shows how this is done at the beginning of each unit of the course.

Example 1

Unit 1: Speaking and listening skills
Learning outcomes

The aim of this section is to engage you in activities that will empower you to:

(a) Speak confidently and fluently (*khuluma ngokuzethemba*);
(b) Open and close conversations (*qala futhi uphethe ingxoxo*); and
(c) Engage in debates or arguments without being emotional (*inkulumo mpikiswano engenakho ukuphakama kwemimoya*).

One of the guiding assumptions that informed the development of the DLI course material was that academic literacy and other generic skills, together with knowledge, transfer across languages (Goldenberg, 2008; Cummins, 2000). This view suggests that if students understand and know how to perform a skill that they acquire in their L1, they might then be able to transfer this knowledge to an L2 environment. Hence, in areas such as grammar, which are also taught in L1, equivalent terminology is used in the DLI material to facilitate the students' understanding of such knowledge in L2 (see Example 2).

Example 2

Parts of speech (Izingcezu zenkulumo)

(1) Noun/*ibizo*: a word that names a person, place, thing, idea, creature, quality or action, for example, soldier, university, thought, love, honesty, cup, wind.
(2) Verb/*isenzo*: a word that describes an action (doing something) or a state (being something), and indicates the time/tense, for example, listening, drive, believe, is, will rise.
(3) Conjunction *umxhumanisi*: joins two words, phrases or sentences together, for example, so, and, but, because, or.

One of the academic and literacy competencies that is transferable is the use of what is called *cohesion* or *transitional* words. Since students often struggle to master this skill in their L2, it was considered useful to present an example in L1 with the hope that it would facilitate understanding in L2. In addition, the same skill was assessed in both languages, as indicated in Example 3.

Example 3

Answer either question 2A or question 2B

Cohesion or transitional words: indicate the function of the underlined, bold words in the sentences that follow by choosing from either (a) listing and addition, (b) contrast, (c) time sequence, (d) reason or (e) emphasis. Write only the number and the corresponding letter, e.g. 1. D.

Question 2A
I-yoghurt *ikhulula umgudu wokudla*

LINGENILE *ihlobo kanti lokhu kusho ukuthi abaningi bazoshintsha nendlela abebedla ngayo ebusika. Baningi abashintsha i*-lifestyle *yabo bathutheleke nasejimini (1)* **uma** *kungena ihlobo ngoba befuna ukunciphisa amafutha azo zonke izicofucofu ebezidliwa ebusika.*

I-yoghurt *ingenye yohlobo lokudla abaningi abazitika ngayo ukuziba iphango (2)* **ngoba** *bengafuni ukudla okuzobakhuluphalisa...*

[Adapted from *Ilanga leTheku*, 4 September 2008. Available at www.ilanga.co.za]

Question 2B
(1) I feel fluoride should not be added to drinking water **until** we are sure it is safe.
(2) **Owing to** extensive research, it has emerged that fluoride is the sixth most poisonous cause of water pollution in the world.

[Adapted from *Read Well: Skills for Better English 1* (Cretchley & Stacey, 1986)].

As Poole (2005: 52) explains, in settings where English language teachers and students share a common language (other than English) and culture, such as in South Africa, Tanzania and China, there is a tendency to either code-switch or simply use the native language in order to overcome any communicative difficulties. Therefore, tasks in bi-/multilingual material can be developed such that they encourage students to communicate among themselves in small informal study groups or in formal tutorial groups in either their L1 and/or in both their L1 and L2. Following the three stages of tasks in developing materials (pre-task, during-task and post-task) provides endless opportunities for the use of L1 as a resource to facilitate effective teaching and learning of L2 and academic literacy skills (Ellis, 2006). Based on this understanding, the pre-task stage of the DLI course includes the use of information that is either translated by the researcher or given in its original translated form (see Example 4, from Ndebele, 1998).

Example 4

Impumelelo ye-Afrika kwezesayensi ayigcini emandulo. Ngisanda kuzwa ukuthi iKreepy Krauly, lobuya bucwazicwazi obasungulwa, obugcina iziziba zomhlaba jikelele zibenyezela, basungulwa ngo-1974 eNingizimu Afrika unjiniyela osebenzisa amandla amanzi (hydraulics engineer), *uFerdinand Chauvier. Kanti futhi sino-Afronaut Mark Shuttleworth ogabavula ashone ezinkanyezini enza imizamo yokuvala igebe lolwazi elikhona kwezedijithali, ukusetshenziswa kwemithombo evulekile yohlelo olufakwa kukhompyutha* (software) *eyenziwe ekhaya, ...*

Africa's scientific successes are not limited to our past. I recently found out that the Kreepy Krauly, that brilliant invention that keeps pools the world over sparkling, was invented in 1974 in South Africa by hydraulics engineer Ferdinand Chauvier. And of course we have Afronaut Mark Shuttleworth charging across galaxies in his quest to bridge the digital divide, using home grown, open-source software that will not cost us an arm and a leg to buy in dollars or pounds ....

The task activities of the DLI material include the use of formal and informal group work to enable the students to draw from their primary language to facilitate their private discussions of the task provided. For instance, Example 5 below gives an instruction on a group task that students have to brainstorm before presentation to their lecturer and classmates. However, the post-task activities are geared to make students use the target language (L2) when making class presentations and submitting written work.

Example 5

Task 5: Argumentative/persuasive presentation

Working in groups or pairs, choose an invention in science, technology or engineering and discuss whether you think it has been good or bad/ has advantages or disadvantages for the people, economy or environment. Present your views in front of the class. Be prepared to defend your views because your audience will have the opportunity to ask you questions.

It was also deemed essential that students be familiar with and understand words in the instructions they are likely to encounter in tests and assignments in their content subjects. As a result, a glossary of 'instruction' words is provided in two languages, while the explanation is in L2 to facilitate the students' understanding (see Example 6).

Example 6

Instruction words

> Analyse (*hlaziya*): take apart a concept or a process and explain it in detail.
> Compare (*ukufanisa*): show similarities and differences between two processes.
> Enumerate (*bala*): provide a list that is in the correct order.
> Prove/justify (*bonakalisa ngobufakazi*): give evidence or provide reasons why.
> Trace (*funa umkhondo womsuka*): find the origin of a process and explain it.

It is also important for academics, and specifically for engineering students and professionals, to be able to present, defend and challenge spoken and/or written arguments. This is, however, not an easy competency and may take considerable time to develop because it requires semantic and syntactic knowledge as well as the use of functional language (Price, 2007: 318). To facilitate an understanding and sharpening of this academic competency, the material provides students with a sample of a written argumentative text that is presented in both isiZulu and English in a form of code-switching (see Example 7, Mbatha, 2008).

Example 7

> *SEZIZININGI izinkinga* [There are many problems] that have been identified by *abantu abaningi uma sikhuluma nge* [many people with regard to] co-hosting. *Kungicacelile ukuthi baningi abantu abawabonayo ama*-challenges *imisakazo yethu ebhekene nawo* [It became clear to me that there are many people who can see the challenges our radio stations are faced with] in as far as this practice is concerned. [...] This observation *yenze ukuthi ngifise ukubheka* some of *ama*-formats *akhona ngoba phela inkinga iqala khona lapho* [made me curious about different formats because that is where the problem lies].

[Adapted from *Ilanga leTheku,* 21 February 2008. (My translation)]

Research Methodology

The number of student participants and the focus of the study on language attitudes made it necessary to select questionnaires as the main research tool. The first questionnaire assessed the language attitudes of 300 students upon their arrival at university and before their participation in the DLI pilot course (February 2008). The second questionnaire evaluated the attitudes of the same students immediately after participation in the DLI pilot course (May 2008). The last questionnaire, similar to the first, was completed by a sample of 87 students from the same initial cohort after a further period of three semesters (March 2010) to assess if there were any changes in terms of their language attitudes after a long time spent in the university environment (see Appendices A and B).

The questionnaires consisted of mostly closed questions and a few open questions. The closed questions required the respondents to indicate their opinions by locating their responses on a rating scale. However, in order to minimise bias, both negative and positive statements were included. Open questions in one questionnaire were intended to allow the participants the opportunity to express their views in their own words so as to offset the bias and limitations that might have been created through the use of closed questions.

As this was a study on bilingual education, the development of questionnaires in two languages was considered appropriate. Consequently, the students' questionnaires were formulated in both isiZulu and English throughout. In the same vein, students were allowed to respond to open questions in either English, isiZulu or a combination of both. The translation of questions was made to allow bilingual students to refer to the isiZulu version if they did not understand the English version very well. The questions were, however, not directly translated from the source language into the target language. Additional steps, such as back translation and the involvement of more than one translator, were undertaken to protect the validity of the research tool.

Findings

This section provides a comparative statistical analysis of the findings of the three questionnaires of the study. The results of the initial questionnaire reveal that although English was identified as the main language of instruction, isiZulu (L1) was the preferred language of learning among the majority of isiZulu-speaking participants, particularly at the foundation level of their studies. This is evident in that 78% of students acknowledged that they used L1 as a learning resource among themselves in group discussions and 72% of the same cohort used it to understand what they heard and read in their studies (as indicated in Table 8.1).

Table 8.1 First student questionnaire, responses to questions 8–10

	Strongly agree		Agree		Unsure		Disagree		Strongly disagree	
	No.	%	No.	%	No.	%	No.	%	No.	%
8. In group discussions I learn better when we use both English and isiZulu.	120	40	114	38	18	6	24	8	24	8
9. To better understand what I read and hear in English, I think about it in my home language.	126	42	90	30	21	7	42	14	21	7
10. In lectures, students should use English throughout, even in the group discussions.	72	24	78	26	24	8	51	17	75	25

Other studies among isiXhosa-speaking students (Aziakpono & Bekker, 2010; Dalvit & De Klerk, 2005) show that there is similar support for the use of isiXhosa alongside English in education and this is also the case for other African languages, as Parmegiani and Rudwick show in Chapter 7.

The results of the second questionnaire (see extract in Table 8.2) reveal that the majority of students (86%) found that the use of the DLI material during their lectures suited them. Therefore, the use of the DLI pilot course was favourably received because it was in line with the students' preferred style of learning.

Table 8.2 Second student questionnaire, responses to questions 5–7

	Strongly agree		Agree		Unsure		Disagree		Strongly disagree	
	No.	%	No.	%	No.	%	No.	%	No.	%
5. I found the mixing of languages in the guide suitable to my style of learning.	159	53	99	33	12	4	21	7	9	3
6. The guide enabled me to understand and use English better.	204	68	84	28	12	4	0	0.0	0	0.0
7. I experienced effective teaching and learning.	111	37	147	49	24	8	18	6	0	0.0

In addition, when comparing responses to question 5 (I found the mixing of languages in the guide suitable to my style of learning, in Table 8.2) in relation to the teacher composition at school level of different groups of students, responses showed no difference in the groups. There was however a trend towards most agreement on this question in the group who had African teachers and least in those with Coloured teachers (compare Table 8.3a and 8.3b). This is consistent with the results on demographics that show that the majority (66%) of student participants were taught by Black teachers only.

However, the use of isiZulu in the piloted engineering course had a positive impact in terms of changing the attitudes of the participants towards its use in lectures. The students' responses to the first questionnaire displayed a preference for the informal use of their L1 as a learning resource, but this did not initially translate into positive attitudes concerning the formal use of their L1 in higher education. This is because the majority (62%) of the students initially indicated that they viewed English as the only language suitable for instruction in higher education. There was also no clear support for the use of isiZulu during assessments, with 43% in support, 51% against and 6% undecided. Yet after participation in the DLI pilot course, 77% of students indicated that they learned to value the role of their L1 in education. After participation in the DLI course, a group of the students (6%) said

Table 8.3a Racial composition of teachers at high school

	Racial composition of teachers at high school	N	Mean rank
I found the mixing of languages in the guide suitable for my style of learning	Coloured	75	51.12
	African	198	49.02
	White	9	39.83
	Indian	18	44.58
	Total	300	

Table 8.3b Mixing of languages in the guide

	I found the mixing of languages in the guide suitable for my style of learning
Chi-Square	0.743
Df	3
Asymp. Sig.	0.863

they found the use of L1 in education helpful were, interestingly, from racially mixed schools, and indicated that neither they nor their school teachers had ever used L1 as a learning resource. This suggests that the DLI course helped bring about a positive change of attitude towards the use of African languages in higher education. There was, however, no significant difference in responses to the same question when compared with the racial mix of the last school attended between those who went to Coloured schools and those who attended Black schools ($p = 0.243$), see Table 8.4a and 8.4b. This suggests that either the DLI pilot course or students' exposure to the new educational environment cancels out the previous school environment.

The formal use of L1 in education was preferred more in the first semester of study and less in the final semester. While the early results indicate a lack of decisiveness as to which language is most suitable for use in tertiary education, this was however not the case at a later stage. Responses to the first questionnaire showed that 62% of students identified English as the only language suitable for use in education. At the same time, 64% of students felt that isiZulu could be used successfully in education. However, responses to the third questionnaire revealed that a higher percentage (75%) of student participants felt English ought to be the only language of

Table 8.4a Racial composition of students at high school

	Racial composition of students at high school	N	Mean rank	Sum of ranks
I learnt to value the role of my home language in education	Coloured	51	41.91	712.50
	African	237	49.92	3943.50
	Total	288		

Test Statistics(a)

Table 8.4b Value the role of the home language in education

	I learnt to value the role of my home language in education
Mann–Whitney U	559.500
Wilcoxon W	712.500
Z	−1.168
Asymp. Sig. (2-tailed)	0.243

Grouping variable: Racial composition of students at high school education. A far lower number (25%) of students saw the need for L1 in education at final year level. Furthermore, the majority (56%) did not support the use of L1 during assessment activities. This suggests that L1 is favoured as a resource only when it serves to bridge the learning gap between university and school, which is nonetheless a strong motivation for using it.

Most importantly, post-DLI responses indicated that 89% of students claimed that the course material contributed towards the better development of their academic literacy and communication skills. These findings are in line with the view expressed by Koch and Burkett (2005: 1091) that South African research on the attitudes of Black African language speakers towards mother-tongue instruction indicates a strong preference for it so long as it provides quality L1 education while at the same time developing English proficiency. This implies that once Black African languages are formally integrated with English in the development of teaching and learning materials (such as textbooks and study guides), they might be accepted by many stakeholders, such as academics and students. Moreover, the fact that more of the study's participants felt positive (from 77% to 86%) about the role of L1 after they had taken the DLI pilot course suggests that the research approach that includes participants' practical experience with mother-tongue instruction – as was adopted in this investigation into attitudes – is a critical factor in changing stakeholders' attitudes to languages. Similarly, the increase (from 64% to 77%) in the number of students who support the use of Black African languages in education is linked with the high number (87%) of students who said they were satisfied with the quality of the DLI course material (Ngcobo, 2009).

Conclusion

The findings of this study suggest that in an educational context where the community's L1 is used more frequently than their L2, attitudes towards L1 in education can be expected to be positive. Furthermore, actual experience of mother-tongue instruction can change language attitudes, as opposed to surveying attitudes towards the use of Black African languages where the respondents have been exposed only to teaching and learning resources that make sole use of English. The findings help inform researchers as to how future sociolinguistic investigations should be conducted, namely, that communities need to be provided with a personal experience of effective bi-/multilingual programmes or courses on which to base their feelings about the use of Black African languages in education. The area that requires further research, however, is the link between the perceptions and actual academic performance of participants in a bi-/multilingual course.

Acknowledgements

The information used in this chapter is part of a PhD thesis in Linguistics that was pursued at the University of KwaZulu-Natal (Howard Campus) under the supervision of Professor Heike Tappe.

The research was also undertaken as an institutional project at the Mangosuthu University of Technology that was registered with the research directorate and funded by the National Research Foundation from 2008–2009.

Note

(1) This category is required for demographic data reporting to the Department of Higher Education and Training. The use of the categories Black, White, Coloured, Indian and Other does not imply acceptance of these racial categories.

References

Alanis, I. (2000) A Texas two-way bilingual program: Its effects on linguistic and academic achievement. *Bilingual Research Journal* 24 (3), 225–248.

Aukerman, M. (2007) A culpable CALP: Rethinking the conversational/academic language proficiency distinction in early literacy instruction. *The Reading Teacher* 60 (7), 626–635.

Aziakpono, P. and Bekker, I. (2010) The attitudes of isiXhosa-speaking students toward language of learning and teaching issues at Rhodes University, South Africa: General trends. *Southern African Linguistics and Applied Language Studies* 28 (1), 39–60.

Baker, C. (2001) *Foundations of Bilingual Education and Bilingualism* (3rd edn). Clevedon: Multilingual Matters.

Bangeni, B. and Kapp, R. (2007) Shifting language attitudes in a linguistically diverse learning environment in South Africa. *Journal of Multilingual and Multicultural Development* 28 (4), 253–269.

Cummins, J. (1998) Immersion education for the millennium: What have we learned from 30 years of research on second language immersion? In M.R. Childs and R.M. Bostwick (eds) *Learning through Two Languages: Research and Practice. Second Katoh Gakuen International Symposium on Immersion and Bilingual Education* (pp. 34–47). Japan: Katoh Gakuen.

Cummins, J. (2000) *Language, Power and Pedagogy: Bilingual Children in the Crossfire*. Clevedon: Multilingual Matters.

Cummins, J. (2001) *Negotiating Identities: Education for Empowerment in a Diverse Society* (2nd edn). Los Angeles, CA: Association for Bilingual Education.

Cummins, J. (2003) BICS and CALP: Origins and rationale for the distinction. In C.B. Paulston and G.R. Tucker (eds) *Sociolinguistics: The Essential Readings* (pp. 322–328). Boston: Blackwell.

Cummins, J. (2009) Fundamental psycholinguistic and sociological principles underlying educational success for linguistic minority students. In A. Mohanty, M. Panda, R. Phillipson and T. Skutnabb-Kangas (eds) *Multilingual Education for Social Justice. Globalising the Local* (pp. 21-35). New Delhi: Orient Blackswan.

Condelli, L. and Wrigley, H.S. (2005) *Real World Research: Combining Quantitative and Qualitative Research for Adult ESL*. London: National Research and Development Centre for Adult Literacy and Numeracy.

Cretchley, G. and Stacey, J. (1986) *Read Well: Skills for Better English 1*. Johannesburg, RSA: Sached Trust/Ravan Press.

Dalvit, L. and De Klerk, V. (2005) Attitudes of Xhosa-speaking students at the University of Fort Hare towards the use of Xhosa as a language of learning and teaching (LOLT). *Southern African Linguistics and Applied Language Studies* 23 (1), 1–18.

Department of Education (Republic of South Africa) (2002) *Language Policy for Higher Education*. Pretoria: Government Press.

Deyi, S., Simon, E., Ngcobo, S. and Thole, A. (2007) Promoting the multilingual classroom: Why the significance of multilingualism in higher education? *Paradigms* 14, 10–20.

Edelsky, C. (1996) *With Literacy and Justice for All: Rethinking the Social in Language and Education* (2nd edn). London: Taylor and Francis.

Ellis, R. (2006) The methodology of task-based teaching. *Asian EFL Journal* 8 (3), article 6.

Garrett, P., Coupland, N. and Williams, A. (2003) *Investigating Language Attitudes: Social Meanings of Dialect, Ethnicity and Performance*. Cardiff: University of Wales Press.

Gómez, L., Freeman, D. and Freeman, Y. (2005) Dual language education: A promising 50–50 model. *Bilingual Research Journal* 29 (1), 145–164.

Goldenberg, C. (2008) Teaching English language learners: What the research does and does not say. *American Educator* 33 (2), 8–44.

Heugh, K. (2002) A history of mother tongue and bilingual education in South Africa. In T. Bekett (ed.) *Reports on Mother Tongue Education with Special Reference to South Africa and Belgium*. International workshop, 14–15 May 2001. University of Cape Town and University of Antwerp: PRAESA.

Heugh, K. (2005) Mother-tongue education is best. *HSRC Review* 3 (3), 6–7.

Hibbert, L. (2011) Language development in higher education: Suggested paradigms and their applications in South Africa. *Southern African Linguistics and Applied Language Studies* 29 (1), 31–42.

Hoffman, C. (2001) Towards a description of trilingual competence. *International Journal of Bilingualism* 5 (1), 1–17.

Hornberger, N.H. (2003) Literacy and language planning. In C.B. Paulston and G.R. Tucker (eds) *Sociolinguistics: The Essential Readings* (pp. 449–459). Malden: Blackwell.

Koch, E. and Burkett, B. (2005) Making the role of African languages in higher education a reality. *SAJHE* 19 (6), 1089–1107.

MacSwan, J. and Rolstad, K. (2003) Linguistic diversity, schooling, and social class: Rethinking our conception of language proficiency in language minority education. In C.B. Paulston and G.R. Tucker (eds) *Sociolinguistics: The Essential Readings* (pp. 329–340). Malden: Blackwell.

Matjila, D.S. and Pretorius, E.J. (2004) Bilingual and biliterate? An exploratory study of Grade 8 reading skills in Setswana and English. *Per Linguam* 20, 1–21.

Mbatha, Z. (2008) *EZEMISAKAZO NO* [RADIO MATTERS] with Zowakha Mbatha. See http://www.ilanganews.co.za/ (accessed 3 March 2008).

Mesthrie, R., Swann, J., Deumert, A. and Leap, W.L. (2000) *Introducing Sociolinguistics*. Edinburgh: Edinburgh University Press.

Ngcobo, S. (2009) Lecturers' and students' reflections on a bilingual programme. In B. Leibowitz, A. Van der Merwe and S. Van Schalkwyk (eds) *Focus on First-Year Success: Perspectives Emerging from South Africa and Beyond* (pp. 209–225). Stellenbosch: Sun Media.

Ndebele, N. (1998) *Remembering Ancient Sciences. (Ukukhumbula Isayensi Yamandulo)*. See http://www.outlet.co.za (accessed 16 July 2009).
Nunan, D. (2006) Task-based language teaching in the Asian context: Defining 'task'. *Asian EFL Journal* 8 (3), article 5.
Plüddemann, P. (2011) Crossing new frontiers with translanguaging wagon. *LEAP news*, 29 March 2011, Praesa.
Pretorius, E.J. (2002) Reading ability and academic performance: Are we fiddling while Rome is burning? *Language Matters: Studies in Language Matters of Southern Africa* 33, 189–195.
Price, L. (2007) Lecturers' vs. students' perceptions of the accessibility of instructional materials. *Instructional Sciences* 35, 317–341.
Poole, A. (2005) Focus on form instruction: foundations, applications, and criticisms. *The Reading Matrix: An International Online Journal* 5 (1), 47–56.
Ryan, E.B., Giles, H. and Hewstone, M. (1988) The measurement of language attitudes. In A.N. Dittmar and K.J. Mattheier (eds) *Sociolinguistics: An International Handbook of Science of Language* (Vol. 2, pp. 1068–1081). Berlin, DE: De Gruyter.
Scott, I. (2009) First-year experience as terrain of failure or platform for development? Critical choices for higher education. In B. Leibowitz, A. Van der Merwe and S. Van Schalkwyk (eds) *Focus on First-Year Success: Perspectives Emerging from South Africa and Beyond* (pp. 17–35). Stellenbosch, RSA: Sun Media.
Short, D. and Fitzsimmons, S. (2007) *Double the Work: Challenges and Solutions to Acquiring Language and Academic Literacy for Adolescent English Language Learners – A Report to Carnegie Corporation of New York*. Washington: Alliance for Excellent Education.
Stubbs, M. (2002) Some basic sociolinguistic concepts. In L. Delpit and J.K. Dowdy (eds) *The Skin That We Speak* (pp. 63–85). New York: The New Press.
Triandis, H. (1971) *Attitude and Attitude Change*. New York: John Wiley and Sons.
Watson, K. (2007) Language, education and ethnicity: Whose rights will prevail in an age of globalisation? *International Journal of Educational Development* 27 (3), 252–265.
Weideman, A. (2006) Transparency and accountability in applied linguistics. *Southern African Linguistics and Applied Language Studies* 24 (1), 71–86.
Zwiers, J. (2005) The third language of academic English. *Educational Leadership* 62, 60–63.

Appendix A: Questionnaire 1

Section 1: Personal information (*Okumayelana nawe*)

The first set of questions is meant to gather some background information about the student who answers this questionnaire. Mark with a cross (X) where possible.

Isigaba sokuqala semibuzo sihlose ukuthola ulwazi mayelana nomfundi ophendula imibuzo yalolucwaningo. Khombisa ngophawu oluwumbaxa (X).

(1) Age (*Ubudala*).

| 16–19 | 20–24 | Over 25 |

(2) Gender (*Ubulili*).

Male	Female

(3) Home language (*Ulimi lwami*).

isiZulu	isiXhosa	Tshivenda
siSwati	seSotho	Other

(4) The racial composition of students from your last high/secondary school.
Uhlanga lwabafundi esikoleni owagogoda kulo izifundo zikamatekeletsheni.

Coloured	African
esixubile	abomdabu

(5) The race of teachers at the school where you matriculated.
Uhlanga lothisha enaninabo esikoleni owagogoda kuso umatekeletsheni.

Coloured	African	White	Indian
abaxubile	abomdabu	abamhlophe	abaseNdiya

(6) The type of place where your last school was situated.
Uhlobo lwendawo lapho waqeda khona isikole.

Rural	Semi-rural	Township/location	Suburb/city	Semi-urban

(7) What language(s) did your high school teachers use to teach you most of your subjects?
Iluphi ulimi olwalusetshenziswa kakhulu ngothisha basesikoleni sakho ekufundiseni izifundo ezahlukene?

isiZulu	English	IsiZulu and English	Other

Section 2: Language attitudes (*Okumayelana nezilimi*)

(8) In group discussions I learn better when we use both English and isiZulu.
Ngifunda kangcono uma singabafundi sihlangene ngezifundo sixuba isiNgisi nesiZulu.

Strongly agree	**Agree**	**Unsure**	**Disagree**	**Strongly disagree**

(9) To better understand what I read and hear in English, I think about it in my home language.

Ukuze ngiqonde kahle engikufundayo noma engikuzwayo okungesiNgisi ngikucabanga ngolimi lwami.

| Strongly agree | Agree | Unsure | Disagree | Strongly disagree |

(10) In lectures, students should use English throughout, even in the group discussions.
Ulimi okufanele lusetshenziswe zikhathi zonke ngabafundi isiNgisi.

| Strongly agree | Agree | Unsure | Disagree | Strongly disagree |

(11) English is the only language that is suitable for use as the language of instruction in higher education.
IsiNgisi isona kuphela esimele ukusetshenziswa emanyuvesi.

| Strongly agree | Agree | Unsure | Disagree | Strongly disagree |

(12) It is possible for Black African languages to become languages of education.
Izilimi zabantsundu zingakwazi ukusetshenziswa kwezemfundo.

| Strongly agree | Agree | Unsure | Disagree | Strongly disagree |

(13) Switching from one language to another by a teacher is a bad thing.
Akukuhle uma uthisha exuba izilimi.

| Strongly agree | Agree | Unsure | Disagree | Strongly disagree |

(14) The use of isiZulu during lessons helps me understand better.
Uma uthisha echaza nangesiZulu ngiyasizakala.

| Strongly agree | Agree | Unsure | Disagree | Strongly disagree |

(15) I have difficulty following lessons that are presented in English alone.
Kuba nzima ukuqonda kahle uma isifundo singesiNgisi kuphela.

| Strongly agree | Agree | Unsure | Disagree | Strongly disagree |

(16) It would help me if examinations and test instructions could be translated into isiZulu.

Kungasiza uma imibuzo yokuhlolwa ingachazwa nangesiZulu.

| Strongly agree | Agree | Unsure | Disagree | Strongly disagree |

(17) The development and promotion of Black African languages in higher education should be regarded as important.
Ukuthuthukiswa nokugqugquzelwa kwezilima zabantsundu kumele kuthathwe njengento ebalulekile emanyuvesi.

| Strongly agree | Agree | Unsure | Disagree | Strongly disagree |

Thank you.
Ukwanda kwaliwa ngumthakathi.

Appendix B: Questionnaire 3

Section 1: Personal information (*Okumayelana nawe*)

The first set of questions is meant to gather some background information about the student who answers this questionnaire. Mark with a cross (X) where possible.
Isigaba sokuqala semibuzo sihlose ukuthola ulwazi mayelana nomfundi ophendula imibuzo yalolucwaningo. Khombisa ngophawu oluwumbaxa (X).
(1) Age (*Ubudala*).

| 16–19 | 20–24 | Over 25 |

(2) Gender (*Ubulili*).

| male | female |

(3) Home language (*Ulimi lwami*).

| isiZulu | isiXhosa | Tshivenda |
| siSwati | seSotho | Other |

(4) The racial composition of students from your last high/secondary school.
Uhlanga lwabafundi esikoleni owagogoda kulo izifundo zikamatekeletsheni.

| Coloured | African |
| *esixubile* | *abomdabu* |

Section 2: Bilingual learner guide evaluation questionnaire

Cross (X) ONE of the options at the end of each statement that represents your most honest response to the given statement. The numbers stand for:

Phambanisa umdwebo (X) ekupheleni kwesitatimende ngasinye ukutshengisa umbono wakho weqiniso ngokuthi ukhethe uhlamvu olulodwa. Izinhlamvu zimele lokhu:

5 = Strongly agree (*Ngivuma ngokungananazi*); **4** = Agree (*Ngiyavuma*); **3** = Unsure (*Angizazi*); **2** = Disagree (*Angivumi*); and **1** = Strongly disagree (*Angivumi sanhlobo*).

(5) I found the mixing of languages in the guide suitable to my style of learning.
Ukuxutshwa kwezilimi encwadini kuyazwana nendlela engifunda ngayo.
5 4 3 2 1

(6) The guide enabled me to understand and use English better.
Incwadi yenze ngikwazi ukusiqonda kalula isiNgisi. 5 4 3 2 1

(7) I experienced effective teaching and learning.
Ngifunde ngedlela egculisayo. 5 4 3 2 1

(8) The guide helped me develop the desire to continue learning English in the future.
Ngikhuthazekile ukuqhubeka nokufunda isiNgisi nangokuzayo. 5 4 3 2 1

(9) I learnt to value the role of my home language in education.
Ngifunde ukuhlonipha iqhaza elingabanjwa ulimi lwami kwezemfundo.
5 4 3 2 1

(10) I had opportunities to develop my English vocabulary.
Ngithole ithuba lokukhuphula ulwazi lwamagama esiNgisi. 5 4 3 2 1

(11) I had opportunities to develop my isiZulu vocabulary.
Ngithole ithuba lokuthuthukisa ulwazi lwamagama esiZulu. 5 4 3 2 1

(12) The guide helped me develop competence in the skills of reading, writing and thinking, as is required in my content subjects.
Ngikwazile ukuthuthukisa amakhono okufunda, ukubhala nokucabanga okudingakalayo ezifundweni zami. 5 4 3 2 1

(13) I felt free to express myself in class.
Ngizizwe ngikhululekile ukuphawula egunjini lokufunda. 5 4 3 2 1

(14) Overall, I was satisfied with the quality of the subject's guide.
Ngenelisekile ngebhukwana lalesisifundo. 5 4 3 2 1

Section 2

The next five questions require detailed answers. Feel free to explain in either isiZulu or in English.
Imibuzo emihlanu elandelayo idinga izimpendulo ezingokugcwele. Ungasebenzisa noma uluphi ulimi phakathi kwesiZulu nesiNgisi.

(15) What do you think are the strengths of this subject's learner guide?
Yini encomekayo ngencwadi yalesi sifundo?

----

(16) What are the weaknesses of this subject's learner guide?
Yini engeyinhle ngencwadi yalesi sifundo?

----

(17) What suggestions do you have for improving this subject's guide?
Iziphi izincomo ongazibeka ukuze isifundo sithi ukuthuthukiswa?

----

(18) What are the most valuable things you have learnt through your participation in this type of subject that uses two languages?
Iziphi izinto ezibalulekile ongathi uzizuzile ngokuba yingxenye yalesi sifundo esixuba izilimi?

----

(19) Any general comments?
Okunye ongathanda ukukubeka?

Thank you very much for your co-operation in completing this questionnaire.
Siyabonga kakhulu ngosizo lwakho ekuphenduleni lemibuzo.

9 Tertiary Educators' Reflections on Language Practices that Enhance Student Learning and Promote Multilingualism

Nomakhaya Mashiyi

Introduction

There is a growing body of existing knowledge on the difficulties experienced by Black students who study in a second language at South African universities (Posel & Casale, 2011) and on the initiatives aimed at 'affirming the linguistic hybridity' of such students in order to improve success (Ramani & Joseph, 2006: 449). The current study contributes to the existing body of knowledge on linguistic diversity in South African higher education by examining the reflections of tertiary educators on how they exercise their agency to promote teaching and learning through bi-/multilingualism.

Whereas previous chapters focused on student learning and language use, this chapter contributes to the important debate on multilingualism in the South African higher education sector by examining the language practices of lecturers whose linguistic profiles match those of their students. As Kotzé points out in Chapter 2, 'the ironic situation exists that in many, if not most, instances the teacher and the class share the same home language', but that this language is avoided (to an extent) in favour of English. The rationale behind this project is to determine the extent to which multilingualism is taken up in practice and to understand the effects of employing other languages for teaching and learning, as perceived by language practitioners and content subject lecturers. An existing assumption regarding languages other than English in the South African context is that African languages are deficient and cannot serve as media of instruction, that multilingualism is a problem and that multilingual education is difficult to implement (Heugh, 2000). This is despite a National Constitution that embraces multilingualism. The South African government has made commendable strides in its attempts at advancing multilingualism in education by developing a policy framework for higher education that is aimed at promoting African languages, including, for example, the 2002 *Language Policy for Higher Education* (Department of Education, 2002). The study described in this chapter brings to the fore practitioners' voices in the debate on the implementation of multilingualism in higher education.

The literature on multilingualism reveals the complexity that has characterised language policy implementation in multilingual contexts, also in South Africa, as Kotzé (Chapter 2) and Maseko (Chapter 3) point out. Mwaniki (2012) argues that while language choice may privilege access for some, it does the opposite for others. Studying in an unfamiliar language, as opposed to studying in their first language, presents learners/students with serious challenges and this is contrary to the principles of social justice. Trudell (2010: 337) asserts that cognitive, pedagogical and non-pedagogical reasons can be offered for using the languages best understood by the learner/student, and that the African elite have the power to influence language choice in education because they have access to resources and can formulate arguments that promote their own values. Marshall (2010: 41) states that multilingual students, that is, those who use foreign languages at a university in British Columbia, Canada, are often confronted with a 'deficit remedial English as a second language (ESL) identity' that is based on a language orientation that views their multilingual identities as a problem and not as an asset. This is also true in South Africa, where the majority of university students, often Black, are offered tuition in English, their second language. Consequently, they experience severe challenges with the language and have to be given extra language support to 'improve' their chances of success at university. Hibbert (2011) claims that a traditional model that frames students as deficient is unlikely to make a difference in student performance. A diversity-compliant, inclusive model that is multimodal, multiliterate, context-embedded, that focuses on discourse as socially constituted and constituting, that takes into account the wider multilingual context and diverse classroom cultures and that is dialectical and interactive would contribute to affirming students' diverse linguistic identities. Preece (2010: 21) argues for the creation of multilingual spaces in

English-medium London universities in which the linguistic diversity of non-traditional, minority ethnic students is embraced. This would counter the perception of there being 'remedial' language students in the sector. This recommendation is particularly relevant in South African universities, where second language students are often subjected to remedial English language programmes that stigmatise them as deficient in the English language and fail to acknowledge or take into account the multilingual capital that these students bring with them into higher education. Higher education could serve as a multilingual space that affirms the linguistic diversity of students, thus promoting student access and retention. The aim of this research is to identify those spaces and how they can be created by lecturers to optimise the use of linguistic diversity in teaching and learning, in line with Benson's (2010: 323) call for the reconstruction of multilingual pedagogy that capitalises on the strengths of students, teachers and linguistic communities.

In this chapter, I explore the extent to which tertiary educators at an African University (AU) (a pseudonym for a comprehensive institution in South Africa in which the majority of students and lecturers speak isiXhosa and seSotho) use the available implementation space to enhance learning through multilingualism. I also describe their positive experiences.

Theoretical Background

The reported study was informed by the 'continua of biliteracy' model (Hornberger, 2003), a multilingual approach to language planning, and the ecology of language metaphor (Haugen, cited in Dil, 1972). These two frameworks, which are premised on a view of multilingualism as a resource, were applied to examine the agentive role of tertiary educators in promoting multilingualism. The 'ecology of language' metaphor comprises three different but related ideological themes, namely, language endangerment, language evolution and language environment. Haugen (cited in Dil, 1972: 325) defines *language ecology* as 'the study of interactions between any given language and its environment', where the *environment* includes psychological and sociological aspects. The ecology metaphor emphasises the *reciprocity* between language and the environment. Languages grow, evolve, change, live and die in relation to other languages and in relation to the environment. Some languages become endangered, and the 'ecology movement' not only describes the losses but also tries to counter them.

The continua of biliteracy model is a framework for situating research, teaching and language planning in multilingual settings (Hornberger, 2003). In this model, *biliteracy* is defined as 'any and all instances in which communication occurs in two (or more) languages in and around writing' (Hornberger, 1990: 213). As discussed in Hibbert and van der Walt (Chapter 1), the continua cluster of the model is made up of four nested sets of intersecting continua, that is, the context, media, content and development of biliteracy (Hornberger, 1989; Hornberger & Skilton-Sylvester, 2000). The *development* of biliteracy occurs along the intersection of the first- and second-language receptive–productive skills and oral–written language skills continua, through the medium of two or more languages. In contexts that include micro and macro levels that are characterised by varying mixes along the monolingual- bilingual- and oral-literate continua, the content ranges from minority to majority perspectives and experiences, literary to vernacular styles and genres, and de-contextualised to contextualised language texts. Full biliterate development and expression is possible when the user is exposed to more language learning contexts, and the contexts of use create opportunities for the user to draw from the whole of each continuum (Hornberger, 2003: 323–324). According to Hornberger (2003: 326), 'the continua of biliteracy model incorporates the language evolution, language environment, and language endangerment themes of the ecology of language metaphor'. Figure 9.1 below depicts power relations in the continua model.

Ricento and Hornberger (1996) maintain that teachers exercise their language policy power through the language choices they make – either by incorporating minority languages into their teaching, thus using multilingualism as a resource, or by not using them at all. Hornberger and Johnson (2007: 527) claim that *'local* [my emphasis] educators are not helplessly caught in the ebb and flow of shifting ideologies in language policies – they help develop, maintain, and change that flow'. As curriculum implementers, lecturers use their judgment and discriminatory powers to decide how best to use language/s to help students achieve learning outcomes. Ricento and Hornberger (1996: 418) regard teachers as being at the heart of language policy and not merely as tools for implementing language policies that have been crafted by government 'experts'. They are 'change agents' who 'can transform classrooms, thereby promoting institutional change that can lead to political and, ultimately, broader social change'. Ricento and Hornberger (1996: 417) also maintain that policy change occurs as a result of the different interpretations that policies go through as they move through the different administrative levels.

Context

In South Africa, English is a minority language (Alexander, 1989) but is perceived as a language of power that is employed in high-domain functions

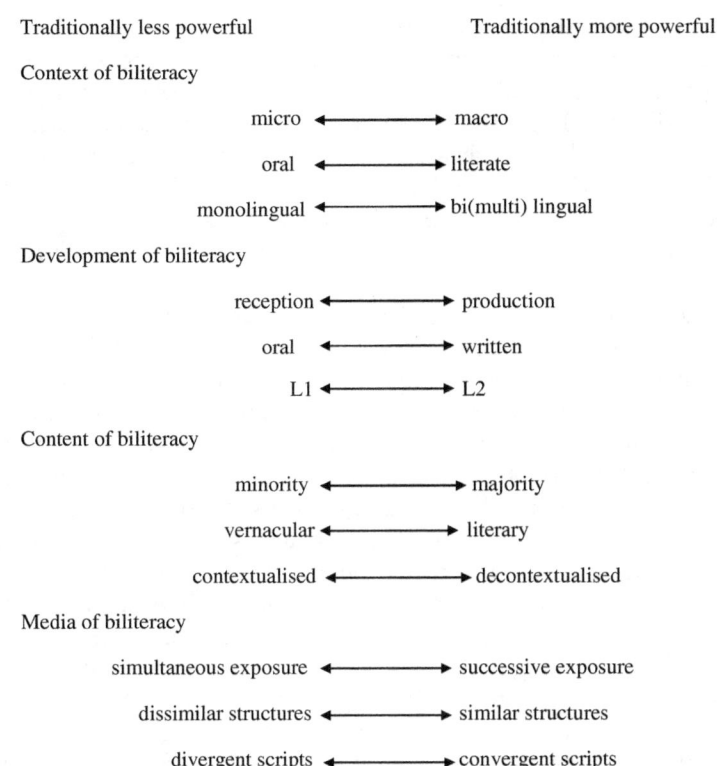

Figure 9.1 Power relations in the continua model (Hornberger, 2003: 326)

such as education, government and politics. In contrast, indigenous languages such as isiXhosa, seSotho and isiZulu, which are spoken by the majority of the population in South Africa, do not have the same currency as English because of the global and local economic power of English, which is used as a *lingua franca*.

The AU language policy (African University Language Policy, 2007) is supportive of multilingualism. In its preamble, the policy underscores the university's commitment to promoting multilingual proficiency and encouraging full participation in a multilingual society. The policy further states that the university, though accommodative of other languages, promotes the *exclusive use* of English as the language of learning and teaching (LoLT). The university *encourages* the use of other regional languages, such as isiXhosa, as supplementary LoLTs and commits to promoting adequate resourcing in order to sustain parallel media of instruction. The policy further mentions the provision of translation services and the optimal use of the language laboratory as a means to provide language services at the university. Steps to promote multilingualism would include the provision of short courses in isiXhosa, English and Afrikaans to students, academics and members of the public. As an indication of the university's acceptance of diversity and multilingualism, sign language courses are also offered. Although the university acknowledges the multilingual character of the university in its policy statement, it cites the acquisition of *effective English literacy* as its major objective.

In practice, the language used mainly for communication within the university is isiXhosa, as most of the students are isiXhosa speaking. When conversing among themselves, students code-switch between English and isiXhosa/seSotho. Inside the lecture halls, English remains the most commonly used medium of instruction, but lecturers who speak isiXhosa/seSotho permit the use of these languages. The staff complement at the AU reflects a diverse linguistic background – with some speaking seSotho, isiXhosa, Afrikaans, Shona, isiNdebele and Indian languages, inter alia. However, the AU databases could not provide the individual linguistic profiles of the 754-strong academic staff complement. AU has 23,820 students, whose linguistic profiles are not indicated on the institution's databases.

Spaces for promoting multilingualism within the university are utilised intermittently. Consequently, multilingualism is implemented in a patchy way as the university has not crafted a formal strategy for implementing multilingualism. Successful implementation is crucial for both student success and the continued vitality of African languages, as Kotzé (Chapter 2) and Maseko (Chapter 3) show. Some examples of the university's practices are that English is employed exclusively for compiling newsletters, notices on the intranet and press releases, the signage on campus is in English, and meetings are conducted in English – a situation that is in direct contrast to the campus described by Parmegiani and Rudwick in Chapter 7. It is only on rare occasions, such as one professor's 2011 graduation acceptance speech, which was delivered in isiXhosa, that indigenous languages are employed for high-order functions.

Research Methodology

This investigation falls within an interpretivist research paradigm. An interpretivist paradigm views reality as subjective and constructed, thus resulting in the existence of many truths. Discourse is dialogic and creates reality, and communication is transactional (Lather, 2006).

Thick descriptions of the phenomenon under investigation are given in order for the researcher to make sense of the phenomenon, providing the researcher with an opportunity to uncover the lecturers' versions of reality, and to also use discourse analysis, a discursive method of analysis that goes beyond the focus on content by integrating context with content.

In the study I conducted, focus group interviews were used to investigate the language practices of lecturers with the aim of addressing the following questions.

(1) What is the repertoire of language practices that tertiary educators use to enhance learning, and to what extent do their practices reflect the ecology metaphor?
(2) What positive experiences are reported by lecturers who use English and the students' L1 for teaching and learning?

Five academics from the faculties of Education, Business Science and Law took part in the study. The participants were studying Communication Skills in English, Consumer Studies, Street Law, Educational Foundations and Business Administration.

Data collection

Focus group interviews were conducted to collect data. Focus groups are usually small and may not be representative of the population because of the small sample size. Information collected may be biased and it may be difficult to bring together potential participants who live in geographically dispersed areas. To counter the challenges associated with focus group interviews, the participants were brought together and interviewed at the same time. Permission to conduct the study was sought from the university and participants were assured of anonymity and confidentiality. The response to each question was recorded as the discussion unfolded. Following the focus group interview session, my reflections on the data, as the researcher/interviewer, were captured and integrated into the critical interpretation.

Analysis of findings

Niewenhuizen (2007: 99) pointed out that qualitative data analysis is based on an interpretive philosophy and can either follow a deductive or an inductive approach. An inductive analysis unravels dominant themes inherent in the data 'without the restraints imposed by a more structured theoretical orientation'. A deductive approach employs categories of information that were distilled from the data in advance. This reliance on pre-determined categories of analysis can create blind and blank spots, which may compromise the credibility of one's study. Both approaches were employed in this study with a view to capturing dominant themes emerging from the data.

Discourse analysis (DA) was used as a lens to analyse the data. DA 'focuses on the meaning of the spoken and written word, and the reasons why it is the way it is' (Niewenhuizen, 2007: 102). As an approach to data analysis, DA is concerned with 'studying and analyzing written texts and spoken words to reveal the discursive sources of power, dominance, inequality and bias, and how these sources are initiated, maintained, reproduced and transformed within specific social, economic political and historical contexts' (Niewenhuizen, 2007: 102). It uncovers ideological assumptions in written and oral texts and is aimed at resisting and overcoming various forms of power (Niewenhuizen, 2007). The lecturers' utterances during the focus group interviews were analysed to uncover underlying messages, themes and assumptions regarding language use for teaching and learning in the context of higher education.

Discussion of Findings

The results of the study are presented and discussed using key concepts that form the building blocks of the continua biliteracy model, the ecology metaphor and the literature review. The theme appears first, then the example from the data, followed by the discussion.

Code-switching

Code-switching refers to 'the alternate use of two [or more] languages within the same utterance or during the same conversation' (Hoffman, 1991: 110). This strategy is used in explaining and clarifying subject content, assisting learners in understanding and interpreting material, confirming understanding and encouraging participation, classroom management and for social functions such as humour, and as a marker of bilingual identity (Uys & van Dulm, 2011: 67). In practice, the L1 is used as a resource to mediate learning in L2 contexts (Brock-Utne, 2005; Mashiyi, 2011; Probyn, 2001; Setati *et al.*, 2002). In de-segregated high schools in South Africa, code-switching and code-mixing are frequently used, an indication that there is language maintenance in these spaces and that African languages are not under threat of extinction (Ndlangamandla, 2010).

In the following excerpt, the lecturer employed code-switching to encourage and promote student participation (the 'E' is an identification device):

E: English is the official MOI [medium of instruction]. Because I speak the same L1 as my students, I occasionally allow them to use the vernacular to promote discussion.

The language used by the lecturer above reflects unequal power relations between the lecturer and the students. She 'occasionally allows' students to use the vernacular and 'insists' that students use English only for reporting and written work. The lecturer sets the agenda for language use by either sanctioning or promoting the use of the different languages. Teaching mainly occurs in English as it is the official medium of instruction and isiXhosa serves as a tool for promoting understanding. In this case, it is the language policy provisions and the shared linguistic profiles that drive classroom practice.

Code-switching also promotes sense-making and access to the curriculum, as the following lecturer indicates:

C: When questions during lessons are not answered, or I see that the question was not grasped even after rephrasing it, I code-switch. I code-switch when I want to promote understanding and application of knowledge gained.

The extract above illustrates that it is the lecturer who has the prerogative to decide when code-switching can be used to facilitate learning. The lecturer's language choices can either silence voices that would normally contribute to class discussions, were it not for the lack of English language skills, or encourage lively debate and discussion through the use of other languages available to students.

The excerpt below illustrates the extent to which some lecturers open up spaces for the use of other languages by taking into account contextual factors, such as the students' linguistic profiles, the linguistic profiles of the target communities and course demands:

B: The main LoLT is English in courses where the students come from diverse linguistic backgrounds e.g. Computer and the Law – promotion of inclusivity is another concern. In other courses where I share an L1 with the students e.g. Street Law, I mostly use isiXhosa, because the students themselves are expected to use isiXhosa when working with the communities. The course was designed to link the university to the community. Offering this course in English only would be counter-productive. My students and I sometimes use SeSotho when conducting our needs-based workshops on Street Law, depending on the community that we have to empower.

The extract above demonstrates the progressive thinking underlying the lecturer's use of languages in the teaching–learning situation. The context in which learning takes place, student profiles and the learning outcomes that must be achieved take precedence over language policy provisions. Some lecturers employ other languages with caution because English is the official LoLT at the university, and thus unconsciously promote the hegemony of English. However, Johnson (2012: 41) cautions against promoting English at the expense of other languages and) asserts that the 'slavish insistence on English' perpetuates the subjugation theme in Africa.

'Allowing' students to code-switch occasionally in order to promote understanding is itself not enough to promote biliterate development. The extract reveals that English has more currency than isiXhosa and the latter is used as a means to an end, that is, to promote English language learning. Lecturer A had this to say about the practice of employing other languages for teaching and learning:

A: I know that the language of instruction is English. In class I use English, Xhosa and se-Sotho, but my emphasis is on promoting understanding in English I also allow my students to use both isiXhosa and seSotho to facilitate sense-making.

The data indicate that lecturers whose L1s match those of their students regard the students' first language as a resource – they code-switch and translate content with the aim of assisting students to achieve learning outcomes. Ricento and Hornberger (1996: 418) assert that such teachers can be regarded as change agents who 'can transform classrooms, thereby promoting institutional change that can lead to political and ultimately broader social change.'

Code-switching was also employed by lecturers for the following reasons:

(a) It is easier to express yourself and give examples in your own language, enhance understanding of content and improve learning (Lecturers B and C);
(b) To accommodate student diversity (Lecturer B);
(c) To compensate for poor English language proficiency (Lecturer A); and
(d) To unpack difficult aspects of the course and promote peer-assisted learning (Lecturer D).

Reasons (a), (b) and (d) are based on sound pedagogical principles. The first language is usually acquired informally through socialisation and prior knowledge that lays the foundation for subsequent learning. Second, a student-centred approach to teaching and learning does not view student diversity, in particular linguistic diversity, as a problem. Third, collaborative learning does not only promote deep learning, it also encourages student engagement, as the Madiba case study clearly shows (Chapter 5). The third reason (i.e. (c)) is based on a deficit model that views the first language as useful in so far as it assists students in developing their proficiency in English.

Lecturer E cautioned against the uncritical acceptance of code-switching without due consideration of market demands:

E: At this level, only English should be employed as students are being prepared to function optimally in the world of work which puts a high premium on English. Code-switching should be used sparingly in content subjects to promote understanding

The power of English is undisputed in this context. However, lecturers also acknowledged the pivotal role played by the home language in aiding second language acquisition and promoting understanding. The irony is that some lecturers close the spaces for using other languages and opportunities for the languages to grow through use. Using indigenous languages as LoLTs would counter language endangerment and improve proficiency in these languages.

Lecturer C observed that the down-side of code-switching is that *'some students do not bother to learn the language of instruction'*. In the extract below, English is seen as a 'killer language' that threatens to stifle the use of other languages in a multilingual environment:

C: English is given priority in class as it is the MOI. The university's language policy is not known to me, neither can I deduce this from banners, placards and official AU documents as everything is written in English. Signage on campus is done in English only. Other languages are not represented. Even during institutional audits, only English was used, thus excluding other staffers, labourers and administrative workers who may not be very proficient in English.

Language endangerment, in respect to isiXhosa and seSotho, does not pose a threat in the AU context even though there may be a challenge regarding technical vocabulary in some courses. First, most students' linguistic profiles match those of the lecturers, and indigenous languages are employed during teaching to 'enhance learning' and 'promote inclusivity'. Second, outside of the lecture room situation, the most commonly used languages for informal communication and doing business are indigenous languages and

English, and code-switching is employed extensively in these contexts. However, there is little room for isiXhosa and seSotho to develop technical vocabulary for use in the different courses if they are not employed as LoLTs. The pervasive use of code-switching is an indication that, given enough support, multilingual higher education is a very real possibility.

Perceptions of language status

The ecology metaphor emphasises reciprocity between languages and the environment in which they are spoken. Language evolution becomes a reality when all the languages spoken in a particular region are supported and given an equal chance to grow (Hornberger, 2003). The literature reflects that, although positive about the use of African languages alongside English, university students believe that a bilingual policy would not be easy to implement in a multilingual institution. However, multilingual practices such as providing bilingual question papers, bilingual tutor support and isiXhosa definitions of technical terms would facilitate learning (Aziakpono & Bekker, 2010).

The data in this study also indicate that languages other than English in the AU context do not have the same status. Analysis of results reveals inconsistencies in the manner in which some lecturers teach and conduct assessments. They conduct assessments in English only, as prescribed by the university policy, even though they may have facilitated classes by using a code-switching mode.

C: No. I don't use the L1 for teaching. I use English. Xhosa is not developed enough for the subjects that I teach. Assessment of competence gained is done in English only. Occasionally, code-switching is used during lectures to promote learner understanding.

The inconsistency referred to above demonstrates that employing more than one language for teaching and learning has its own challenges. Although some lecturers may be valuing the L1 as a teaching and communication tool, their language choices are constrained by the demands of the workplace, which places more value on English than on indigenous languages.

Lecturer D teaches and assesses in English, mainly because of his beliefs about English:

D: I always present my lectures in English ... I use English only for teaching and assessment. My motivation for doing so is that English is the language of business globally.

His practice is informed by the orientations and discourses that view English as a global language that facilitates cross-cultural communication.

The use of indigenous languages is limited to oral code-switching during lectures (Lecturers D and B) and is sanctioned in writing (Lecturers B and D). Non-standard varieties are permitted in spoken communication only, and writing is viewed as a more powerful medium than spoken communication, as demonstrated in the following excerpts:

(a) Not in writing, but in spoken communication they can use other varieties. I want to make them feel at ease and enhance student learning.
(b) Yes, in spoken communication, but, I am stricter when it comes to writing. Not fussy about the isiXhosa variety. They can use any.
(c) They use the vernacular sometimes during lectures for oral discussion. However, for research development purposes, they are expected to use formal English only – in writing.
(d) I only permit formal English for academic writing purposes. Yes, during a lecture, they can use other varieties.

Depending on the course, both standard and non-standard varieties are permitted (in speech and in writing) in the English Communication Skills classes (Lecturer E). The unequal power relations depicted in the continua model were evident in the data collected; for example, written English communication has more value than speech. Lecturers demand formal English in writing (Lecturers C, B and A); indigenous languages, but non-standard varieties, are mainly used in spoken communication. Students are not required to present their answers in a test in the vernacular for two reasons: the AU's language policy prescribes that English be used as a LoLT, but examiners' and moderators' linguistic profiles may not match those of the test takers. The excerpts above reveal that in some instances, lecturers create spaces for students to use both the powerful and less powerful ends of the continua, for example, through code-switching and the use of non-standard varieties during lectures (Lecturer E).

Lecturer justifications for practice

The fact that some lecturers deviate from the institution's prescribed language policy by employing other languages for teaching is a reflection of the lecturers' 'unstated beliefs' about language(s). These lecturers seem to subscribe to the view that the L1 is a resource and that languages live and grow through use in formal and informal contexts. They blend the powerful and less powerful ends of the continuum to create a rewarding academic experience. They also view formal education as a reflection of society and as such build on students' existing linguistic knowledge.

The data reveal that affirming students' 'linguistic hybridity' enriches the teaching–learning experience; for example, it improves understanding, student motivation, participation and the quality of interactions among the students. These are conditions that are associated with deep learning and meaningful engagement with the subject content, as the following lecturers show:

D: I encourage my students to assist one another using the language they are most comfortable with. This improves the quality of the interactions and promotes understanding.

E: Code-switching improves ... enhances student learning, learner motivation, self-esteem and student performance ... as long as one is mindful of the fact that there are students who do not speak local languages. Interactivity improves and co-operative learning/peer-to-peer learning becomes a reality.

B: Learner understanding improves ... Interactivity ... Students open up, even those who have challenges with English.

C: The effect can be both negative and positive: positive because it (code-switching) promotes understanding of content, negative because some students do not bother to learn the language of instruction.

D: The downside of code-switching is that during examinations students often give the same examples that I had given in class ... in the language that I used during the lecture.

Through their flexible approaches to teaching (use of co-operative and peer-assisted learning (Lecturer C), and allowing L1 students to translate for fellow students whose L1 is different from the majority of the students' and the teachers' (Lecturer B), the possibility of English becoming a barrier to learning is reduced. The data revealed innovative teaching and assessment practices that utilise English and 'community languages', and enhance learning and improve student motivation and achievement in the School of Law, as indicated in the following excerpt:

B: The reports which form part of my assessment strategy are usually presented in English. Student presentations which are often conducted in the languages spoken in the communities are assessed by me. It would be worth our while if some of the courses were to be presented in the vernaculars.

Researcher: Is Street Law presented in the languages spoken in the area?

B: Yes. I believe legal reference materials should be translated from English to the vernaculars to enable communities to access these materials. Pass rates in this course are extremely good and students enjoy the course very much. Some Indian students signed up for this course and because they could not speak isiXhosa, others translated for them. They performed well in the course. There should be a balance between the use of languages in courses such as Street Law ... personally, I would prefer to offer this course in the vernacular.

Lecturer B above displayed eclecticism, creativity and originality in the way he responded to the linguistic diversity in the communities and in the lecture room. He integrated the less powerful ends of the continuum with the more powerful ones. For example, oral presentations in the communities were conducted in the languages spoken in that community, and back in the lecture hall, the reports were written and presented in English. Translations by peers served to ensure that no student was left behind because he/she could not communicate in the languages spoken in the communities.

Regrettably, some lecturers exclude the less powerful ends of the continua from their teaching and focus on the development of students' English language skills. Notwithstanding the fact that the institutions' language policy promotes English while being supportive of other languages, in practice, these lecturers reinforce the existing institutional culture, which places more value on English. They close the available implementation space that diverse student profiles create for multilingualism, thus making it difficult for students to tap into their home languages and use them for learning. As depicted above, the different ways in which lecturers use language for teaching and learning result in different language policy implementation patterns within the same context, as well as varied academic experiences for students.

Language support for students who struggle with English is offered in different ways, that is, content is simplified, questions are re-phrased and paraphrased, and the use of non-standard varieties is also permitted (Lecturers A and D). Some employ student-centred and participatory techniques (Lecturer C). Struggling students are referred to the English for Academic Purposes programme for (English) language support (Lecturer B). There was no mention of language intervention programmes for students who need support in their L1, an indication of either the low status assigned to indigenous languages or the misconception that if students are L1 speakers of any of the indigenous languages, they do not need academic language support in that language. Cope and Kalantzis (2000) argue for a curriculum framework that embraces multiple literacies. This would entail acknowledging previously acquired discourses that students bring into the learning environment and the workplace, thereby creating an opportunity for reflection and the development of metacognitive and metalinguistic abilities (Hibbert, 2011: 36).

In my view, language practitioners and content subject lecturers in bi-/multilingual contexts can exploit a common underlying language proficiency that, according to Cummins (2007), is accessible through both languages and uses the prior knowledge that is embedded in the speaker's first language thereby assisting students to acquire the target language (in this case, English). Therefore, code-switching and translation, which are employed extensively in multilingual settings, should become an integral part of a lecturer's repertoire of strategies in multilingual classrooms.

Conclusion

In summary, the data reveal two distinct and different ways of thinking about language in the AU context. Some lecturers' language practices revealed a perspective that views multilingualism as a resource, and they employed the L1 through code-switching. In linguistically diverse classrooms, lecturers allowed students to translate for those who were not speakers of the dominant African language in the region. By employing these strategies, such lecturers acted as change agents, in that they countered language endangerment (of isiXhosa and Sesotho in this case) and ensured that the students' first/home languages do not die, but live and grow alongside 'killer languages' such as English. They contributed to the development and maintenance of biliteracy or multilingualism by integrating the traditionally powerful and less powerful ends of the continua. Although there were apparent inconsistencies in their practices (e.g. teaching in code-switching mode but assessing in English only, allowing students to use their L1 for discussions but not sanctioning it in writing and insisting that students report in English although they had made the presentations in the languages spoken in the communities), their reported practices reflect a student-centred approach and a strategic move towards embracing linguistic diversity in higher education.

Other respondents, although not opposed to the use of code-switching, were cautious and ambivalent about the extent to which the L1 should be used in higher education, their overriding concern being the fact that English is a tool used for global communication. Also, because of the complexities of implementing multilingualism, for instance, lecturer linguistic profiles not matching those of students, promoting the use of English seemed a practical and viable option.

This study reveals that the ideological assumptions that underpin lecturers' language practices continue to affect the academic project in different ways and have thus contributed to either the use of African languages to support a predominantly English education or the consolidation of the hegemonic status of English. In relation to Question 1, the main findings reveal that the manner in which some lecturers exercise their agency in the lecture hall as implementers of curriculum and language policy leads to different implementation patterns of the university's language policy, with some lecturers providing a rich academic experience for their students through the adoption of standard and non-standard varieties and multilingual practices, such as code-switching and translation. Such practices resonate well with the language ecology metaphor and the continua of biliteracy model because they encourage affirmation of, and use of, the students' multilingual repertoire.

Making use of metaphor, as Carstens and Alston describe in Chapter 11, can aid the understanding of macro-identities across student groups. It can be a valuable device with which to reflect on and strengthen language and teaching practices.

In relation to Question 2, participants in the study identified a number of positive experiences that they had had from utilising home/other languages for teaching and learning alongside English. This finding is similar to that found by Madiba (Chapter 5) and Makalela (Chapter 6), that is, improved understanding, student motivation, pass rates and cross-cultural communication challenge the assumption that bi-/multilingualism is a problem.

The results of the case study, though not generalisable, have serious implications for higher education in South Africa, as they suggest that the multilingual repertoire that students bring to university can be utilised to improve teaching and learning. As the small-scale studies in this book continue to build the big picture of multilingual language use in South African higher education, the urgent need grows for professional development programmes in higher education institutions, specifically to focus on the development of multilingual pedagogy. This would render the transition from high school to university less painful for the majority of Black students in South Africa and result in enhanced student motivation and learning while fostering a nurturing environment for the development of biliteracy/multilingualism.

References

African University Language Policy (2007) See http://www.wsu.ac.za (accessed 2 April 2013).
Alexander, N. (1989) *Language Policy and National Unity in South Africa/Azania*. Cape Town, RSA: Buchu Books.

Aziakpono, P. and Bekker, I. (2010) The attitudes of isiXhosa-speaking students toward language of learning and teaching issues at Rhodes University, South Africa: General trends. *Southern African Linguistics and Applied Language Studies* 28 (1), 39–60.

Benson, C. (2010) How multilingual African contexts are pushing educational research and practice in new directions. *Language and Education* 24 (4), 323–336.

Brock-Utne, B. (2005) Language-in-education policies and practices in Africa with a special focus on Tanzania and South Africa – Insights from research in progress. In J. Zajda (ed.) *International Handbook on Globalisation, Education and Policy Research: Global Pedagogies and Policies* (pp. 549–565). Dordrecht, NED: Springer.

Cope, B. and Kalantzis, M. (2000) *Multiliteracies: Literacy Learning and the Design of Social Futures*. London: Routledge.

Cummins, J. (2007) *Language, Power and Pedagogy: Bilingual Children in the Crossfire*. Clevedon: Multilingual Matters.

Department of Education (2002) *Language Policy for Higher Education*. Pretoria, RSA: Department of Education.

Dil, A.S. (ed.) (1972) *The Ecology of Language: Essays by Einar Haugen* (pp. 325–329). Stanford, CA: Stanford University Press.

Heugh, K. (2000) *The Case Against Bilingual and Multilingual Education in South Africa*. PRAESA Occasional Papers No. 6. Cape Town, RSA: PRAESA.

Hibbert, L. (2011) Language development in higher education: Suggested paradigms and their applications in South Africa. *Southern African Linguistics and Applied Language Studies* 29 (1), 31–49.

Hoffmann, C. (1991) *An Introduction to Bilingualism*. London: Longman.

Hornberger, N.H. (1989) Continua of Biliteracy. *Review of Educational Research* 59 (3), 271–296.

Hornberger, N.H. (1990) Creating successful learning contexts for bilingual literacy. *Teachers College Record* 92 (2), 212–229.

Hornberger, N.H. (2003) Multilingual language policies and the continua of biliteracy: An ecological approach. In N. Hornberger (ed.) *Continua of Biliteracy: An Ecological Framework for Educational Policy, Research, and Practice in Multilingual Settings* (pp. 315–339). Clevedon: Multilingual Matters.

Hornberger, N.H. and Skilton-Sylvester, E. (2000) Revisiting the continua of literacy: International and critical perspectives. *Language and Education: An International Journal* 14 (2), 96–122.

Hornberger, N.H. and Johnson, D.C. (2007) Slicing the onion ethnographically: Layers and spaces in multilingual language education policy and practice. *TESOL Quarterly* 41 (3), 509–532.

Johnson, P. (2012) Slavish insistence on English limits us. *Mail and Guardian*, 31 August to 6 September, p. 4.

Lather, P. (2006) Paradigm proliferation as a good thing to think with: Teaching research in education as a wild profusion. *International Journal of Qualitative Studies in Education* 19 (1), 35–57.

Marshall, S. (2010) Re-becoming ESL: Multilingual university students and a deficit identity. *Language Education* 24 (1), 41–56.

Mashiyi, F.N. (2011) How South African teachers make sense of language. In Education Policies in Practice. Unpublished PhD thesis, University of Pretoria. See upetd.up.ac.za/thesis/available/etd-06012011-142257/.

Mwaniki, M. (2012) Language and social justice in South Africa's higher education: Insights from a South African university. *Language and Education* 26 (3), 213–232.

Ndlangamandla, S. (2010) (Unofficial) multilingualism in desegregated schools: Learners' use of and views towards African languages. *Southern African Linguistics and Applied Language Studies* 28 (1), 61–73.

Niewenhuizen, J. (2007) Analysing qualitative data. In K. Maree (ed.) *First Steps in Research* (pp. 99–122). Pretoria, RSA: Van Schaik.

Posel, D. and Casale, D. (2011) Language proficiency and language policy in South Africa: Findings from new data. *International Journal of Educational Development* 31 (5), 449–457.

Preece, S. (2010) Multilingual identities in higher education: Negotiating the 'mother tongue', posh and slang. *Language and Education* 24 (1), 21–39.

Probyn, M. (2001) Teachers' voices: Teachers' reflections on learning and teaching through the medium of English as an additional language in South Africa. *International Journal of Bilingual Education* 4 (4), 249–266.

Ramani, E. and Joseph, M. (2006) The dual-medium BA degree in English and Sesotho sa Leboa at the University of Limpopo: Successes and challenges. In B. Brock-Utne, Z. Desai and M. Qorro (eds) *Focus on Fresh Data on the Language of Instruction Debate in Tanzania and South Africa* (pp. 4–18). Cape Town: African Minds.

Ricento, T.K. and Hornberger, N.H. (1996) Unpeeling the onion: Language planning and policy and the ELT professional. *TESOL Quarterly* 30 (3), 401–427.

Setati, M., Adler, J., Reed, Y. and Bapoo, A. (2002) Incomplete journeys: Code switching and other language practices in mathematics, science and English language classrooms in South Africa. *Language and Education* 16 (2), 128–149.

Trudell, B. (2010) When Prof speaks, who listens? The African elite and the use of African languages for education and development in African communities. *Language and Education* 24 (4), 337–352.

Uys, D. and Van Dulm, O. (2011) The functions of classroom code-switching in the Siyanda District of the Northern Cape. *Southern African Linguistics and Applied Language Studies* 29 (1), 67–76.

Part 4

Africanisation and Localisation of Content for Cultural Identification

10 An Exemplary Astronomical Lesson that Could Potentially Show the Benefits of Multilingual Content and Language in Higher Education

Lerothodi L. Leeuw

Background and Context

Like many people across the globe, Africans have for many generations been awed by the night skies (Leeuw, 2007). Using their natural astronomical instrument, the eye, they have observed, commented on and named celestial objects of interest to them, in the process of developing an indigenous knowledge system (IKS) of astronomy. Most of the cosmic objects they have observed are very bright and relatively near to Earth and can thus be seen by the human eye of anyone who cares to look up at the night sky, without requiring them to use sophisticated or expensive tools. On the other hand, most modern astronomers use data from large telescopes, some of which are here in Southern Africa, and their studies can deal with the very faintest and most distant observable objects in the universe.

The scholarly study of astronomy that is done with these large telescopes and its teaching in schools and universities is done almost exclusively in English, which is the assumed international and standard language of astronomy and science, and certainly of most scientific journals. Such an approach often disregards the local IKS and builds on a notion that interest in the subject is primarily Western and that there is no similar or even basic interest in the local South African cultures. This approach can alienate some local learners or, at least, result in learners missing the opportunity to build on what they may already know, particularly those who have some home-taught knowledge and introduction to the IKS of the night sky from their own cultures.

Here, I consider a different approach and revisit astronomical nomenclature of the Setswana language of Southern Africa, mentioning our galaxy, some constellations, and the two brightest and nearest astronomical bodies to the Earth (after the Sun), the Moon and Venus, presenting exemplary lessons on them in Setswana and English. The goal of this presentation is to demonstrate the potential benefits of multilingual content or approach in higher education, in response to the call by scholars, such as Maseko (Chapter 3) and Madiba (Chapter 5), to develop concept literacy in a range of content subjects. The presented approach is trans-disciplinary and draws on the Setswana IKS of astronomy. Among other things, I attempt to show the implications of the presentation in (a) broadening access and understanding of scientific concepts, (b) exposing a relatively unpublicised astronomical interest and IKS of the Batswana people and (c) perhaps enhancing intra-cultural and multicultural knowledge and also respect. The presentation is particularly timely now, given the anticipated construction of the world's largest radio telescope, the Square Kilometre Array, and its smaller predecessor, the MeerKAT, which will be built primarily in Southern Africa. The full scientific operations of Southern African Large Telescope, and the very faint and distant celestial objects its telescopes will observe, will be studied by experts, led by a large number of international scientists that should include an increased number of local ones. The work from these telescopes should also result in a growing interest in astrophysics from non-specialists, and creating an accessible context to a broader local audience is therefore also timely. The development of the described astronomical lessons is in the early stages and they have, up to now, only been presented in extra-curricular and conference presentations. Steps are needed toward their structuring into proper teaching and assessment modules and subsequent implementation in the classroom.

Educational and Pedagogical Context

The use of Southern Africa's Setswana astronomical nomenclature in exemplary lessons, as described in this chapter, can be supported by the theory and practice of multicultural education, which can include multilingual education, though such use was traditionally developed and has primarily been studied for social sciences and humanities education (Banks, 1997; Bennett, 2003). As noted by Cumming-McCann (2003: 9), 'the primary goal of multicultural education is to promote the education and achievement of all students', particularly those from disadvantaged backgrounds. She also notes that an additional outcome of multicultural education can be 'to promote human relations, help students feel good about themselves, or to preserve student's native languages and culture'.

As summarised by Cumming-McCann (2003) and Banks (2011), a model for multicultural education curricular infusion developed by Banks (1997, 1998) 'includes four approaches to content integration from least to implement and least likely to lead to the goals of multicultural education, to most challenging, and offering the most potential' (Cumming-McCann, 2003: 10). The approaches can be implemented with the Setswana astronomical nomenclature lessons described in this chapter. They are the contribution, additive, transformative and decision-making or social-action approaches.

In the *contribution* approach, the curriculum is essentially unchanged, and aspects or units, such as heroes of the marginalised culture, may become a focal point for a lesson on a certain day or in a certain month, coinciding with some designated dates or relevant holidays in the year. Outside those dates, little specific attention is paid to the ethnic group. The approach can be implemented easily, but is limited because it does not give opportunity for the ethnic group to see any critical role for themselves in the broader society or curriculum (Banks, 2011; Cumming-McCann, 2003). In the *additive* approach, the curriculum is also mostly unchanged, and certain cultural dimension, such as some ethnic women's rights movements, may be added to a discussion or lesson on women's rights. At its basic level, the approach would be limited and fail to delve into the interplay or interconnectedness of the mainstream topic and added content. The *transformative* approach differs from the first two in that it would give the opportunity for the students to see the subject from several perspectives or frames of reference, perhaps even allow them to delve into the impact or usefulness of the context added to the mainstream subject. In the *decision-making* or *action* approach, as well as the content integration noted above, students have a chance to make a decision or take action based on the added content, and therefore the approach also helps the students develop their thinking skills, empowers them and allows them to acquire a sense of their own role in the knowledge they are acquiring and hence a feeling of efficacy (Banks, 2011; Cumming-McCann, 2003).

170   Part 4: Africanisation and Localisation of Content for Cultural Identification

Exemplary Astronomical Lessons and their Benefits

Our galaxy, the Milky Way or *Molagodimo*

Figure 10.1 shows a digital photographic mosaic of our galaxy, the Milky Way or *Molagodimo,* made by astrophotographer Axel Mellinger between 2007 and 2009 from dark-sky locations in South Africa, Texas and Michigan (Mellinger, 2009a, 2009b). The full view seen in this picture is therefore not one that could possibly be seen at any one location or time on Earth, but rather a mosaic of views from the noted locations and over different times as different parts of the galaxy come into view in the night sky. The map, with our Milky Way galaxy or *Molagodimo* in the centre of the image, is plotted in a Hammer-Aitoff projection, which is an equal-area map of an equatorial form and shows the central part of the Milky Way, with its multitude of stars and dust that will form future stars. As well as stars, dust and nebulae where new stars are forming in our galaxy, the Milky Way's bright neighbouring galaxies, Andromeda and Magellanic Clouds, are also shown, appearing like small stellar patches in this map, off the central part.

Our galaxy, as seen by the human eye or an optical camera, is a myriad of patterns, that is, a multitude of stars among dark patches of dust and gas, that astronomers now understand is forming new stars. Indeed, for the night

Figure 10.1 A panoramic mosaic of the night sky showing our galaxy, the Milky Way or *Molagodimo,* as photographed by Axel Mellinger from dark-sky locations in South Africa, Texas and Michigan, using three optical digital photography colours or filters RGB (Mellinger, 2009a, 2009b)

sky and stars, there is a riddle in the Setswana language of Southern African that says, *'mosese ya ga mmakgathi, maranthatha'* or 'the dress of the painter (a female one) is a myriad patterns'. This Setswana riddle demonstrates an old, though refreshing, interest in the stars and night sky by the Batswana – a fascination that is deeply woven into the language and culture of the people of Southern Africa, rich in idiom, poetry, indirect or evasive speech and educational potential. *Mosese*, or literally 'a dress', is also poetically used to mean a woman, in Setswana. It is wonderfully coincident that the beautiful patterns of this 'dress' or 'woman' is partly made so by stars and cosmic dust, out of which future stars are born. The beauty of the coincidence lies in that *mosese*, or a woman, bears children, and in Setswana culture, traditionally cares for them, providing a perfect analogy for the galaxy (with its stars and dust from which future stars will be born), as seen by the naked eye, and trans-disciplinarily weaves the poetic phrase with the scientific knowledge of its makeup.

The Setswana name for the Milky Way galaxy itself, or *Molagodimo*, means the path (or *mola*) above (or *godimo*). Like the meaning of 'way' in the Milky Way, it is referred to as a 'path' both in English and Setswana because the galaxy, as seen from Earth, looks like a path. This is because Earth, and the Sun around which Earth revolves, sits inside a disk-like part of the galaxy. This disk is made up of a concentration of stars interlaced with dust and is actually the main component of the galaxy. In fact, Earth sits about two-thirds from the centre of this disk-like part of the galaxy; and, when looking along the direction of this disk from the location of the Earth, the disk or, if you like, the galaxy itself, looks like a path. Both these simple English and Setswana names of our galaxy therefore describe the main disk component of the galaxy and how it appears from Earth. The projection of the galaxy, as it would be seen in the Northern and Southern Hemispheres, respectively, can be seen on the left and right of the picture in Figure 10.2.

Our galaxy, the Milky Way or *Molagodimo*, and its constellations

Figure 10.3 shows our galaxy, the Milky Way or *Molagodimo*, as presented in Figure 10.1, but now with Western constellations, which are based on Greek mythology, included to guide the eye toward given directions or locations in the galaxy. Constellations are imaginary pictures that people from many cultures around the world construct about what they believe they see when they look up at certain patterns of stars at the sky. Such images vary from culture to culture, and one of their purposes is to provide a picture of particular locations, following patterns of stars seen in the sky.

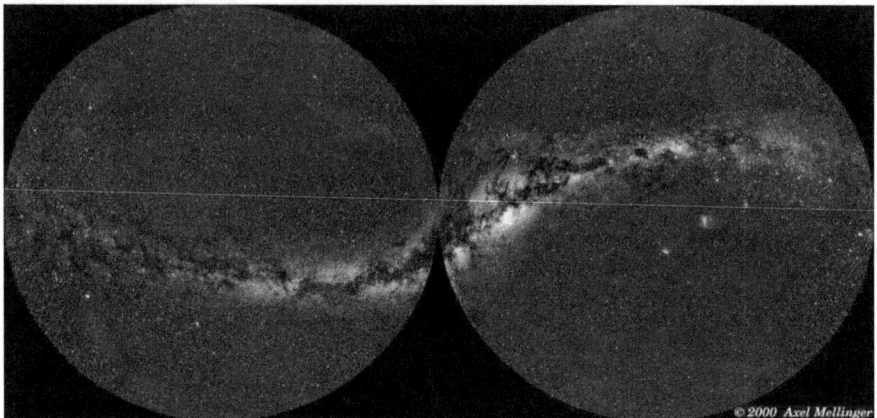

Figure 10.2 A photographic mosaic of our galaxy and other nearby bright celestial objects, as would be seen in the Northern and Southern Hemispheres, respectively, on the left and right of the pictured galaxy. This picture is an all-sky, equidistant azimuthal projection (http://home.arcor-online.de/axel.mellinger/mwpan_old.html)

In some cultures, such as described for the Batswana below, these star names also refer to particular times the stars appear in the sky, revealing a keen interest and knowledge of the sky in the people who named them. However, the constellation names sometimes do not seem to have any clear physical meaning relating to the star patterns they describe. In some cases, constellation names are also given to parts of the sky that show no stars (see Figure 10.4), such as the dark area to the bottom left of the Southern Cross or *Sefapano* that is called *Emu* by the Aborigines or 'Coal Sack' in English. Both the names in this case are derived from the shape and hue of the 'constellation'. All these astronomical names and the constellations they refer to, together with their mythical or physical connections, can be discussed further and used in the lessons I am proposing, and a few are noted with more details below.

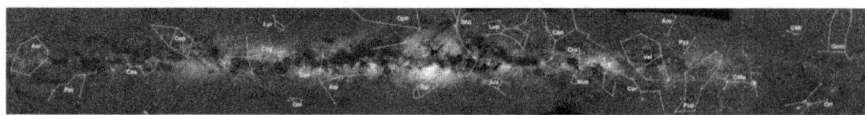

Figure 10.3 Our galaxy, the Milky Way or *Molagodimo*, as presented in Figure 10.1, with Greek-based, Western constellations included to guide the eye toward given directions or locations in the galaxy (http://home.arcor-online.de/axel.mellinger/mwpan_old.html)

Figure 10.4 *Right*: A 28 mm wide-angle Milky Way photograph by Axel Mellinger of the Southern Cross constellation, with the dark Coal Sack or *Emu* to the centre left and reddish Eta Carina Nebula or *Naka* to the bottom right. *Left*: Picture of the bird *Emu*

The Orion constellation with *Dikolobe*

The constellation of Orion, the hunter in Greek mythology, is unique in the night sky for having three straight-lined, bright-blue stars that are visible with the naked eye. In Greek mythology, these three stars are called Orion's belt; while, in the Setswana, they are known as *Dikolobe* (pigs) or, more tellingly, as *Dikolojwane* (piglets). Orion is highest in the sky in November, when the wild pigs in Southern Africa, where the Batswana live, have their piglets, who often run in groups. Therefore, the naming of the stars *Dikolojwane* is coincident with the time of the annual birth of wild piglets and marks this seasonal time for the Batswana.

Almost orthogonal to these three stars are some other less bright stars that are just visible to unaided eyes in very clear, dark skies. In Setswana, these stars are known as *Dintswa* (dogs) that are chasing the pigs, or *Lerumo* (an arrow) that has fallen short of hitting the pigs; while, in Greek mythology, they are known as Orion's belt. The belt has a reddish nebula, one of the few whose hue is visible to the naked eye in clear, dark skies. The nebula is a site of star formation, in fact, about 1500 light-years away, and is the nearest star nursery to Earth. It is an interesting coincidence that *Dikolojwane* (piglets), named by the Batswana for the time when wild piglets are born in Southern Africa, is also related to birth in astrophysical terms – the Earth's closest site of stars being born.

It is worth noting that in addition to Orion's belt and sword, this constellation also has the prominent, bright star with a reddish hue called

Figure 10.5 The constellation of Orion, the hunter in Greek mythology, or in the Setswana, the constellation of *Dikolojwane* (piglets) *le* (and) *Dintswa* (dogs)

Betelgeuse (Alpha Orionis) at the upper left in Figure 10.5 and the blue one called Rigel (Beta Orionis) at the lower right. Astrophysically, Betelguese is known as a the red-giant star, a fairly evolved and much older star than our Sun that is on an evolutionary path similar to it; while Rigel is a blue-giant star, a much younger star than our Sun, and is on a different evolutionary path than it, in which it will burn its gas reserves very fast and live a much shorter life than the Sun will. Also interesting is that the prominent stars in this constellation are at great distances from Earth; therefore, seeing and naming them as a constellation is based on their appearance in the night sky and not on their common physical location in relation to Earth. Furthermore, the appearance of objects in the night sky can be named after different things – historically, culturally or otherwise – as shown by their Greek and Setswana names. These names are useful for helping identify the stars in the night sky and may be linked to the actual time of their annual or nightly appearance; however, the astrophysical details of their physical environment, away from Earth, are a separate matter that needs careful scientific study.

The Moon or *Ngwedi/Mosese*

The actually Setswana names of the Moon, *Ngwedi* and *Mosese*, are also used to mean or refer to, respectively, the female monthly cycle and to a woman's dress. Indeed, references to the Moon are common and deeply woven into Setswana culture (Leeuw, 2007). For example, the Moon is used to represent a woman in wall murals of Batswana homes. In this case, the woman is thought to bring light to a home, but light that is not as scorching as the Sun. Indeed, the Moon is about 500,000 times less luminous than the Sun, and therefore, such interpretation of its light makes sense. Moonlight is also associated with happiness by the Batswana, as at full Moon, children can play outside at night.

Though the references to the Moon are common among the Batswana, they are primarily poetic or emotional. They also provide indication of it being used to mark the passing of time, though with not much physical nuance of where its light comes from, how its phases come about, or what the physical relation of the Moon to Earth is. The Batswana using the phases for telling the passage of time from day to day and month to month is in a way similar to that method used in basic principles of lunar calendars around the world. First, the reference to a woman's monthly cycle of light and happiness hints at this, because it speaks to their cyclic or periodic behaviour, the woman's with its underlying physiological and emotional changes and the Moon's with its physical appearance and gravitational effects on tides and perhaps emotions of people on Earth (e.g. happiness at the light of full Moon). Second, full Moon is said to be when '*Ngwedi a toloka*', literally meaning when the Moon is 'translating' or really 'transitioning', presumably to a new cycle, as marking the end of an old or beginning of a new month or year. Telling time is at the core of any science, civilisation and indeed living, and the Batswana's way of doing this can be exploited in many different ways in lessons.

Venus (goddess of love and beauty) or the 'Evening Star' and 'Morning Star'

Venus, the goddess of love and beauty, according to Greek mythology, is the third brightest celestial object in the sky, after the Sun and the Moon. In Setswana, Venus is *Kopadilalelo* (or, seeker of evening meals) as seen at sunset or *Mphatlalatsane* (the brilliant one) as seen at sunrise. The inner planets, Mercury and Venus, always appear in the west or east with the Sun – never opposite to it. Mercury is dimmer and only visible a few weeks a year, so the brighter Venus is the one called the 'Evening Star' or 'Morning

Star' by the Batswana and many across the globe, depending on when it is sighted in the sky.

Venus does not appear as the 'Evening Star' and the 'Morning Star' on the same day in the sky. In fact, the periods of appearance, as evening and morning stars respectively, last around nine months, with other shorter periods in between. Viewed through a small telescope (e.g. by Galileo in 1610, when he observed these phases), Venus has phases; and, when it is at its brightest, it is actually in a phase of a crescent, which a few say they have observed with the naked eye or seen making shadows.

The orbital (i.e. period with respect to stars as seen from outside Earth) and synoptic (i.e. period with respect to the Sun as seen from moving Earth) periods of Venus are 225 and 584 Earth days. Now, 225 times 13 is about eight times 584 and is five times 365. Thus, Venus orbits the Sun 13 times in eight Earth years, passing Earth five times. The synoptic cycle of Venus takes 584 Earth days, about 263 continuously, as the evening star and then as the morning one, and eight and 50 days in between on the near- and far-side from the Sun. Thus, one reason Venus was thought of as two separate celestial objects by the Batswana and many across the globe is these long separate appearance periods of about 263 days continuously as the evening star and then as the morning one.

Venus is the second-closest planet to the Sun, orbiting it every 224.7 Earth days. Its mean surface temperature is 735 K or 460 degrees Celsius. Venus has few impact craters, demonstrating that the surface is relatively young (about 0.5 billion years) and, perhaps, how Earth was when young. Classified as a terrestrial planet, it is sometimes called Earth's 'sister planet' because they are similar in size, gravity and bulk composition. Perhaps because of its age and temperature, Venus can be thought of as Earth's younger and hotter or more temperamental sister or, as the Batswana call it, *Kopadilalelo* (young seeker of evening meals, the bringer of night) as seen at sunset or *Mphatlalatsane* (the brighter bearer of dawn) as seen at sunrise – the forerunner of night or day time.

Findings and Conclusion

Using Southern Africa's Setswana astronomical nomenclature and IKS in exemplary, multicultural and trans-disciplinary lessons, as described above, is a fairly new idea needing further development. It has up to now only been attempted in extra-curricular (both at high school and university levels) and conference presentations (both with science and language focuses). Steps are needed towards structuring it into proper teaching and assessment modules and subsequent implementation in the classroom. Its content and context can be tailored to participants of different educational levels (from early learning to university levels) and teachers may implement any of the approaches of multicultural education discussed above. Makalela writes in Chapter 6 of an 'Ubuntu language methodology' and the positive value in revealing to students the interconnectedness of language, and how this enhances motivation to learn with 'filters lowered'. This envisaged programme, as I have outlined here, would complement this approach.

Reactions, where the Setswana lessons have been presented, at this stage, mostly in the additive or transformative approaches of multicultural education, have been positive, with excited questions and interest from the participants. Non-Setswana speakers value the Setswana nomenclature when their direct English meaning is explained so that they understand their origin and broader context, such as referring to the Milky Way galaxy as *Mosese* or 'Dress' and Venus as *Kopadilalelo* (young seeker of evening meals, the bringer of night) or *Mphatlalatsane* (the brighter bearer of dawn), thus giving them female human personalities, which is quite different to the approach of Western astronomy, where the heavenly bodies are seen as deities that have nothing to do with Earth. The Setswana speakers value the trans-disciplinary way of linking the Setswana nomenclature to Greek constellations or the physical meaning they are normally presented with in English only, without any context in their own language or culture. The possible implications are that the presentation (a) broadens access and understanding of scientific concepts, (b) exposes a relatively unpublicised astronomical interest and the IKS of the Batswana people and (c) perhaps enhances intra-cultural and multicultural knowledge and also respect. These reactions also need to be properly analysed and contextualised with the relevant pedagogical tools and theory.

References

Banks, J.A. (1997) *Educating Citizens in a Multicultural Society*. New York: Teachers College Press.
Banks, J.A. (1998) Approaches to multicultural curricular reform. In E. Lee, D. Menkart and M. Okazawa-Rey (eds) *Beyond Heroes and Holidays: A Practical Guide to K-12 Antiracist, Multicultural Education and Staff Development*. Washington: Network of Educators on the Americas.
Banks, J.A. (2011) *Multicultural Education: Goals and Dimensions*. Blog. See http://education.washington.edu/cme/view.htm (accessed 10 July 2010).
Bennett, C.I. (2003) *Comprehensive Multicultural Education: Research and Theory* (5th edn). Boston: Allyn and Bacon.
Cumming-McCann, A. (2003) Multicultural education: Connecting theory to practice. *Focus on Basics: Connecting Research and Practice* 6 (B), 9–12.

Leeuw, L. (2007) Setswana astronomical nomenclature. *African Skies/Cieux Africains* 11, 19–20.
Mellinger, A. (2009a) A color all-sky panorama image of the Milky Way. *Publications of the Astronomical Society of the Pacific* (PASP), 121, 1180–1187.
Mellinger, A. (2009b) *Milky Way Panorama 2.0*. Blog. See http://home.arcor-online.de/axel.mellinger/ (accessed 3 September 2012.

11 Literacy Self-Narratives as Constructions of Pre-Service Teachers' Multiliterate and Multilingual Identities

Adelia Carstens and Linda-Anne Alston

Introduction

The main aim of this chapter is to demonstrate, through research conducted among first-year students enrolled for the Bachelor of Education degree at a large residential university in Gauteng, South Africa, that the writing and analysis of literacy self-narratives have multiple benefits. They are useful in assisting BEd *students* to grapple with a variety of literacies, multilingualism and identity and to shape the educational beliefs and practices of these pre-service teachers to 'teach around and across difference' (Miller, 2009: 53). By looking carefully at the identities toward which students gravitate, academic literacy (AL) *lecturers* may uncover how the diverse contexts of literacy development have influenced their students' lives and adapt their classroom practice to accommodate diversity. We also wish to facilitate *curriculum* change (in our AL course) through a participatory approach (Ricento & Hornberger, 1996: 421) in order to optimise learning (Clark & Medina, 2000: 64–65; Williams, 2003: 342, 343).

Context

In Europe and the United States, the expansion of access to higher learning has been in evidence since the 1970s (Coffin *et al.*, 2003; David, 2008; Zipin & Brennan, 2006), while the widening of participation in South Africa came under the spotlight only about 20 years later, with the publication of the *Green Paper on Transformation in Higher Education* (Department of Education, 1996). However, scholarly attention to first-year success at South African institutions of higher learning is fairly recent (Leibowitz *et al.*, 2009). One of the issues in student retention and throughput that has been highlighted is the acquisition of AL – not as a set of generic skills, but as a social practice (Lea & Street, 1998), mediated by membership of a community of practice (Lave & Wenger, 1991). In South Africa, this interpretation of AL has been emphasised by scholars such as Granville and Dison (2009) and Archer (2011). Concerns about the AL levels of teacher trainees have been raised by Seligman (2011a), who published the first comprehensive AL textbook for South African students of education (Seligman, 2011b).

In university classrooms across the world, many lecturers still adhere to 'deficit' approaches to AL. They stereotypically label the majority of non-traditional students as underprepared for tertiary education and unable to master the conventions of academic writing (Turner, 2011: 10), while ignoring the other types of literacy that these students bring to the university, such as competence in understanding and speaking a variety of languages and constructing meaning via other modes than text. Such approaches also conveniently ignore the complex challenges that all freshman students face in moving between different genres, registers and modes, as mentioned by scholars abroad (Devereux & Wilson, 2008: 124) as well as in South Africa (Archer, 2011: 387).

Literacy narrative pedagogy has proven to be useful in understanding the role that experiences of literacy acquisition have played in the development of students' literacy identities and empowers them to become literate in the 'standard' literacies, dominant discourses and technologies required for successful university study. This will be discussed below.

Theory

Literacy self-narratives

In order to discuss the theoretical underpinnings of literacy self-narratives, we need to make clear our understanding of the term *literacy*. Definitions vary from 'common' usages, such as 'the ability to read and write' (Janks,

2010: 2), to 'cavalier usages' (Kress, 2010: 114), such as 'advanced competency or knowledge' in knowledge domains such as environmental studies, finance or medicine (Williams, 2009: 18). According to Williams, 'literacy is connected to the way humans communicate ideas, concepts and emotions to one another' (Williams, 2009: 18), creating representations of their ideas that can be interpreted by others. Drawing on insights from the new literacies (New London Group, 1996), multiliteracies (Newfield & Maungedzo, 2006) and multimodality (Kress, 2010; Kress & Van Leeuwen, 1996, 2001, 2006; Williams, 2009), we have adopted the following working definition:

> Literacy is the ability to use conventional sign systems to compose and interpret texts that communicate ideas from one person to another.

Literacy self-narratives, in the conventional sense, are autobiographic stories 'that foreground issues of language acquisition and literacy' (Eldred & Mortensen, 1992: 513). Probably influenced by the content of canonical literacy narratives, such as Richard Rodrigues's *Hunger for Memory* (1982), these narratives have become associated with 'explicit images of schooling and teaching' (Eldred & Mortensen, 1992: 513).

Scholarly publications on literacy self-narratives published since 1994 have consistently focused on the potential that they have to facilitate social change. According to Kouritzin (2000), they are particularly useful for allowing the voices of the historically marginalised to be heard and may prompt the researcher to reconsider the curriculum. Autoethnography is particularly useful as it 'open[s] up a space of resistance between the individual (auto-) and the collective (ethno-), where the writing (-graphy) of resistance cannot be foreclosed' (Reda, 2007: 177).

In the United States, a considerable amount of critical scholarly work on literacy self-narratives has been done since the 1990s, focusing on a variety of purposes, among which are: (a) making explicit the student's passage through different life worlds 'when the self is on the threshold of possible intellectual, social and emotional development' (Soliday, 1994: 511); (b) helping students and lecturers to grapple with multiculturalism and multilingualism (Ball, 2000; Busch, 2007; Clark & Medina, 2000); (c) building confidence in the L2 classroom (Corkery, 2004, 2005); (d) foregrounding the learner perspective in literacy and language learning (Busch, 2007: 5); and (e) teaching literacy across the curriculum (Coffey, 2011).

Recently, writing educators involved in the National Writing Project (in the US) have started opening up the writing classroom to multimodal composition instead of 'the linear, argumentative and word-processed essay' (Frost *et al.*, 2009: 182) and using methods that engage students in understanding and applying the rhetorical possibilities of different technologies, each with a repertoire of semiotic resources (Frost et al., 2009: 181–182). Frost et al.'s research linked the composition of multimodal literacy narratives with writing traditional essays. This resonates with our view of the value of building confidence by drawing upon students' repertoire of languages and literacies and then gradually introducing them to the genres and modes of the academy.

A new literacies framework to embed literacy narrative pedagogy

Although a significant body of research literature on literacy narratives exists, an adequate model for teaching literacy self-narratives in higher education has not yet been fully developed (Coffey, 2011: 95). A useful starting point is Barton and Hamilton's (2000) framework, which comprises four main components: literacy practices, literacy domains, literacy events and sponsors. *Literacy practices* are regular activities patterned by social institutions and power relationships (Barton & Hamilton, 2000: 8). Literacy practices typically involve *literacy events* and manifest in a range of semiotic systems (Barton & Hamilton, 2000: 9). These practices are exercised in *literacy domains*, such as home, school and the workplace. *Sponsors* are 'agents, local or distant, concrete or abstract, who enable, support, teach and model, as well as recruit, regulate, suppress or withhold, literacy' (Brandt, 2004: 19). Hamilton (2000) preferred to use the more generic term *participants* when analysing self-narratives, since it includes the narrator as agent. The term *participant* can be linked to Williams' (2003) notion of *identities*, which refers to the images that students portray of themselves and other participants. In this chapter, we depart from Williams' (2003: 844) basic categorisation of the identities that student writers (as narrators) assume for themselves.

In the remainder of this chapter, the methodology and findings of the first phase of our research project on literacy self-narratives will be discussed, with a focus on the social construction of multilingual and multiliterate *narrator identities*.

Methodology

Data-gathering procedure

The current AL curriculum of the module in question, Literacies in Education, draws upon the procedure used by Frost et al. (2009) during their teaching of first-year composition. Their students first had to compose 'a multimodal profile essay describing and commenting on one individual's experiences with literacy' (Frost *et al.*, 2009: 183), followed by a traditional written essay, based on the same content.

All our students who were registered for the English track of Literacies in Education were required to compose a multimodal narrative on their *personal* (multi-) literate and multilingual histories, using at least two modes of expression. Thereafter, the multimodal narrative was transmediated to a monomodal written essay. Scaffolding included class discussion of the notions 'literacy' and 'literacies', reading of published literacy narratives and group discussions to learn more about the literacies that other cultural groups bring to the university. An important characteristic of the autobiographical narrative, that is, relating a uniquely personal experience while also reflecting societal discourses, was effectively illustrated by the published literacy self-narrative of Emmanuel Mgqwashu (Mgqwashu, 2009), now a professor of English Studies at the University of Natal. This served as a model text for both the English and Afrikaans tracks. Individual, task-specific planning for the multimodal and the written essay included the design of a literacy timeline or mind map, with key words on practices, domains, events and sponsors. The following essay prompt was given to the students:

> Write an essay of 700 to 1000 words telling the story of how you acquired one or more types of literacy that has/have special meaning for you.

From the total population of 554 students registered for the English track, 153 students (four out of 12 class groups) were conveniently sampled to submit their essays for research purposes. They were taught by Linda-Anne Alston and another lecturer, Yolandi Woest, who volunteered to assist with data-gathering and coding. With the exception of 19, all students voluntarily signed a letter of consent to allow their essays to be analysed. All students submitted a hard copy of the essay for grading purposes, while only those who signed the consent letter were requested to send an anonymous electronic version of the essay to a dedicated email address. Eventually, only half ($n = 57$) of the students who signed the consent letters submitted their essays electronically. Possible explanations for the low participation rate are a lack of confidence in their writing abilities and a lack of familiarity with using email and attachments. A concomitant drawback of the procedure was that the electronically submitted essays did not mirror the demographics of the sampled classes. While only 38% of the sampled class groups comprise White students (thus 62% are Black, Coloured and Indian), 58% of those who submitted their essays electronically indicated 'White' as their racial identity. The male–female profile in the sample closely reflects the profile of the total English cohort. Table 11.1 summarises the personal profiles of the students who submitted electronically.

Table 11.1 Profile of the students who volunteered their literacy self-narratives for research purposes and who submitted electronically

Profile characteristic	Summary of data
Race	34 White
	19 Black
	3 Coloured
	1 Indian
Gender	46 female
	11 male
Type of high school previously attended	33 urban
	13 rural
	4 township
	5 combination of the above
	2 attended school in other African countries
Home language	28 English
	7 Sepedi
	6 Afrikaans
	3 IsiNdebele
	3 Setswana
	2 German
	2 IsiZulu
	1 each of IsiXhosa, Sesotho, SiSwati, Xitsonga, Urdu, Greek
Literacy practice reported on	31 verbal literacy
	2 musical literacy
	5 kinaesthetic literacy (drama)
	3 visual literacy
	4 computer literacy
	1 subject literacy
	1 religious literacy
	10 combinations of technological, musical, verbal, kinaesthetic and visual literacies

Data analysis procedure

Instead of using narrative analysis, which includes reading and making notes in recursive cycles (Cole & Knowles, 2001: 99; Lieblich *et al.*, 1998), we preferred qualitative content analysis, which is a more linear and structured approach, sometimes used in narrative research dealing with identity (Murray, 2009: 47, 51).

The 57 essays (of the original 62, five were inadvertent duplicates) were analysed using the qualitative data analysis program AtlasTi version 6.1. The coders departed from the set of categories defined by Barton and Hamilton (2000), as well as a basic set of narrator codes derived from Williams (2003). Coding was done in four cycles (Saldanha, 2009: 45–146): First, a set of initial codes was recorded and defined in a qualitative codebook (Creswell, 2009: 187), and a sample of five essays were analysed. These essays comprised part of the corpus of 57 essays that was coded according to the process of constant comparison. Two more cycles involving all three coders followed, with a final moderation round by the primary researcher.

As a result of the richness of the data, it was decided to focus the initial phase of the data analysis on *the literacy identities that students construct for themselves* (Petersen & Henderson, 2008; Williams, 2003) and deal with sponsor identities in a later round of analysis.

Findings and interpretation

Eighteen narrator codes (labels for different literacy identities) emerged from the data, as summarised in Table 11.2.

Each essay was then read slowly, and with attention, to identify its 'narrative structure' (as described by Williams, 2003: 343) or 'macro-literacy identity' (the term we coined). Plant names were found to be meaningful in labelling the macro-identities. The idea was sparked by a scholarly article on biological predisposition towards sensitivity, which distinguishes two types of children: *dandelion children* and *orchid children*. Orchid children are predisposed to be susceptible to their environments, while dandelion children thrive, irrespective of their circumstances (Ellis *et al.*, 2011: 1). Using plant names as metaphors for literacy identities had additional benefits in the context of teacher education. Among these advantages is the ability of metaphors to capture complex constructs and facilitate reflection. De Guerrero and Villamil (2001: 13), who analysed the use of metaphor in second- and foreign-language instruction within the framework of socio-cultural theory, indicated that 'it is important for working and prospective teachers to become aware of the powerful and extensive way in which metaphors shape educational beliefs and practices'.

In the essay corpus, eight macro-identities were identified. To test the intuitive assignment of categories, the frequencies of the narrator codes (from a set of 18) for each essay that belongs to a particular macro-identity were calculated, and fairly distinct clusters of micro-identities emerged. Table 11.3 summarises these clusters, together with the socio-demographic composition of each category. Below the table, each macro-identity is discussed

Table 11.2 Narrator codes used in the final analysis

Code	No. of occurrences	Definition: A person who ...
1. MAchiever	61	Performs a literacy activity exceptionally well and receives some kind of acknowledgement or shows some evidence of excellence
2. MConfident user	48	Demonstrates or expresses satisfaction with his/her level of learning at a particular time
3. MCoper	28	Successfully deals with difficulties during his/her literacy development and acts to overcome them
4. MEnthusiast	178	Shows excitement about learning a particular literacy skill
5. MExperimenter	24	Tries out new ways of doing, especially in order to gain experience
6. MFailure/fool	22	Feels inadequate, insufficient or falls short in terms of acquiring a particular literacy
7. MInsecure learner	5	Lacks confidence in the ability to master the particular type of literacy
8. MLearner/developer	110	Makes a conscious attempt at gaining mastery of a particular skill or literacy
9. Multilingual/multiliterate	35	Provides evidence of the mastery of more than two languages and/or literacies
10. Nerd/geek	7	Is not sociable resulting from a strong academic or work-related focus
11. Perseverer	45	Remains constant to the cause of acquiring a particular literacy in the face of obstacles or discouragement
12. Prodigy	7	(Child who) is particularly skillful for his/her age
13. Reluctant learner	27	Is hesitant to learn a particular literacy because he/she does not want to or is unsure whether it is the right thing to do
14. Struggler	89	Tries very hard to acquire a particular literacy in the face of problems or when it is difficult.
15. Sufferer	14	Has a physical/mental condition that hinders literacy development
16. Survivor	16	Demonstrates the spirit and perseverance to conquer difficulties
17. Teacher	13	Assists others to become literate
18. Victim	6	Has been prevented from acquiring a particular literacy, by another person, institution or system

Table 11.3 Summary of macro-identities, components and socio-demographic spread

Macro-identity	Definition of macro-identity	Micro-identity components Bold = shared by all the categories, Not bold: shared by more than two thirds	No of instances per demographic category B = Black C = Coloured I = Indian W = White F = Female M = Male
Dandelion	Learner who has comfortably adapted to a variety of contexts or environments	**Multilingual/ multiliterate learner** **Struggler** **Learner** Achiever Enthusiast	CF 2 BF 2 IF 1 WF 7
Ivy	Self-motivated and confident learner	**Enthusiast** **Learner** Confident user Achiever Perseverer	BF 1 WF 5 WM 2
Resurrection plant	Learner who has suffered from a condition that inhibited literacy learning, but has overcome it	**Reluctant learner/ failure** **Struggler** **Enthusiast** **Coper** Perseverer/survivor	CF 1 BF 1 WF 3 WM 1
Sensitive plant (touch-me-not)	Conscientious and introspective person who has learnt through practice	**Experimenter** **Learner** Teacher	WF 4
Venus fly trap	Learner who has engaged with a literacy practice as a hobby and prefers to do it in solitude	**Enthusiast** **Learner** **Achiever** **Nerd**	WF 3 BF 1

(Continued)

Table 11.3 (continued) Summary of macro-identities, components and socio-demographic spread

Macro-identity	Definition of macro-identity	Micro-identity components Bold = shared by all the categories, Not bold: shared by more than two thirds	No of instances per demographic category B = Black C = Coloured I = Indian W = White F = Female M = Male
Sunflower	Positive learner who has excelled from a young age and basks in the sun of his/her achievements	**Prodigy** **Enthusiast** **Learner** **Achiever**	WF 3
Cactus	Learner who has survived despite hardships and a lack of resources	**Struggler** **Learner** **Coper/perseverer** Failure/reluctant learner Enthusiast	BF 5 BM 3 WF 2
Unidentified herbaceous plant	Indefinite narrator identity	Indefinite clustering	BF 3 BM 4 WF 3 WM 1

with reference to its prototypical build-up of micro-identities and examples from the relevant essays.

Dandelion

The dandelion (*Taraxacum officinale*) is a plant with yellow-rayed flowers and deeply notched basal leaves, of which the parachute-shaped seeds are blown about by the wind – often for considerable distances. Similarly, the dandelion learner is extremely mobile and easily adapts to almost any environment. Eleven narrators were categorised as dandelions. The forces behind dandelions' mobility and adaptability are their eagerness to learn and their resilience. The author of essay 1 is a prototypical dandelion. Her mother tongue and linguistic identity is Afrikaans, and her racial identity is Coloured.[1] She is fluent in Sesotho because her nannies spoke their mother tongue to her as a toddler, and at school she befriended many Black children who spoke Sesotho. She prefers to write academically in English, although at the university where she studies, she has the right to write in Afrikaans or English. For her, the next challenge is to learn to write in Sesotho, and to speak isiZulu fluently, as some of her friends are speakers of isiZulu.

The dandelions of essays 35 and 53 also tell stories of multilingualism, and mobility between vastly different languages, such as Greek, English and German (35); and Urdu and English (53). The narrator of essay 10 tells the story of how she, as a Setswana mother-tongue speaker, first attended a Setswana pre-school in a rural village in the North-West Province, then an English medium pre-school in a township north of Pretoria, and Grade 1 in a former Model C school with an Afrikaans mother-tongue teacher, teaching through the medium of English. She started high school in a Model C school on the western side of Pretoria, with English being taught by a mother-tongue speaker of isiZulu whom she had difficulty understanding. Finally, she attended a Model C school in Pretoria North, where she had a Sepedi-speaking English teacher who struggled to teach English poetry, and then again an Afrikaans-speaking English teacher, who rekindled her love of language and literature.

Among the other dandelions are three students who recount their musical literacy (narrator No. 14) and dance literacy (narrators No. 26, 45 and 51), including how they mastered various genres, joined various dance groups and participated in numerous performances. The dandelion category also includes four essays that recount multiliterate histories: narrator No. 25: verbal, musical and computer; narrator No. 30: verbal, drama and music; narrator No. 47: verbal, mathematical and music; and narrator No. 57: drama, dancing and visual.

Common among dandelion narrators is that all of them experienced difficulties in learning aspects of the particular literacy at some stage of their literate lives. In the case of the multilingual dandelions, the difficulties include struggling with writing in English, Sesotho and isiZulu as a result of suffering from Attention Deficit Disorder (narrator No. 1, whose mother tongue is Afrikaans); struggling to understand an unfamiliar medium of instruction in pre-school (English) and the English of non-mother-tongue teachers (narrator No. 10, a mother-tongue speaker of Setswana); struggling with German in a parallel medium English/German school in Grade 4 (narrator No. 35, whose mother tongue is Greek); and struggling with English grammar and pronunciation (narrator No. 53, whose mother tongue is Urdu). Given their eagerness to learn, and their resilience, all these learners were able to overcome their problems and succeeded in their ultimate goal: to obtain university exemption.

Ivy

The ivy (*Hedera*) is a self-driven learner. Like the ivy plant, which is a climbing or trailing plant that grows enthusiastically in sun or shade, the ivy learner is an enthusiastic and eager learner who becomes confident in a particular literacy through practice and dedication. Ivies have the ability to persevere in order to reach their literacy goals irrespective of the literacy practice they engage in. Narrator No. 4 tells the story of a student who started working on computers at the age of six. He started off by playing games, then learnt to surf the internet and use MSOffice and then took Computer Technology as a subject, ending top of his class. Narrator No. 62 tells a similar story. At first, he just sat and watched his father work on the computer; then imitated him, becoming more and more fascinated by computers. He learnt everything he could about computers and is now *'staying in* [sic] *the forefront of technological innovations'*. The same pattern of development emerges from the essays by narrators 6, 56 and 58 (verbal literacy focus), narrator No. 11 (dance literacy), and narrator No. 19 (subject-related literacy in geography).

Apart from being self-driven learners, ivies are also reflective learners. Their self-narratives either implicitly or explicitly reflect the awareness that learning and achievement are reciprocal: Hard work ensures achievement, and achievement instils enhanced motivation to study.

Resurrection plant

The resurrection plant (*Myrothamnus flabellifolius*) absorbs water when the soil is moist, and as the soil dries, it folds up its stems into a tight ball. When the rains return, the stems unfold and growth resumes. The resurrection plant learner is a person who has been subjected to intense physical or emotional suffering and has managed not only to overcome the problem but to adapt to a normal schooling routine. Three narrators tell how they have suffered from dyslexia (Nos 3, 15 and 20) and how difficult reading and writing in English have been for them. For instance, narrator No. 3 opens her narrative as follows: *'"I can't, I don't know" was my answer for many questions ... Being dyslexic seemed like it was the end of the world'*; and concludes with *'By the time I was in matric I was one of the top students in some subjects'*. She was also awarded 'an Excellent Academic Certificate'. Narrator No. 15 writes about hearing loss as a result of recurring ear infections; No. 21 tells how her dancing career was cut short as a result of a knee injury; and No. 33 relates the story of pregnancy in high school, and how the freedom to read what she found interesting (short stories, pregnancy and baby magazines, etc.) improved her reading development. Narrator No. 48 gives the reader a look into the literate life of a learner whose brain hemispheres *'did not synchronise'*.

Notwithstanding their debilitating conditions, these learners' narratives tell stories of support by teachers, doctors, friends, family members and therapists. The narrator of essay 15 writes, *'Fortunately for me, I had my families [sic] support and the support from friends. They all treated me as if I had nothing wrong with me'*.

One possible explanation for the absence of learners from poor rural areas in the resurrection plant category is that learners suffering from such conditions in underprivileged schools and communities might not have been (accurately) diagnosed, and the narrator might not have received the same nurturing or intensive, remedial and medical help as privileged children. Other contributing factors could be the difference between school culture and home and community culture: School culture exposes learners with disabilities, while home and community culture encourages non-disclosure because of the shame that perceived (or real) physical, psychological and educational deficiencies may bring to families.

Sensitive plant (touch-me-not)

The sensitive plant, also known as touch-me-not (*Mimosa pudica*) has compound leaves with leaflets that fold and droop when touched. Two of the four essays that fall into this category deal with visual literacy (12 and 28); one reflects on visual and kinaesthetic (drama) literacy (55), and another deals with a type of religious literacy (essay 31). Sensitive plant learners are introverted learners who wish to retract into a quiet space when practising their preferred literacy, like the narrator of essay 12: *'When I was a young girl, I often spent a lot of time alone, because for some reason I enjoyed my own company more than that of a group of people'*. In essay 28, the narrator expresses a similar desire for solitude: *'When I draw, I feel like I go into my own world where nothing else really matters'*.

Sensitive plant learners are eager and diligent, but need freedom to apply creatively what they have learnt. The narrator of essay 12 writes about her appreciation for the fact that her art teacher motivated her to *'think out of the box'*. The sensitive plant narrator of essay 55 contrasts the influence that two of her art teachers had on her. The O-levels teacher bombarded her with rules, while in A-levels, she was allowed to practice what was *'exciting and different'*, and her art teacher understood her style of art *'instead of trying to hold me back with rules'*.

Because of their need for creativity, sensitive plants delight in experimentation. The author of essay 12 writes that her teacher's inspiration led her *'to trying complete different mediums and using different materials such as painting, charcoal, sculpture with clay and plaster of Paris, glass, etc.'* She reflects on her experimentation as follows: '[If] *you wish to create something that will be thought provoking, one needs to use materials that no one has ever used before. ... So I began to step out of my comfort zone, and cross boundaries for the sake of creating an original piece of work*'.

Sensitive plants also delight in sharing what they have learnt with others (they easily assume the role of a teacher). It is therefore no surprise that they would choose teaching as a career. The narrator of essay 55 links her literacy story in art to her chosen profession in the following way:

> I visited an orphanage near my school very often. The children were very unenthusiastic to learn anything. I wanted to inspire them and encourage them to want to work like my art teacher inspired me. I wanted them to experience the opportunities to be creative and to be an individual in the same way I was. That's what encouraged me to become a teacher.

Interestingly, all the sensitive plants in the corpus are White females. Possible explanations for the absence of Black (including Coloured and Indian) students may be a general lack of resources outside the domain of formal schooling, which denies them opportunities to experiment with technological literacies and artistic literacies such as art, drama and music. The absence of males across the racial spectrum may perhaps be attributed to a general reluctance among boys to admit to a sensitive and artistic nature, for fear of being labelled 'sissies' or 'gays'.

Venus fly trap

The Venus fly trap (*Dionaea muscipula*) is an insectivorous plant with hinged, two-lobed leaf blades with bristles on the edges that close, entrap and devour insects. Venus fly trap learners can be bookworms or computer nerds. They usually become immersed in the literacy practice at a young age, as stated by the following narrators:

Narrator no. 16: 'At a very young age I got taught how to read.'
Narrator no. 24: 'My parents introduced me to reading from a very young age.'

Similar to sensitive plants, Venus fly traps prefer solitude to 'buzz'. They usually spend a great deal of time practising their literacy, often as a hobby, which later becomes an addiction.

Narrator no. 54 recounts:

In these story time sessions I would be able to escape to another world through my imagination where anything was possible and it was in my control whether negative aspects existed or not.

In essay 43, the narrator says:

The library literally became school for me because I'd go there instead of class at times because I read books like they were running away from me. Books at the time were like food to me and I couldn't go without reading.

The Venus fly trap is normally extremely enthusiastic about his/her literacy hobby, typically learns through exploration, and often becomes very adept at performing the particular literacy practice. As a result of their introverted behaviour, Venus fly traps are often characterised as 'nerds' or 'geeks', as demonstrated by narrator No. 16: *'I was no longer seen as a popular. I had become a book worm and got labelled a geek. The glasses I was forced to wear didn't exactly help either'*.

Sunflower

Sunflowers (*Helianthus annuus*) have large, yellow-rayed flower heads that follow the sun. Sunflower learners have excelled in a particular literacy practice from a young age. They delight in portraying themselves as child prodigies. The narrator of essay 13 relates how she *'started to sing from a very young age and played the flute from the age of 8'*; while the narrator of essay 38 boasts that she was the first of her cousins to know the alphabet.

Sunflowers are typically from privileged backgrounds and have grown up in families that are highly literate in the practice about which they write, as is evident from the above quotes. They draw inspiration and motivation from the support given by significant others. For instance, narrator No. 42 relates how, as a very young girl, she was inspired by her grandfather, a landscape artist, and how her motivation grew from his appreciation for her first charcoal drawing: *'When I was done he looked at me and smiled as if it was a Picasso masterpiece'*. The author of essay 13 gives a particularly vivid and detailed account of the musical accomplishments of close family members, starting with her grandfather, who was a well-known bass baritone singer. She fondly remembers how her mother accompanied her while playing musical instruments, while *'always watching and believing that I could be the best'*.

A similar recognition of the role her mother played in her literacy career is given by the author of essay 38: *'She would spend hours on end listening to me read anything that I could find, be it school books or magazines. She would also read to me every single day. She emphasized the importance of being able to read and write immensely'*. Apart from her mother, she also lists by name the various teachers in her school career who had recognised her passion for reading and creative writing, formed caring relationships with her, and went out of their way to create learning opportunities for her.

Sunflowers thrive on the recognition and accolades they receive for their achievements. The three narrators in this category were recipients of numerous distinctions and awards. They clearly delight in public display of their abilities and achievements. Narrator No. 38 writes, *'I couldn't wait for my grade 3 teacher, Mrs X, to call me to the front of the classroom every Friday to read my story'.*

Although a frequency of three out of 57 is hardly generalisable, it is worthy of mention that all three of the sunflower narrators are White females – one English and two Afrikaans mother-tongue speakers. If students with this demographic profile are representative of the category, it would not be surprising. The majority of Black first-year Education students are first-generation university students whose parents often have not had the resources to engage their children in literacy practices that carry social and cultural capital in Western societies. Furthermore, it is quite plausible that the absence of White males can be ascribed to culturally determined shyness about admitting to artistic or literary endeavours.

Cactus

The cactus (family *Cactacea*) is a succulent, spiny plant that mostly grows in arid regions, where it is usually subject to drought. Cacti are typically adapted to conserve water. Similarly, the cactus learner is a tough learner who has demonstrated that he/she can survive despite unfavourable circumstances and a lack of resources. The majority of the cacti in our corpus started out as reluctant and unsuccessful learners, but owing to their hardiness, combined with enthusiasm and internal motivation, they persevered through difficult times, developed coping strategies and finally reached their ultimate literacy goal: to gain entrance into university.

The struggling and suffering related in the narratives of the cacti seem different from the types of struggle and suffering narrated by members of the majority of other categories: First, where students from privileged backgrounds take laptops, PCs, music centres and smart phones for granted, some cacti find it worth mentioning that they had a radio and a television in the home (narrators No. 7, 40 and 41). Second, whereas narrators in the Venus fly trap category reminisce on how stories were read to them as small children, cacti reflect a deprivation of such stimuli. This reality is recounted by the narrator of essay 23: *'I was from a family where they were all illiterate in reading, so there was no person to help me, and that made me to hate reading because I thought it was a family curse'.* A third obstacle in the literacy lives of some cacti is the lack of alignment between the mother tongue of the learner and the medium of instruction. In essay 17, the narrator, whose mother tongue is Xitsonga, remembers her Grade 4 teacher telling the class that they were going to learn only through the medium of English from then onwards, and that she could not give them Xitsonga interpretations of what she said, since she was a speaker of Tshivenda. Another learner reflects on how she started her academic career in a school with German as medium of instruction, then attended two Afrikaans-medium schools consecutively, followed by an English/German medium school, and later, an Afrikaans-medium school again – all in different parts of the country (narrator No. 37). Unlike the dandelions' testimony that learning took place despite displacement, the cacti's struggle to become literate dominates over the learning that took place. A fourth contrast between cacti and the majority of other categories is the status of the available resources and infrastructure for learning: Where libraries, computers, therapists' consulting rooms, art studios and so on feature prominently in the sunflower, resurrection plant, sensitive plant, ivy and Venus fly trap essays, the essays of cacti unveil a different reality. The narrator of essay 60 paints a picture of a dysfunctional school:

> Teachers at X High would normally spend their working hours in the staff room eating, gossiping or chating [sic] amougst [sic] themselves about their personal affairs. Whilst learners caused corruption [sic] in the school by vandalising school property by breaking windows, tables, chairs and break fence to bunk classes, learners smoking publicly outside toilets and others gambling.

Some of the cacti find meaning in their hardships and literacy struggles. Thus, the writer of essay 7 comments on her narrative as follows: *'and in a strange way I am very great full [sic] of how and where I grew up. I would have possibly not worked so hard to get to university. Even though I obtained code 4 for my academic literacy test I wrote when I got to university'*. Narrator No. 23 writes that *'it also made me to realize that I am from a bad background of reading, so I should not underestimate reading but I must read more and more to improve my reading'*.

It is not surprising that 8 of the 10 cacti are Black students. In the Faculty of Education at the university where the research was conducted, 64% of all first-year students studying on full bursaries are Black (excluding Coloured and Indian), indicating a lack of means within this group to pay tuition fees. It could be inferred that many Black students grew up in dire circumstances, without support to acquire the literacies that carry social capital.

Unidentified herbaceous plant

We also found some essays that cannot be characterised. Metaphorically speaking, they are 'unidentified herbaceous plants'. Some of these essays are hybrids, demonstrating characteristics of more than one literacy identity; while others are so incoherently written that categorisation is not possible. The narrators' difficulty in expressing meaning in English is evident in the conclusions to some of their essays, as illustrated by the following reflection by narrator No. 2:

> For all that journey of my life it was not easy but I strived for what I want. Because I knew that one day I will get everything right. So we as a nation if we can strive for what we believe is right we are going to build the nation before us.

Our deduction about poor writing skills as a problematic factor is underscored by the fact that more than half of the unidentified herbaceous plants had obtained a score of 1 or 2 (on a 5-point rating scale) on the compulsory AL test they had written at the beginning of 2012.

After the data analysis, member-checking sessions were held to honour our ethical commitment to the Ethics Committee of the Faculty, provide students with a metacognitive learning opportunity and triangulate our research results. We framed our feedback in terms of the research process, as the subsequent study unit in the AL curriculum was to deal with reading academic articles. Each student received a printed summary of the characteristics of the seven macro-identities (excluding the unidentified herbaceous plant), and we showed them pictures of each plant to enhance motivation and facilitate recall. After the explanation, students were given the opportunity to ask questions. Finally, they were provided with a checklist containing the seven macro-types and were requested to tick the box next to the macro-identity that resonated best with the identity they construed for themselves after the information session. Very close alignment was found between the findings of the study and the students' self-categorisation in the case of the dandelion, ivy and resurrection plant identities, but there were small discrepancies (4%–5%) regarding the Venus fly trap, sunflower and cactus identities. In comparison, a fairly large discrepancy occurred in the sensitive plant category: 11% more students aligned themselves with the sensitive plant identity during member-checking than were reflected by the written essays. This discrepancy can perhaps be explained by the fact that 19% of the essays could not be categorised and that a considerable number of the unidentified herbaceous plant learners might have categorised themselves as sensitive plants. Another possible explanation is a reluctance to reveal sensitivity in the self-narratives.

Conclusion

The main finding of the research is that a distinctive set of literacy profiles are prevalent across language and cultural groups and across literacy practices – as was also found by Parmegiani and Rudwick (Chapter 7). These macro-identities are a composite of micro-identity traits that reflect biological characteristics, environmental influences, social discourses and constructions of the self. Metaphor is a useful device for understanding these complex constructions and to introduce education students to the educational applications of metaphor as a cognitive-linguistic device.

The outcomes of the research have implications for classroom practice as well as curriculum design. Lecturers should interrogate their own assumptions about 'being literate', and value their students' contributions to discourses of language and literacies to allow 'the productive and creative agency of all students' (Mills, 2011: 122). This fits in with the findings of Mashiyi (Chapter 9) and her call for a learner-centred approach to multilingual learning and teaching. With this approach, lecturers act as change agents, countering language endangerment and allowing African languages to flourish alongside 'killer languages' such as English.

Syllabus themes dealing with literacy narratives should problematise over-simplistic categorisations, such as 'academically literate' versus 'non-academically literate', as imposed by compulsory tests of AL levels. Such an approach is also in line with the continua of biliteracy, as discussed by Hibbert and van der Walt (Chapter 1) and Mashiyi (Chapter 9). Lecturers should make a concerted effort at making it clear that literacy is a matter of degree, rather than one of all or none. To affect this, tutorial sessions could be loosely structured around textual problems identified in students' literacy self-narratives, and lecturers should remain cautious of reverting to modernist practices such as error analysis.

Since 23 essays (43% of the corpus) refer to contexts of multilingualism, and narrate events associated with becoming literate in languages other than the mother tongue, overt strategies should be devised to accommodate the needs of these students. This may include classroom strategies such as the following, adapted for the university context from Stein (2008: 16):

- The class divide themselves into language groups that all speak the same language(s).

- Each person in the group tells, performs or presents his/her literacy story multimodally in a common language.
- Each group chooses the best story in the group to perform to the class in the original language, which is interpreted by someone else in English (English translations could also be used on PowerPoint slides).
- After each storytelling event, learners (in groups) talk about the meanings that they derive from the story.
- Individual students, groups or the entire class choose a story, and write it in English.

Another suggestion for classroom practice and materials design is to replicate our member-checking exercise and to request learner groups, constituted on the basis of self-categorisation, to compile inventories of preferred and dispreferred teacher actions for their particular macro-identity. Responses should be shared with the whole class. More attention could be paid to using metaphor as a categorisation device for reflection on teaching practices. Metaphorical labels should resonate with learners' life-worlds in order to help them make sense of complex, abstract concepts and new experiences.

Time could also be devoted to the interrogation of sponsor identities. As far as we could ascertain, no attempt has been made, locally or abroad, towards an auto-ethnographic understanding and description of the roles that different categories of sponsors – teachers, parents, other family members and friends – play in the literacy development of learners. After analysing the essay corpus in terms of sponsor identities, we hope to address this gap and to suggest curriculum changes, as well as classroom exercises, that will help teacher trainees to reflect critically on the roles that sponsors play in the literacy development of learners.

We believe that such exercises resonate with the 'diversity-compliant inclusive curriculum model', as expounded by Kotzé and Hibbert (2010: 16):

- A focus on discourse as socially constituted and constituting, instead of a focus on correctness, preferred knowledge, attitudes and beliefs.
- Critical engagement, active text production and a strong performance orientation, instead of the transmission of 'vacuum-packed knowledge bites'.
- Dialectical and interactive, instead of a unidirectional monologue.
- Context-embedded critical enquiry, instead of discreet skills taught as a decontextualised list.
- Multimodal instead of monomodal.

One of the remaining challenges is to align our entire curriculum with this model.

Note

(1) 'The term 'Coloured' refers to a controversial category for people who did not fit into the Apartheid government's race-based categories as they were of mixed racial background. It has remained in use and is a title carried with pride by many 'Coloured' people who developed their own culture and art forms during segregation. This could be likened to the re-appropriation of the term 'Nigger' by intellectual African Americans (see the writings of Houston A. Baker and Henry Louis Gates).

References

Archer, A. (2011) Clip-art or design: Exploring the challenges of multimodal texts for writing centres in higher education. *Southern African Linguistics and Applied Language Studies* 29 (4), 387–399.
Ball, A.F. (2000) Preparing teachers for diversity: Lessons learned from the US and South Africa. In C. Lee and P. Smagorinsky (eds) *Worlds of Meaning: Vygotskyan Perspectives on Literacy Research* (pp. 314–359). Cambridge: Cambridge Press.
Barton, S. and Hamilton, M. (2000) Literacy practices. In D. Barton, M. Hamilton and R. Ivanic (eds) *Situated Literacies: Reading and Writing in Context* (pp. 7–15). London: Routledge.
Brandt, D. (2004) *Literacy in American Lives*. Cambridge: Cambridge University Press.
Busch, B. (2007) *Language Biographies for Multilingual Learning*. PRAESA Occasional Paper No. 24. Cape Town, RSA: PRAESA.
Clark, C. and Medina, C. (2000) How reading and writing literacy narratives affect pre-service teachers' understandings of literacy, pedagogy, and multiculturalism. *Journal of Teacher Education* 51 (1), 63–76.
Coffey, M. (2011) *Literacy Narratives Across the Curriculum*. Master's Dissertation, Oregon State University, USA.
Coffin, C., Curry, M., Goodman, S., Hewings, A., Lillis, T. and Swann, J. (2003) *Teaching Academic Writing: A Toolkit for Higher Education*. London: Routledge.
Cole, A.L. and Knowles, J.G. (2001) *Lives in Context: The Art of Life History Research*. Walnut Creek, CA: Altamira.
Corkery, C. (2004) *Narrative and personal literacy developing. a pedagogy of confidence-building for the writing classroom*. Doctoral Thesis: University of Maryland, USA.
Corkery, C. (2005) Literacy narratives and confidence building in the writing classroom. *Journal of Basic Writing* 24 (1), 48–67.
Creswell, J.W. (2009) *Research Design: Qualitative, Quantitative, and Mixed Methods Approaches*. Thousand Oaks, CA: SAGE.
David, M. (2008) *Widening Participation in Higher Education*. See http://www.tlrp.org/pub/documents/HEcomm.pdf (accessed 15 June 2012).
De Guerrero, M. and Villamil, O.S. (2001) *Metaphor analysis in second/foreign language instruction: A sociocultural perspective*. Paper presented at the AAL Annual Meeting, St. Louis, Missouri, 24 February 2001. See www.eric.ed.gov/ERICWebPortal/recordDetail?accno=ED461990 (accessed 15 June 2012).
Department of Education (1996) *Green Paper on the Transformation of Higher Education*. See http://www.info.gov.za/greenpapers/1996/highereduc.htm (accessed 5 March 2012).
Devereux, L. and Wilson, K. (2008) Scaffolding literacies across the Bachelor of Education program: An argument for a course-wide approach. *Asia-Pacific Journal of Teacher Education* 36 (2), 121–134.

Eldred, J.C. and Mortensen, P. (1992) Reading literacy narratives. *College English* 54 (5), 512–539.
Ellis, B.J., Shirtcliff, E.A., Boyce, W.T., Deardorff, J. and Essex, M.J. (2011) Quality of early family relationships and the timing and tempo of puberty: Effects depend on biological sensitivity to context. *Development and Psychopathology* 23, 85–99.
Frost, A., Myatt, J.A. and Smith, J. (2009) Multiple modes of production in a college writing class. In A. Herrington, K. Hodgson and C. Moran (eds) *Teaching the New Writing. Technology, Change and Assessment in the 21st Century Classroom* (pp. 181–197). New York: Teachers College Press.
Granville, S. and Dison, L. (2009) Research and the first-year student: Opportunities for learning. In B. Leibowitz, A. van der Merwe and S. van Schalkwyk (eds) *Focus on First-Year Success. Perspectives Emerging from South Africa and Beyond* (pp. 181–193). Stellenbosch, RSA: SUN Media.
Hamilton, M. (2000) Expanding the new literacy studies: Using photographs to explore literacy as social practice. In D. Barton, M. Hamilton and R. Ivanič (eds) *Situated Literacies: Reading and Writing in Context* (pp. 16–34). New York: Routledge.
Janks, H. (2010) *Literacy and Power*. New York: Routledge.
Kotzé, E. and Hibbert, L. (2010) Are multilingual education policies pipe dreams? Identifying prerequisites for implementation. *Alternation* 17 (1), 4–18.
Kouritzin, S. (2000) Bridging life to research: Life history research in ESL. *TESL Canada Journal* 17, 1–35.
Kress, G. (2010) *Multimodality. A Social Semiotic Approach to Contemporary Communication*. London: Routledge.
Kress, G. and Van Leeuwen, T. (1996) *Reading Images: The Grammar of Visual Design*. London: Routledge.
Kress, G. and Van Leeuwen, T. (2001) *Multimodal Discourse. The Modes and Media of Contemporary Communication*. New York: Routledge.
Kress, G. and Van Leeuwen, T. (2006) *Reading Images. The Grammar of Visual Design* (2nd edn). New York: Routledge.
Lave, J. and Wenger, F. (1991) *Situated Learning: Legitimate Peripheral Participation*. Cambridge: Cambridge University Press.
Lea, M.R. and Street, B. (1998) Student writing and faculty feedback in higher education: an academic literacies approach. *Studies in Higher Education* 23 (2), 157–165.
Leibowitz, B., Van der Merwe, A. and Van Schalkwyk, S. (eds) (2009) *Focus on First-Year Success. Perspectives Emerging from South Africa and Beyond* (pp. 181–193). Stellenbosch, RSA: SUN Media.
Lieblich, A., Tuval-Mashiach, R. and Zilber, T. (1998) *Narrative Research: Reading, Analysis and Interpretation*. Thousand Oaks, CA: SAGE.
Mgqwashu, E. (2009) On becoming literate in English: A during- and post-apartheid personal story. *The Language Learning Journal* 37 (3), 293–303.
Miller, J. (2009) Teaching with an accent: Linguistically diverse pre-service teachers in Australian classrooms. In J. Miller, A. Kostogriz and M. Gearon (eds) *Culturally and Linguistically Diverse Classrooms* (pp. 36–55). Bristol: Multilingual Matters.
Mills, K.A. (2011) *The Multiliteracies Classroom. New Perspectives on Language and Education Series*. Bristol: Multilingual Matters.
Murray, G. (2009) Narrative inquiry. In J. Heigham and R.A. Croker (eds) *Qualitative Research in Applied Linguistics* (pp. 45–65). Basingstoke: Palgrave MacMillan.
New London Group (1996) A pedagogy of multiliteracies: Designing social futures. *Harvard Education Review* 66 (1), 60–92.

Newfield, D. and Maungedzo, R. (2006) Mobilising and modalising poetry in a Soweto classroom. *English Studies in Africa* 49 (1), 60–92.
Petersen, S. and Henderson, R. (2008) *Pre-Service Teachers Developing Literacy Identities.* Paper presented at the National Conference for Teachers of English and Literacy, Adelaide, 6–9 July 2008. See http://www.englishliteracyconference.com.au/files/documents/Petersen-Henderson-Pre-service%20teachers.pdf (accessed 24 March 2012).
Reda, M.M. (2007) Autoethnography as research methodology? *Academic Exchange Quarterly* 11 (1), 177–182.
Ricento, T.K. and Hornberger, N.H. (1996) Unpeeling the onion: Language planning and policy and the ELT professional. *Tesol Quarterly* 30 (3), 401–427.
Rodrigues, R. (1982) *Hunger of Memory: The Education of Richard Rodriguez.* New York: Bantam.
Saldanha, J. (2009) *The Coding Manual for Qualitative Researchers.* London: SAGE.
Seligman, J. (2011a) Academically lost in translation. *Mail and Guardian,* 4 November 2011. See http://mg.co.za/article/2011-11-04-academically-lost-in-translation (accessed 18 November 2011).
Seligman, J. (2011b) *Academic Literacy for Education Students.* Cape Town, RSA: Oxford University Press.
Soliday, M. (1994) Translating self and difference through literacy narratives. *College English* 56 (5), 511–526.
Stein, P. (2008) *Multimodal Pedagogies in Diverse Classrooms: Representation, Rights and Resources:* London: Routledge.
Turner, J. (2011) *Language in the Academy: Cultural Reflexivity and Intercultural Dynamics.* Bristol: Multilingual Matters.
Williams, B.T. (2003) Heroes, rebels, and victims: Student identities in literacy narratives. *Journal of Adolescent and Adult Literacy* 47 (4), 342–345.
Williams, B.T. (2009) *Shimmering Literacies. Popular Culture and Reading and Writing Online.* New York: Peter Lang.
Zipin, L. and Brennan, M. (2006) Meeting literacy needs of pre-service cohorts: Ethical dilemmas for socially just teacher educators. *Asia-Pacific Journal of Teacher Education* 34 (3), 333–351.

12 African Languages in Higher Education: Lessons from Practice and Prospects for the Future

Christa van der Walt and Liesel Hibbert

Introduction

Higher education in Africa, and possibly in other developing countries, is in a difficult position in that it is expected to be at the forefront of critical thinking about contemporary issues while being accountable to regional and national governments. African governments increasingly see higher education institutions as crucial for economic survival and job creation (as shown by Bitzer, 2002: 155), explicitly demanding international competitiveness and local responsiveness. An example in the South African context is the Draft Strategy for Human Capital Development for Research, Innovation and Scholarship, developed by the Department of Science and Technology, which states:

> Commitment Six of the HRD-SA [Human Resource Development Strategy for South Africa] foregrounds the improvement of the technological and innovation capability and outcomes within the public and private sectors (including persons in employment) to enhance South Africa's competitiveness in the global economy, and its ability to meet

its human development priorities. (Department of Science and Technology, 2012: 7)

Steering its way between global and local agendas is an energy-sapping challenge for South African higher education and Bitzer points out that:

> Education is supposed to solve the problems of environmental destruction, unemployment, major diseases such as HIV/AIDS, increasing inequality in wealth, and the social and personal disruption caused by constant technological change and so forth. (Bitzer, 2002: 160)

The Draft Strategy (Department of Science and Technology, 2012: 8) underlines this challenge to produce graduates for a particular vision of South African society by stating that, '[m]odern, knowledge-intensive economies require high-level skills that will continually generate quality research and innovation in pursuit of socio-economic development and to support the country's global competitiveness'. As is the case with other African countries, access to global markets and stages is used as the main reason for the continued use of colonial languages, particularly in education and training.

Higher education all over the world is expected to have an international presence and to manage an increasingly multilingual student population. The solution for teaching, learning and research on multilingual campuses is seen to be the use of English (as shown by Van der Walt, 2013). However, it is important to keep in mind that the challenges in Africa, specifically with regard to the use of minoritised languages in education, are different to those in, for example, the Netherlands or Mexico. Although minoritised languages are also in a difficult position in such countries, high status alternatives to English are readily available and such languages are used as academic languages at primary and secondary school levels. The use of Dutch or Spanish in education is supported by a long history of standardisation and the availability of print and electronic sources in these languages. The situation in most African countries is different, with minoritised languages spoken by the majority of the population, without their being used beyond the very lowest levels of primary schooling. Gadelii (2004: 31), in his overview of the use of African languages in different domains, concludes that 'African languages dominate in preschools and adult literacy programmes, whereas they are rare in secondary schools, let alone universities'.

As the previous chapters in this book show, attempts to incorporate African languages in higher education classrooms go against very powerful perceptions and practices (see Part 3 of the book in particular). The purpose of this chapter is to link these attempts to global debates and issues in multilingual higher education by showing how the authors address and manage issues of linguistic diversity and increased access to higher education.

Language Planning and Policy

When global competitiveness is linked to the use of English in particular, the perception that English is the only alternative as a language of learning and teaching (LoLT) in education is supported, thereby reducing multilingual language-in-education policies to little more than 'pretty' words on impressive documents. As Kotzé (Chapter 2) cautions, the potential for language shift and death is high in this situation. When such policies are supported by perceptions that African languages are not 'developed' or cannot support academic learning, their use in education becomes difficult. This is the point made by Parmegiani and Rudwick (Chapter 7) when they refer to students' 'skepticism towards using [isiZulu] as a medium of instruction'. However, these attitudes and negative perceptions cannot be used as an excuse to continue the exclusive use of English, since attitudes can be changed when African languages are given a place in higher education classrooms, as Ngcobo (Chapter 8) shows.

Unlike established European languages, African languages require a concerted effort to consolidate various terminology projects as the first step towards cementing their place in academic texts. The way in which this has been done and continues to be done, with Madiba's work (Chapter 5) being one of the most recent examples, will be discussed next as a necessary precursor to the development of a uniquely South African multilingual higher education.

In order for a language to become 'intellectually modernised, such that it can be used in the "controlling domains of language" including higher education, much work (corpus development) has to be done by the universities and colleges' (Alexander, 2007: 35). It has been argued that while the African languages of South Africa 'have written forms, literary works, dictionaries and terminology lists, they are lagging far behind in the area of modem terminology as compared to the neo-colonial languages' (Finalyson & Madiba, 2002: 40). Unlike the case of Afrikaans, apartheid-era language policy did little to develop African languages to meet the demands of academic disciplines, in that the indigenous languages of the country were never intended for use in higher functions such as higher education.

Although there are many grassroots initiatives in progress, one of the ground-breaking success stories in South Africa is the work done by Esther

Ramani and Michael Joseph. According to Ramani *et al.* (2007: 207), 'African languages in their current state can be used as media of instruction if the focus is on getting learners to engage with cognitively-challenging tasks for grasping new concepts'. Indeed, the emphasis that is often placed on the need for semantic and lexical development in African languages can result in the role of corpus planning being accorded undue importance. An approach to language planning that takes the perspective of language development as a pre-requisite to language use is, according to Ramani *et al.* (2007: 207), 'quite contrary to the way human languages develop, namely in response to conceptual and communicative needs'. The dual-medium BA degree in Contemporary English Languages Studies (CELS) and Multilingual Studies (MUST) recently implemented at the University of Limpopo is an example of the manner in which pedagogic processes can drive corpus planning. While CELS is both taught and assessed in English, MUST is taught and assessed in Sesotho sa Leboa. A shortage of materials and terminology in Sesotho sa Leboa was identified as a major challenge to the implementation of the programme. However, this obstacle has in part been overcome by the involvement of teachers and students in resource creation by means of translation of academic texts and task-based activities.

The development of terminology was approached by using three strategies:

- The first strategy used, particularly at the start of the project, was that of transference, where terms were borrowed from English without any adaptation of the word to Sesotho sa Leboa.
- The second strategy, which is used most commonly across African languages, is transliteration, by means of which English words are borrowed and 'morphologically and phonologically adapted' (Ramani *et al.*, 2007: 213); for example, the English term *sample* is adapted to *sampolo*. Part of this strategy included finding Sesotho equivalents but imbuing them with a specifically academic meaning.
- The third strategy is that of omission, where ambiguity or redundancy is avoided by not translating every English item.

Ramani *et al.* (2007: 218) conclude that 'the terminology evolved over a period of time as part of curriculum development', an important sign that terminology development cannot be used as an excuse for avoiding African languages in academic contexts.

Applying the development of terminology to electronic media can be seen in the work done at the University of Cape Town, as described by Madiba (Chapter 5). The fact that students can contribute and extend the terminology as proposed by Madiba is important because it invites and encourages engagement, which may increase the use of African language terms, leading to context-sensitive language use that enhances learning (Kosch & Bosch, Chapter 4).

The importance of this work and others like it, however, must be linked to the world represented by such words. Leeuw (Chapter 10) shows that terminology development can (and should) be more than direct translations of English words. Terms expressed in African languages can represent indigenous knowledge systems that provide a much-needed alternative to Western thought, while connecting learners and students to local contexts. While it is necessary to acknowledge Horsthemke's (2004) criticism of the perception that indigenous knowledge is in direct opposition to so-called Western thought, it is important to recognise that culturally familiar perceptions and practices can be empowering, as Higgs (2003: 17) argues. What is more, when education builds on a powerful oral tradition, the use of African languages in classroom discussions and presentations can support what Canagarajah (1999: 91) calls 'counter discourses' that 'forestall cultural reproduction'. The naming of natural phenomena as evidence of indigenous *'knowledge of persons, places, or things'* (Horsthemke, 2004: 34, emphasis in the original) is demonstrated by Leeuw (Chapter 10), not only as quaint or exotic, but also as presenting an alternative world view that is supported by the culturally familiar. In this venture, local languages and language practices are foregrounded and become prerequisites for successful learning. The way in which multilingual South African higher education, as showcased in Chapters 2–10, is directed by theoretical frameworks that acknowledge the cultural embeddedness and multilingual nature of its campuses will be discussed next.

Sociocultural Approaches to Multilingual Learning and Teaching: the Development of Biliteracy

Sociocultural approaches to multilingual education, with a focus on local contexts, are useful in challenging, and possibly reframing, accepted monolingual models (Hornberger, 2002) that have dominated higher education generally. The necessary ideological and implementation spaces for transformation are slowly opening up as a result of policy decisions taken in parliament (see Kotzé & Hibbert, 2010 for further details). In the past, institutions of higher education in South Africa were clearly defined sites of learning that promoted the values and beliefs of relatively homogenised social, cultural and linguistic groups. The present higher education context is representative of the complex social, linguistic and cultural diversity that characterises South African society today.

The case studies presented in this publication represent what is termed 'multilingualism from below' (Cuvelier, 2010), in other words, multilingual teaching and learning strategies that go against dominant views and official, top-down policies. Hornberger's 'onion' metaphor (Hornberger & Johnson, 2007) aptly describes how policy can be influenced through the careful documentation of real-life case studies and practices on the ground. The strategically applied pedagogical initiatives by a new generation of academics, as presented here, show that, as in other parts of the world, linguistic diversity is the norm and is thriving in institutions of higher learning. This new generation of academics, particularly speakers of minoritised languages, have documented the application of their multilingual identities to classroom practices.

The difficulty that many African-language speakers experience on entering the English-dominated environment of higher education is underscored by Gee's notion of primary and secondary discourses in that it is beneficial if secondary discourses (such as words, deeds and values) are compatible with one's primary discourses (Gee, 2008). Academic success is thus relative to the level of mastery that a student acquires in the secondary discourse of academic literacies, which are specific genre-based ways of expressing oneself. As Ramphele (1995: 209) has pointed out, the dominance of English as academic language in institutions of higher education establishes English as an effective gatekeeper to academic success by imperceptibly creating 'circles of privilege' that facilitate the promotion of students from dominant groups within the environment of higher education. The notion of 'circles of privilege' proposed by Ramphele is not unlike Bourdieu's 'profits of distinction', which he describes as the material and symbolic profits that 'scarce cultural capital secures in class divided societies' (Bourdieu, 1986: 245). Mother-tongue proficiency in English is considered a powerful form of cultural capital in the academic context in South Africa. Possession thereof produces notions of profit or privilege that distinguish and maintain inequitable hierarchies in the linguistically diverse context of higher education. However, the next generation of academics, particularly when they are able to use African languages, create new dynamics of power that deny simplistic links between English and dominance. Van der Walt (2013: 8) argues that '[a] reductionist view [of language and power] does not take the covert prestige and speakers' power into account when a junior employee can use Xhosa to narrow the status gap between herself and her Xhosa-speaking supervisor'.

A poststructuralist perspective considers identity as being constructed and validated in multiple and fluid processes of dynamic social interactions in which language constitutes a powerful marker of individual and cultural affiliation. Gee (2008: 175) describes the acquisition of secondary discourses, such as that of the academic institution, as 'taking on an identity that transcends the family or primary socializing group'. The acquisition of academic discourse can thus be considered, in an ideal situation, as a process during which distinct identity positions are negotiated and appropriated both in terms of the discourse of the institution and the student's perception of self in relation to the discourse being acquired. The process of identity construction is complex and influenced by a variety of variables that have few obvious links with academic work (Carstens & Alston, Chapter 11).

Linguistic and cultural diversity brings to the educational context a range of values, beliefs and behaviours encompassed in the primary discourse or home identities of each student. Expressed through the medium of language, primary discourses serve as a framework for the acquisition and learning of secondary discourses (Gee, 2008). The significant symbolic value of language as a regulator of the status quo in postmodern society (Pennycook, 1994) raises sociocultural concerns regarding minority language rights. By drawing on language competencies that were developed in particular communities, the alienation and lack of integration experienced by many first-year students can be mitigated. An explicit recognition of local and community 'funds of knowledge', as promoted by Moll (2007: 274) and Leeuw (Chapter 10), strengthens existing knowledge and provides different perspectives on mainstream and dominant classroom discourses, challenging students and academics to develop critical distance to 'accepted wisdom' and institutionalised practices.

Building on existing multilingual practices in higher education is imperative for the training of professionals who will have to function in multilingual communities. This means that the use of African languages is not only important to access the academic content in higher education (i.e. as an *entrance mechanism* to successful learning), but also for the world of work (i.e. as an *exit* or *graduation requirement*). A similar acknowledgement of the community in which higher education functions is evident in the requirement that all first-year students at the University of KwaZulu-Natal are required to pass a first-year course in isiZulu. Maseko (Chapter 3) describes the way in which a journalism course at a South African university includes the study of isiXhosa culture and language, thereby acknowledging both the community in which the university functions and the multilingual community in which graduates will have to work. At the University of Stellenbosch, Afrikaans–English bilingual students in the Education Faculty are required to develop a command of isiXhosa for use in multilingual school classrooms, while isiXhosa–English bilingual students are expected to develop a command of Afrikaans for similar purposes. The promotion of African languages in the context of higher education therefore validates not only the student's cultural orientations, but also the community's role when graduates return to them to do their jobs.

Makalela's case study (Chapter 6) demonstrates how students' cultural orientations are extended to other African languages, which is part of a bigger process whereby the artificial distinctions between African languages are systematically dismantled. Makalela concludes that, '[t]he students realised that death, wedding, initiation and burial procedures (e.g. readings from a primary school authoring teacher's text entitled *Moeno le Setšo sa Bakgakga*) were not as different as they initially thought in these two language clusters [Sotho and Nguni languages]'. This similarity, including the realisation that societal multilingualism needs to be reflected in academic programmes for the teaching of African languages, is also at the heart of the model for teaching African languages proposed by Kosch and Bosch (Chapter 4, p. 61). As they point out, '[i]n a multilingual context such as South Africa where individuals need to communicate across speech communities, the 'basket module' approach with its multiple languages enables the student to gain insight into '"synergies and cross-fertilisation of languages which are a feature of 'true' multilingualism" (Ouane, 2009: 59)'.

The introduction of multilingual pedagogies in higher education is qualitatively different from practices that have developed in school programmes, mainly because higher education students have developed literacies to a high level and can therefore draw on home language literacies to varying extents. Sociocultural approaches to biliteracy (Hornberger, 1989, 2002, 2003) and pluriliteracy (García, 2009; García *et al.*, 2007) are shown to act as effective frameworks for the creation and identification of spaces and opportunities in which language change can facilitate the way to achieving large-scale implementation strategies.

Hornberger (2002) states that traditional approaches to educational policy and practice have viewed each continuum in terms of polar opposites, for example, literate contexts as opposed to oral contexts or written development to that of oral development, in which one end of each continuum is assigned greater power than the other. The continua of the biliteracy model has proven an effective heuristic to understanding ways of creating ideological spaces for multiple languages and literacies in South African classrooms and communities (Bloch & Alexander, 2003). Spaces and opportunities are created in multilingual academic materials that encourage comparison and analysis across languages, as proposed by Madiba (Chapter 5). By comparing terminology in different African languages to their English equivalent, the sociocultural approach of biliteracy addresses 'the need to contest the traditional power weighting of the continua by paying attention to and granting agency and voice to actors and practices at what have traditionally been the less powerful ends of the continua' (Hornberger & Skilton-Sylvester, 2000: 99). This is also the explicit purpose in Mashiyi's contribution (Chapter 9), where the continua of biliteracy act as the justification for improving student performance. That such efforts would not automatically meet with students' approval (as Mashiyi finds) is to be expected, since perceptions of the so-called inferiority of African languages are inculcated already at primary school level.

Drawing on biliteracy studies by Hornberger and the New Literacy studies, García (2009) unpacks monoglossic ideologies that have traditionally approached bilingualism as the sum of two discrete languages and proposes that 'in the 21st century we must go beyond the traditional models of subtractive and additive bilingualism to understand the more hybrid language practices of bilinguals' (García, 2009: 378). García *et al.* (2007) propose a 'pluriliteracies' approach that 'builds on and extends the continua of biliteracy and the concept of multilingual literacies by integrating key insights from other literatures' (García *et al.*, 2007: 10). In other words, a pluriliteracies approach to education focuses on the interrelatedness of multimodal sociocultural literacy practices that challenge traditional boundaries of language separation.

A significant aspect of plurilingual education is that of 'translanguaging', which can be described as the 'blending of language separation with language integration' (García *et al.*, 2007: 304). The practice of translanguaging in learning environments draws on the resources of two or more languages to construct meaning and mediate understanding. García *et al.* argue that 'translanguaging is not about code-switching, but rather about an arrangement that normalizes bilingualism without diglossic functional separation' (2007: 14). García (2009) refers to studies in translanguaging in a New York kindergarten and the European School of Brussels, which highlight the manner in which children tend naturally toward the practice of translanguaging in order to co-construct meaning, negotiate meaning and include others in integrated language group contexts. García concludes that 'monoglossic ideologies' (2009: 308) have stigmatised translanguaging practices in the past and thus encouraged the shift by minority communities to dominant languages and monolingualism (Kotzé, Chapter 2). That this should happen, in an era of growing sociocultural and linguistic super-diversity (Blommaert, 2010) in the 21st century, goes against the emergence of complex forms of multilingualism that challenge traditional perspectives on language practice in diverse multicultural contexts.

Going Against the Grain: Developing a Multilingual Pedagogy for South African Higher Education

The use of translanguaging and multilingual practices in higher education, despite resistance from students, and possibly fellow lecturers, is not an easy road for the academics who describe their orientations and strategies in this volume. Their commitment is an act of what Canagarajah (2004: 282) calls *appropriation*: 'infusing the established conventions with one's own discourses in a direct act of resistance'. The fact that attitudes towards African languages in education can change over time is shown by Ngcobo (Chapter 8) where students at first resisted the use of African languages as a resource for learning, but then, towards the end of their course, registered more positive attitudes, even among those 'from racially mixed schools, [who] indicated that neither they nor their school teachers had ever used L1 as a learning resource' (this volume). There is little doubt that there is a long way to go and it is clear that piecemeal attempts to support multilingualism will not engender long-term change.

Kembo (2000: 286) warns that '[i]f the people of Africa want to give themselves a realistic opportunity to develop to their full potential educationally, economically, and politically, and to contribute to the resolution of their many problems, the issue of language in education must be addressed'. Working against dominant practices and ideas of what languages can and cannot do, as well as perceptions of the relative value of a language, is essentially a subversive process, termed micro-policy practice by Baldauf (2006), where the needs of students are accounted for by adapting 'accepted' practices to ensure that learning takes place.

Four multilingual teaching practices are discussed in the next section, but they represent only the tip of the iceberg and much more research is necessary to investigate practices like the style and formatting of multilingual texts (see for example Sebba, 2012), bilingual assessment strategies (see for example Van der Walt & Kidd, 2012) and the use of electronic translations for languages that are unfamiliar to the lecturer or the students. These strategies and orientations cannot be seen in isolation, because students and lecturers work in contexts where the dominant languages of learning and teaching, English and to a lesser extent Afrikaans, carry the promise of a job, economic progress and upward social mobility. Many attempts to include marginalised languages have been 'failed experiments', as Michael-Luna and Canagarajah (2007) call their attempt to encourage students to use vernacular discourses in academic contexts. Despite using such discourses online, their students were not willing to use them in class because of their perceptions about the authoritative rigidity of academic conventions. However, recording these practices raises awareness of multilingual pedagogies, which in turn stimulates research and may change monolingual orientations.

If one had to conceive of a multilingual pedagogy for South African higher education, or as Makalela (Chapter 6) calls it, an Ubuntu (language) methodology, translanguaging will have to be accepted as the driving principle: using one language to make meaning in another (Williams, 2002: 2). In most cases African languages are used to understand English academic texts, with production (in writing) almost exclusively in English. The case studies in this volume show planned and purposeful integration of African languages into higher education and as such they are not representative of higher education pedagogy and practice. They do, however, constitute guidelines for what a multilingual pedagogy would entail and can be seen as the one end of a continuum of multilingual education practices: starting with some acknowledgement of minoritised languages at one end, to the full acknowledgement of bi/multilingualism in speaking and writing at the other end. The strategies that are discussed next show this progression:

> Awareness raising → code-switching → the use of interpreters → using more than one language in assignments and examinations

Although these strategies are, by far, not the only translanguaging strategies that can be used in the classroom, they are the ones described in this book and elsewhere as multilingual education practices that are currently used in South Africa

Awareness-raising

If one were to follow Van der Walt's suggestion (2013: 141) for the introduction of multilingual practices, there needs to be an initial process of awareness-raising of other languages and the role they can play in education before these languages are introduced in the classroom. If lecturers and students already use code-switching inside and outside the classroom, its importance for learning would need to be discussed if it is to be used in a planned and responsible way (see Van der Walt *et al.*, 2001). Managing students' perceptions about the inclusion of African languages in higher education is important if monolingual orientations are to be reversed. Parmegiani and Rudwick (Chapter 7) mention the 'general scepticism' towards the use of African languages in education when they are presented in opposition to English. The construction of African languages as 'whole bounded systems' (Heller, 2007) not only prevents students from understanding 'the close linguistic relationship that exists among African languages in southern Africa' (Dowling & Maseko, 1995: 101), but also creates the impression that the use of say, isiZulu, would imply a choice *against* other African languages, which may raise the spectre of conflict. The simplistic notion of English as a national, unifying language then seems like a more neutral choice. The result, as Parmegiani and Rudwick (Chapter 7) point out, is that:

> These students' investment in their mother tongue as a marker of cultural and ethnic identities, combined with their scepticism towards language policies aimed at raising the status of African languages, points to a scenario where African languages continue to be extensively used in informal domains, while English continues to be the undisputed intranational lingua franca in formal domains.

It is therefore crucial that both lecturers and students have opportunities to discuss and critique the role and potential benefits of multiple languages in education, before such strategies are introduced.

Code-switching

The use of code-switching in education has been an area of significant research in South Africa (Adendorff, 1993; Probyn, 2009; Setati *et al.*, 2002; Van der Walt, 2009). Code-switching is defined as 'alternations of linguistic variety within the same conversation' (Myers-Scotton, 1993: 1). Classroom observation indicates that students rely on their peers a great deal during lectures for assistance in understanding and following instructions (Terzoli *et al.*, 2005). Peer-interaction in the classroom commonly takes place through the medium of a shared African language, interspersed with English terms and concepts. The predominant use of code-switching among African language students highlights the manner by which knowledge and new information is mediated in terms of that which is known, in other words, through a language that is familiar and relevant to students' life-world experiences. Mashiyi (Chapter 9) reports that lecturers use code-switching to promote discussion, understanding, peer-assisted learning and, most importantly, to encourage links with the community served by a particular course. As noted earlier, the responsibility of higher education institutions to educate and train professionals who have to serve local communities *in local languages* is conveniently forgotten when the virtues of English are extolled. A challenge to this orientation can also be seen in Maseko's description

(Chapter 3) of isiXhosa cultural and language education in a journalism course.

The use of code-switching as a contextual cue in learning (Gumperz, 1982: 98) can serve as a powerful scaffolding tool for acquisition of knowledge and learning, while at the same time acting as an affective variable that helps to validate the identities of African-language speaking staff and students in an English-dominated context of higher education. As informal communication strategies, code-switching and translanguaging are ubiquitous in South African classrooms, from primary through secondary to higher education level. When used in a planned manner, as part of a multilingual pedagogy, code-switching (as an element of translanguaging) is also one of the easiest ways to introduce other languages in the classroom, particularly when the lecturer shares a home language with the majority of the students. Ngcobo (Chapter 8) emphasises the importance of exposing students to such multilingual strategies and concludes that 'actual experience of mother-tongue instruction can change language attitudes, as opposed to surveying attitudes towards the use of Black African languages where the respondents have been exposed only to teaching and learning resources that make sole use of English'.

In view of the fact that urban users of African languages often use hybrid forms of these languages, it is important to reconsider the use of the term *code-switching* in the light of Canagarajah's (2011: 403) term *codemeshing*. He contrasts the idea of *code-switching* as moving between two separate systems with that of *codemeshing*, where languages are treated 'as part of a single integrated system'. This view aligns more closely with the situation described by Parmegiani and Rudwick (Chapter 7), where 'students also commented that the standard varieties of the African languages are often removed from their communicative needs and their sense of self'. Parmegiani and Rudwick's premise (Chapter 7), that multilingual speakers own an extensive repertoire of languages, dialects and registers, rather than just the one 'whole bounded system' we refer to as 'mother tongue', seems accurate and may also reflect the situation at other higher education institutions. Such a situation is more likely to result in codemeshing as described by Canagarajah (2011: 403).

Using interpreters in the classroom

The use of interpreters via the 'Whispered Interpreting System' (Van Rooyen, 2005: 85) started as a pilot project at the North-West University in Potchefstroom. It has since grown to provide simultaneous interpretation in 1500 classes per week in 2011. The system is also being piloted at the

University of Johannesburg, the University of Stellenbosch and the University of the Free State. Sustained research to assess improvements in learning is being done at all these institutions, with varying degrees of success. Van Rooyen (2005) reports moderate improvements in performance by students who use the service (it is voluntary), but the biggest obstacle seems to be students' perceptions of the usefulness of their home languages in academic contexts (Beukes & Pienaar, 2006). Again, the introduction of multilingual education strategies may need to be framed in a discussion about the rationale for these practices, coupled with a critical analysis of language and power in higher education.

Assignments and tests in more than one language

Some higher education institutions, mostly historically Afrikaans institutions, have formulated language policies that allow students to use choose Afrikaans or English in assignments and tests. In these cases, lecturers are generally bilingual and in some cases students may also switch their preferred study language for a variety of reasons. Van der Walt and Dornbrack (2011) report that, in their study, students provided a number of reasons for switching from one language to another when answering questions in tests and examinations.

At the moment, South African higher education lecturers are still predominantly White, Afrikaans- and English-speaking, with the result that the use of an African language for assignments and tests (except in Departments of African languages) is not widespread. The introduction of translanguaging strategies, as described in this volume by Makalela, Madiba, Ngcobo and Mashiyi, may be the precursor to the increased use of African languages in formal, written assessments.

Conclusion: Affirming Linguistic Hybridity in South African Higher Education Practice

A major challenge facing institutions of higher education in South Africa today is to meet the developmental needs of government, private sector, local communities and society in general. Normative responses to cultural diversity, often framed in the curricula of remedial programmes designed for under-prepared students, are couched in 'deficit-driven notions of instructional design in which some populations of students are described as suffering from cultural deprivation, living in a culture of poverty or being part of the underclass' (Gutierrez et al., 2009: 218). Recurriculation, which embraces the development of African languages for use in high status functions, thus helps to affirm the identity of African language speakers. The recognition that students' and lecturers' identities and beliefs are 'complex constructions' (Carstens & Alston, Chapter 11), is a prerequisite for successful recurriculation to implement multilingual policies. By participating in and contributing to issues of community development, responsive recurriculation within vocation-specific fields of study, such as those proposed by Maseko (Chapter 3), as well as in subject areas as proposed by Leeuw (Chapter 10), may result in the development of a new generation of professionals better equipped to apply their knowledge and to communicate in their professions with clients, patients and particularly learners. The inclusion and promotion of the country's official languages thus respond to the national need for the human resources required for transformation and development.

PanAfrican partnerships, such as the African Academy of Languages (ACALAN), established in 2001 with the approval of the Organisation of African Unity Heads of State and Government, have identified the need to 'conceive and develop a language policy, relevant and efficient enough to quickly contribute to the Renaissance and the Unity of Africa' (Alexander, 2009). The overarching role of ACALAN is the management of linguistic diversity on the African continent according to the principles of additive bilingualism in which African languages are seen in a symbiotic and equitable relationship with English and other dominant European languages of Africa, such as French. One of the core issues of the ACALAN is the role of language policy in education and the concomitant promotion of African languages at all levels of education. Institutions of higher learning are seen to play a significant role in creating the necessary conditions and capacity to drive language development programmes in Africa. Investment in struggling African Language Departments is required in order to support the development of competent and skilled language practitioners. Sociocultural responses to recurriculation of African languages at higher education level need to take the lived experiences of multilingual students into account, as Kosch and Bosch (Chapter 4) argue. Rather than maintaining the prevailing misconception that African language speakers have one, dominant language and many additional languages, their approach raises 'awareness of differences and similarities between the languages' by making it possible for students to compare different African languages.

Bourdieu's (1977: 651) notion of discourse acting as 'a symbolic asset which can receive different values depending on the market on which it is offered' is relevant here. Formal education acts as a powerful market regulator by creating, maintaining and challenging the economic value of cultural and symbolic capital in modern society. Economic and cultural responsiveness to recurriculation underpins the creation of a vital link between African languages and the economy by developing their use as languages of teaching and learning and by promoting African language scholarship.

References

Adendorff, R. (1993) Code-switching amongst Zulu-speaking teachers and their pupils: its functions and implications for teacher education. *Southern African Journal of Applied Language Studies* 2 (1), 3–26.

Alexander, N. (2007) The role of African universities in the intellectualisation of African languages. *Journal for Higher Education in Africa* 5 (1), 29–44.

Alexander, N. (2009) Afrikaans as a language of reconciliation, restitution and nation-building. Paper presented at the Roots-conference held at the University of the Western Cape, 22–23 September 2009.

Baldauf, Jr R.B. (2006) Rearticulating the case for micro language planning in a language ecology context. *Current Issues in Language Planning* 7 (2–3), 147–170.

Beukes, A. and Pienaar, M. (2006) Some factors influencing the use of simultaneous interpreting as an alternative to parallel-medium teaching in tertiary education. *Journal for Language Teaching* 40 (2), 127–138.

Bloch, C. and Alexander, N. (2003) A luta continua: The relevance of the continua of biliteracy to South African multilingual schools. In N. Hornberger (ed.) *Continua of Biliteracy. An Ecological Framework for Educational Policy, Research, and Practices in Multilingual Settings*. Clevedon: Multilingual Matters.

Blommaert, J. (2010) *The Sociolinguistics of Globalization*. Cambridge: Cambridge University Press.

Bourdieu, P. (1977) The economics of linguistic exchanges. *Social Sciences Information* 16 (6), 645–668.

Bourdieu, P. (1986) The forms of capital. In J.G. Righandson (ed.) *Handbook of Theory and Research for the Sociology of Education*. Westport, CT: Greenwood Press.

Bitzer, E. (2002) Teaching in a globalised African context: Reflections from the 45th World Assembly on Education for Teaching. *South African Journal of Education* 22 (3), 155–161.

Canagarajah, A.S. (1999) *Resisting Linguistic Imperialism in English Teaching*. Oxford: Oxford University Press.

Canagarajah, A.S. (2004) Multilingual writers and the struggle for voice in academic discourse. In A. Pavlenko and A. Blackledge (eds) *Negotiation of Identities in Multilingual Contexts* (pp. 266–287). Clevedon: Multilingual Matters.

Canagarajah, A.S. (2011) Codemeshing in academic writing: Identifying teachable strategies of translanguaging. *The Modern Language Journal* 95 (3), 401–417.

Cuvelier, P. (2010) Foreword. In P. Cuvelier, T. du Plessis, M. Meeuwis, R. Vanderkerckhove and V. Webb (eds) *Multilingualism from Below* (pp. xxii–xvi). Pretoria, RSA: Van Schaik.

Department of Science and Technology (2012) *Draft Strategy for Human Capital Development for Research, Innovation and Scholarship*. Pretoria, RSA: State Printers.

Dowling, T. and Maseko, P. (1995) African language teaching at universities. In K. Heugh, A. Siegrühn and P. Plüddemann (eds) *Multilingual Education for South Africa* (pp. 100–106). Johannesburg, RSA: Heinemann.

Finalyson, R. and Madiba, M. (2002) The intellectualisation of the indigenous languages of South Africa: Challenges and prospects. *Current Issues in Language Planning* 3 (1), 40–61.

Gadelii, K.E. (2004) Annotated statistics on linguistic policies and practices in Africa. See http://www.sprak.gu.se/digitalAssets/1310/1310354_annotated-statistics.pdf (accessed 15 January 2014).

García, O. (2009) *Bilingual Education in the 21st Century: A Global Perspective*. Oxford: Wiley-Blackwell.

García, O., Bartlett, L. and Kleifgen, J. (2007) From biliteracy to pluriliteracies. In P. Auer and L. Wei (eds) *Handbook of Multilingualism and Multilingual Communication*. Berlin/New York: Mouton de Gruyter.

Gee, J.P. (2008) *Social Linguistics and Literacies: IDEOLOGIES in Discourses* (3rd edn). New York: Routledge.

Gumperz, J. (1982). *Discourse Strategies*. Cambridge: Cambridge University Press.

Gutierrez, K., Morales, P. and Martinez, D. (2009) Re-mediating literacy: Culture, difference, and learning for students from nondominant communities. *Review of Research in Education* 33, 212–245.

Heller, M. (ed.) (2007) Bilingualism as ideology and practice. *Bilingualism: A Social Approach* (pp. 1–22). New York: Macmillan.

Higgs, P. (2003) African philosophy and the transformation of educational discourse in South Africa. *Journal of Education* 30, 5–22.

Hornberger, N. (1989) Continua of biliteracy. *Review of Educational Research* 59 (3), 271–296.

Hornberger, N. (2002) Multilingual language policies and the continua of biliteracy: An ecological approach. In O. García and C. Baker (eds) (2007) *Bilingual Education: An Introductory Reader*. Clevedon: Multilingual Matters

Hornberger, N. (2003) Introduction. In N. Hornberger (ed.) *Continua of Biliteracy. An Ecological Framework for Educational Policy, Research, and Practices in Multilingual Settings*. Clevedon: Multilingual Matters.

Hornberger, N. and Skilton-Sylvester, E. (2000) Revisiting the continua of biliteracy: International and critical perspectives. *Language and Education* 14 (2), 96–122.

Hornberger, N.H. and Johnson, D.C. (2007) Slicing the onion ethnographically: Layers and spaces in multilingual language education policy and practice. *TESOL Quarterly* 41 (3), 509–532.

Horsthemke, K. (2004) 'Indigenous knowledge' – conceptions and misconceptions. *Journal of Education* 32, 31–48.

Kembo, J. (2000) Language in education and language learning in Africa. In V. Webb and K. Sure (eds) *African Voices: An Introduction to the Languages and Linguistics of Africa*. Oxford: Oxford University Press.

Kotzé, E. and Hibbert, L. (2010) Are multilingual educational policies pipe dreams? Identifying prerequisites for implementation. *Alternation* 17 (1), 4–26.

Michael-Luna, S. and Canagarajah, A.S. (2007) Multilingual academic literacies: Pedagogical foundations for code meshing in primary and higher education. *Journal of Applied Linguistics* 4, 55–77.

Moll, L.C. (2007) Bilingual classroom studies and community analysis: Some recent trends. In O. García and C. Baker (eds) *Bilingual Education: An Introductory Reader* (pp. 272–280). Clevedon: Multilingual Matters.

Myers-Scotton, C. (1993) *Social Motivations for Code Switching: Evidence from Africa*. Oxford: Oxford University Press.

Ouane, A. (2009) My journey to and through a multilingual landscape. In K. Kwaa Prah and B. Brock-Utne (eds) *Multilingualism: An African Advantage* (pp. 53–61). Cape Town, South Africa: Centre for Advanced Studies of African Society.

Pennycook, A. (1994) *The Cultural Politics of English as an International Language.* London: Longman.
Probyn, M. (2009) Smuggling the vernacular into the classroom: Conflicts and tensions in classroom codeswitching in township/rural schools in South Africa. *International Journal of Bilingual Education* 12 (2), 123–136.
Ramani, E., Kekana, T., Modiba, M. and Joseph, M. (2007) Terminology development versus concept development through discourse: Insights from a dual-medium BA degree. *Southern African Linguistics and Applied Language Studies* 25 (2), 207–223.
Ramphele, M. (1995) *Mamphela Ramphele: A Life.* Cape Town, RSA: David Philips.
Sebba, M. (2012) Researching and theorising multilingual texts. In M. Sebba, S. Mahootian and C. Jonsson (eds) *Language Mixing and Code-Switching in Writing* (pp. 1–26). New York: Routledge.
Setati, M., Adler, J., Reed, I. and Bapoo, A. (2002) Incomplete journeys: Code-switching and other language practices in mathematics, science and English language classrooms in South Africa. *Language and Education* 16 (2), 128–149.
Terzoli, A., Dalvit, L., Murray, S., Mini, B. and Zhao, X. (2005) Producing and sharing ICT-based knowledge through English and African languages at a South African university. *South African Journal of Higher Education* 19 (Special Issue), 1486–1498.
Van der Walt, C. (2009) The functions of code switching in English language learning classes. *Per Linguam* 25 (1), 30–43.
Van der Walt, C. (2013) *Multilingual Higher Education: Beyond English Medium Orientations.* Bristol: Multilingual Matters.
Van der Walt, C. and Dornbrack, J. (2011) Academic biliteracy in South African higher education: Strategies and practices of successful students. *Language, Culture and Curriculum* 24 (1), 89–104.
Van der Walt, C. and Kidd, M. (2012) Acknowledging academic biliteracy in higher education assessment strategies: A tale of two trials. In A. Doiz, D. Lasagabaster and J.M. Sierra (eds) *English-Medium Instruction at Universities: Global Challenges* (pp. 27–43). Bristol: Multilingual Matters.
Van der Walt, C., Mabule, R. and De Beer, J.J. (2001) Letting the L1 in by the back door: Code-switching and translation in science, mathematics and biology classes. *SA Language Teaching Journal* 35 (2–3), 123–134.
Van Rooyen, B. (2005) The feasibility of simultaneous interpreting in university classrooms. *Southern African Linguistics and Applied Language Studies* 23 (1), 81–90.
Williams, C. (2002) *Extending Bilingualism in the Education System.* Report by the Education and Lifelong Learning Committee, National Assembly for Wales. See http://www.assemblywales.org/3c91c7af00023d820000595000000000.pdf (accessed 15 January 2014).

Subject Index

Academic literacy, 4, 5, 10,12, 30, 36, 38, 109, 113, 115, 118, 123–129, 136, 179, 195
Access, 4, 6, 8, 21, 25, 27, 28, 30, 39, 51, 58, 64, 71, 74, 75, 84, 108, 112, 113, 116, 119, 124, 146, 147, 153, 159, 160, 168, 177, 180, 203, 204, 208
Achievement, 22, 158, 169, 190
Acquisition, 5, 8, 9, 12, 23, 27, 39, 43, 73, 96, 97, 120, 150, 155, 180, 181, 208, 214
Additional language, 26, 27, 29, 30, 33, 34, 35, 38, 39, 40, 43, 44, 78, 89, 93, 94, 108, 112, 216
African language studies, 10, 29, 38, 39, 40, 41
African Languages, 6–11, 13, 16, 24, 25, 28–44, 49–65, 76, 88–90, 93–95, 97–103, 107–110, 112, 113, 115–120, 123, 133, 135, 136, 141, 142, 146, 150, 152, 156, 161, 197, 202–217
Afrikaans, 6, 15, 19, 24, 28, 29, 36, 37, 58, 80, 89, 94, 150, 183, 184, 189, 194, 195, 204, 208, 209, 211, 215
Arabic, 4
Assessment, 53, 65, 84, 85, 95, 124, 127, 134, 136, 156, 158, 168, 177, 211, 215
Astronomical nomenclature, 168, 169, 176
Astronomy, 11, 35, 167, 168, 177

Bi-/multilingual education, 10, 16, 23, 25, 26, 27, 63, 74, 91, 92, 109, 124, 125, 126, 127, 132, 146, 169, 206, 212, 215

Bilingualisation policy, 107, 108, 111, 113
Bilingualism, 18, 23, 27, 37, 89, 90, 91, 92, 127, 210, 216
Biliteracy, 3, 5, 7, 8, 9, 10, 12, 23, 108, 147, 148, 149, 152, 160, 161, 197, 206, 209, 210
Biliteracy model, 9, 147, 148, 152, 161, 209
Biliterate, 111, 148, 154

Code switching, 5, 7, 10, 84, 92, 131, 152–158, 160, 210
Cognition, 35, 69
Cognitive, 7, 17, 22, 23, 26, 27, 60, 71, 73, 124, 125, 126, 127, 146, 197, 205
Colonial, 4, 16, 17, 18, 203, 204
Colonization of the mind, 110
Communication skills, 10, 94, 124, 136, 151, 157
Communicative, 12, 31, 35, 37, 42, 60, 89, 90, 91, 92, 94, 100, 107, 109, 112, 114, 115, 129, 205, 214
Community, 3, 9, 11, 24, 25, 36, 41, 44, 58, 62, 98, 110, 119, 124, 136, 153, 158, 159, 180, 191, 208, 209, 213, 216
Community language, 9, 124, 158
Competence, 31, 35, 42, 143, 156, 180
Compulsory, 64, 196, 197
Concept literacy, 68, 69, 70, 71, 72, 74, 75, 77, 78, 84, 168
Constitution, 15, 19, 20, 65, 70, 89, 108, 146
Context, 3, 5, 6, 11, 12, 23, 31, 32, 33, 34, 35, 36, 38, 39, 40, 41, 54, 58, 60, 61, 64, 70, 71, 72, 73, 74, 82, 90, 91, 92, 93, 97, 98, 101, 102, 107, 108, 111, 113, 115, 125, 127, 136, 146, 148,

Context (*Continued*)
149, 151, 152, 153, 154, 155, 156, 157, 159, 160, 167, 168, 169, 177, 179, 180, 185, 187, 197, 198, 202, 205, 206, 207, 208, 209, 210, 211, 214, 215
Continua, 5, 6, 9, 107, 108, 119, 147, 148, 149, 152, 157, 159, 160, 161, 197, 209, 210
Continua of biliteracy, 147, 148, 161, 197, 210
Correspondence, 51, 52, 53
Cultural, 57, 64, 72, 93, 94, 96, 97, 98, 99, 100, 101, 102, 112, 115, 118, 119, 157, 161, 168, 169, 174, 176, 177, 181, 183, 185, 194, 197, 206, 207, 208, 209, 210, 213, 214, 215, 216
Curriculum, 8, 10, 11, 12, 33, 38, 40, 41, 53, 60, 63, 64, 92, 148, 153, 159, 161, 169, 179, 181, 182, 196, 197, 198, 205

Darwinism, 18, 19, 22, 25
Degree, 4, 5, 17, 41, 51, 100, 101, 117, 176, 179, 197, 205, 215
Democracy, 15, 16, 25, 28
Discourse, 3, 5, 6, 9, 18, 23, 24, 36, 56, 58, 74, 81, 84, 111, 146, 150, 151, 152, 157, 160, 180, 183, 197, 198, 206, 207, 208, 211, 216
Dual-language instruction, 10, 124

Ecology, 90, 147, 148, 151, 152, 156, 161
Economic, 3, 4, 22, 23, 24, 25, 44, 51, 54, 70, 75, 81, 82, 83, 84, 108, 119, 149, 152, 202, 203, 211, 216
Education policies, 3, 15, 17, 23, 92, 204
Embeddedness, 206
English, 3, 4, 6, 7, 8, 9, 10, 15, 16, 17, 19, 20, 21, 22, 23, 24, 28, 29, 31, 35, 36, 37, 38, 39, 44, 54, 58, 59, 60, 62, 64, 68, 69, 70, 73, 75, 76, 77, 78, 79, 80, 81, 83, 84, 85, 89, 90, 94, 95, 107, 108, 109, 110, 111, 112, 113, 114, 115, 116, 117, 118, 119, 120, 123, 125, 127, 129, 131, 132, 133, 134, 135, 136, 140, 141, 143, 144, 145, 146, 147, 148, 149, 150, 151, 153, 154, 155, 156, 157, 158, 159, 160, 161, 167, 168, 171, 172, 177, 183, 184, 189, 190, 194, 195, 196, 197, 198, 203, 204, 205, 206, 207, 208, 209, 211, 212, 213, 214, 215, 216
English medium, 116, 189
English for academic purposes EAP, 159
Environment, 4, 8, 12, 26, 37, 40, 61, 63, 64, 70, 71, 73, 74, 77, 97, 102, 111, 125, 128, 130, 132, 135, 147, 148, 155, 156, 160, 161, 174, 181, 185, 187, 188, 197, 203, 207, 210
Epistemological, 101
Ethnicity, 112, 118

French, 4, 7, 16, 17, 72, 216,
First language, 6, 17, 19, 34, 36, 42, 44, 58, 69, 84, 110, 146, 154, 155, 160

Globalisation, 13, 40, 139, 162
Graduate, 61, 203, 208, 209

Heteroglossia, 73, 93
Home language, 8, 20, 22, 26, 27, 38, 39, 78, 90, 91, 94, 95, 98, 100, 133, 135, 140, 142, 143, 145, 155, 159, 160, 184, 209, 214, 215

Identity, 4, 6, 38, 89, 91, 93, 97, 107, 111, 112, 113, 115, 116, 119, 146, 152, 179, 183, 184, 185, 187, 188, 189,196, 197, 198, 207, 208, 216
Identity construction, 107, 112, 113, 119, 208
Indigenous, 8, 11, 16, 17, 19, 22, 28, 29, 30, 31, 32, 33, 34, 35, 36, 37, 41, 42, 44, 55, 58, 59, 89, 98, 100, 149, 150, 155, 156, 157, 159, 167, 204, 206
Indigenous African languages, 28, 29, 30, 31, 32, 33, 34, 35, 37, 41, 44, 55, 89, 98, 100
Indigenous knowledge system, 11, 58, 167, 206
Institutional Policy, 10, 41, 42
Instruction, 10, 19, 29, 30, 31, 36, 42, 51, 53, 58, 59, 60, 63, 68, 72, 88, 94, 108, 110, 111, 119, 120, 123, 124, 130, 131, 132, 134, 136, 141, 146, 149, 150, 153, 154, 155, 158, 185, 189, 195, 204, 205, 213, 214, 215
Interpreting, 7, 43, 125, 152, 214

Isindebele viii, 8, 31, 50, 52, 55, 66, 94, 95, 129, 139, 150, 184
isiXhosa, 9, 10, 19, 24, 29, 37, 38, 39, 40, 41, 44, 50, 52, 54, 56, 63, 75, 76, 78, 94, 95, 97, 133, 140, 142, 147, 149, 150, 153, 154, 155, 156, 157, 159, 160, 184, 208, 214
isiZulu, 9, 10, 19, 44, 50, 52, 54, 55, 56, 63, 65, 94, 97, 98, 107, 108, 109, 110, 111, 112, 113, 114, 115, 116, 117, 118, 119, 120, 124, 127, 131, 132, 133, 134, 135, 140, 141, 142, 143, 144, 149, 184, 189, 204, 208, 213

Knowledge, 9, 11, 12, 25, 39, 40, 41, 44, 54, 57, 58, 59, 61, 62, 64, 68, 90, 128, 131, 145, 153, 154, 158, 160, 167, 168, 169, 171, 172, 177, 181, 198, 203, 206, 208, 213, 214, 216

Language ecology, 147, 161
Language groups, 49, 62, 65, 101, 197
Language integration, 210, 124
Language of learning and teaching (LoLT), 4, 7, 8, 9, 20, 22, 27, 35, 36, 38, 44, 109, 110, 111, 112, 113, 115, 116, 117, 118, 119,149, 153, 154, 155, 156, 157
Language policy, 6, 20, 23, 24, 29, 32, 34, 36, 37, 38, 69, 89, 94, 146, 148, 149, 153, 154, 155, 157, 159, 161, 204, 216
Language practices, 8, 11, 90, 91, 92, 113, 119, 120, 145, 151, 160, 161, 206, 210
Linguistic, 6, 7, 9, 15, 18, 19, 22, 23, 24, 25, 28, 32, 33, 35, 36, 37, 38, 39, 40, 43, 54, 56, 57, 58, 64, 65, 68, 69, 71, 72, 73, 74, 76, 89, 90, 91, 92, 93, 95, 97, 100, 101, 102, 108, 117, 123, 125, 126, 137, 145, 146, 147, 150, 153, 155, 157, 158, 159, 160, 189, 197, 204, 206, 207, 208, 210, 213, 215, 216
Linguistic failure, 123
Linguistic repertoire, 74, 90, 95, 108
Literacy, 4, 5, 6, 10, 12, 23, 25, 30, 31, 36, 38, 68, 69, 70, 71, 72, 74, 75, 77, 78, 84, 109, 113, 115, 118, 119, 123, 124, 125, 126, 127, 128, 129, 136, 150, 168, 179, 180, 181, 182, 183, 184, 185, 186, 187, 189, 190, 191, 192, 193, 194, 195, 196, 197, 198, 203, 210

Medium of instruction, 31, 51, 58, 59, 68, 88, 108, 111, 119, 150, 153, 189, 195, 204
Mobility, 4, 6, 89, 119, 188, 189, 211
Mother-tongue, 10, 33, 35, 36, 37, 39, 40, 52, 58, 59, 94, 110, 112, 124, 136, 189, 194, 207, 214
Multiculturalism, 29, 37, 41, 181
Multilingual approach, 16, 62, 147
Multilingual concept literacy, 69, 74, 78
Multilingual dispensation, 15
Multilingual glossaries, 41, 68, 69, 70, 71, 72, 73, 74, 77, 78, 84
Multilingual proficiency, 28, 149
Multilingual settings, 147, 160
Multilingual society, 23, 28, 50, 149
Multilingual teaching, 3, 12, 13, 49, 65, 207, 211
Multilingualism, 7, 12, 16, 17, 19, 20, 24, 26, 27, 29, 30, 32, 36, 37, 38, 39, 41, 42, 43, 44, 60, 61, 69, 72, 77, 89, 94, 96, 101, 102, 112, 145, 146, 147, 148, 149, 150, 159, 160, 161, 179, 181, 189, 197, 207, 209, 210, 211, 212
Multiliteracies, 24, 162, 181, 200
Multimodal, 24, 71, 74, 77, 146, 181, 182, 183, 198, 210
Mutual intelligibility, 99, 100, 101, 102

National language, 38, 77
National policy, 10, 16, 28, 36, 43

Online learning platform, 50, 53

Pedagogic strategy, 69, 90
Policy, 5, 6, 7, 10, 15, 16, 20, 21, 22, 23, 24, 25, 26, 27, 28, 29, 32, 33, 34, 35, 36, 37, 38, 39, 41, 42, 43, 44, 49, 52, 63, 64, 69, 89, 94, 107, 108, 109, 111, 113, 146, 148, 149, 150, 153, 154, 155, 156, 157, 159, 161, 204, 206, 207, 209, 211, 216
Portuguese, 4, 16, 17
Postgraduate, 35, 37, 39, 43, 54
Power relations, 72, 107, 108, 111, 112, 148, 149, 153, 157

Practices, 4, 5, 6, 7, 8, 9, 11, 12, 28, 30, 33, 34, 44, 62, 65, 69, 89, 90, 91, 92, 93, 96, 98, 100, 112, 113, 114, 119, 120, 145, 150, 151, 156, 158, 160, 161, 179, 182, 183, 185, 194, 197, 198, 203, 206, 207, 208, 209, 210, 211, 212, 215
Primary language, 7, 77, 84, 130
Professional, 6, 33, 40, 42, 43, 70, 77, 131, 161, 208, 213, 216
Proficiency, 7, 8, 28, 30, 33, 35, 36, 39, 68, 84, 95, 96, 97, 108, 109, 110
Programmes, 3, 11, 25, 27, 30, 35, 36, 39, 40, 85, 92, 93, 109, 123, 136, 147, 159, 161, 203, 207, 209, 215, 216

Resources, 5, 21, 23, 24, 35, 36, 37, 42, 44, 54, 56, 59, 60, 63, 70, 71, 73, 74, 93, 95, 100, 101, 102, 119, 120, 126, 136, 146, 182, 188, 192, 194, 195, 210, 214, 216
Respect, 26, 37, 40, 56, 85, 95, 97, 98, 101, 113, 155, 168, 176, 177

Scientific concepts, 72, 109, 168, 177
Second language, 21, 23, 60, 90, 91, 94, 123, 124, 125, 145, 146, 147, 148, 155
Secondary, 4, 23, 29, 90, 95, 115, 140, 142, 203, 207, 208, 214
Service delivery, 56
Sesotho, 19, 50, 52, 53, 56, 63, 64, 65, 94, 99, 100, 101, 140, 142, 147, 149, 150, 153, 154, 155, 156, 160, 184, 189, 205
Setswana, 11, 19, 50, 52, 53, 64, 99, 100, 101, 168, 169, 171, 173, 174, 175, 176, 177, 184, 189
Shona, 52, 150,
Siswati, 50, 52, 67, 94, 95, 140, 142, 184
Social justice, 146
Sociocultural, 206, 208, 209, 210, 216
Sociolinguistics, 6, 35, 40, 43, 90, 124
Sotho, 19, 50, 52, 53, 65, 94, 96, 100, 101, 102, 111, 117, 209
Standard, 4, 19, 20, 62, 65, 72, 76, 77, 80, 93, 96, 110, 115, 116, 119, 157, 159, 161, 167, 180, 203, 214
Strategies, 5, 6, 25, 30, 32, 33, 35, 36, 37, 41, 42, 58, 59, 96, 160, 194, 197, 205, 207, 209, 211, 212, 213, 214, 215
Support, 3, 5, 7, 8, 19, 20, 23, 24, 29, 30, 31, 32, 35, 36, 37, 39, 41, 43, 44, 50, 61, 69, 73, 83, 96, 101, 107, 108, 109, 110, 111, 119, 125, 126, 127, 133, 134, 136, 146, 149, 156, 159, 161, 168, 182, 191, 193, 195, 203, 204, 206, 211, 216
Swahili, 17, 52,

Tacit policy of multilingualism, 36
Tertiary level, 23, 52, 65, 68
Translanguaging, 4, 5, 6, 7, 8, 9, 10, 12, 23, 69, 71, 73, 74, 78, 81, 82, 83, 84, 85, 90, 91, 92, 93, 95, 96, 97, 100, 101, 102, 103, 124, 210, 211, 212, 214, 215
Translation, 5, 7, 11, 35, 40, 43, 57, 58, 60, 64, 70, 73, 75, 76, 84, 93, 94, 126, 127, 131, 132, 150, 159, 160, 161, 198, 205, 206, 211
Transnational, 4, 6
Tshivenda, 50, 52, 54, 56, 63, 75, 76, 78, 79, 80, 81, 82, 83, 84, 140, 142, 195
Two-way bilingual education, 23, 27, 123
Two-way programmes, 123

Undergraduate, 35, 52, 54, 55, 57, 123

Variety, 4, 5, 6, 7, 58, 65, 92, 93, 116, 157, 179, 180, 181, 187, 208, 213, 215
Vernacular, 5, 16, 17, 22, 24, 25, 58, 63, 111, 148, 149, 153, 157, 158, 159, 211
Vocational, 29, 40, 44

Xitsonga, 50, 52, 54, 63, 184, 195

For Product Safety Concerns and Information please contact our EU Authorised Representative:

Easy Access System Europe

Mustamäe tee 50

10621 Tallinn

Estonia

gpsr.requests@easproject.com

www.ingramcontent.com/pod-product-compliance
Lightning Source LLC
Chambersburg PA
CBHW070604300426
44113CB00010B/1388